# FEAR OF FALLING

# FEAR OF FALLING

## THE INNER LIFE OF
## THE MIDDLE CLASS

### BARBARA EHRENREICH

PANTHEON BOOKS

New York

*Grateful acknowledgment is made to the following for permission to reprint previously published material:*

*The American Scholar:* Excerpt from "Confessions of a Reluctant Yuppie" by Peter Baida. Reprinted from *The American Scholar,* vol. 55, no. 1 (Winter 1985/86). Copyright © 1985 by Peter Baida. By permission of the publisher.

*The New York Times:* Excerpt from "By Land and Air They Got to the Forbeses" by Patricia L. Browne, May 30, 1987. Copyright © 1987 by the New York Times Company. Reprinted by permission.

*Newsweek, Inc.:* Excerpt from "Troubled Americans" from the October 6, 1969, issue of *Newsweek.* Copyright © 1969 by Newsweek, Inc. All rights reserved. Used by permission.

*Simon & Schuster, Inc.:* Excerpt from *DO IT!* by Jerry Rubin. Copyright © 1970 by Social Education Foundation. Reprinted by permission of Simon & Schuster, Inc.

*The Washington Post:* Excerpts from "What's With Americans?" by Walt Harrington from the July 26, 1987 issue of the *Washington Post.* Copyright © 1987 by the *Washington Post.* Reprinted by permission.

LIBRARY OF CONGRESS CATALOGING-IN-PUBLICATION DATA

Ehrenreich, Barbara.
Fear of falling: the inner life of the middle class/
by Barbara Ehrenreich.
p.   cm.
Bibliography: p.
Includes index.
ISBN 0-394-55692-5
1. Middle classes—United States—Attitudes.   I. Title.
HT690.U6E47   1989
305.5′5′0973                                        88-43202

# CONTENTS

# CONTENTS

# ACKNOWLEDGMENTS

Many innocent people must be implicated in this unortho-
dox undertaking. John Ehrenreich collaborated with me on the
article that laid the formal groundwork for my thinking about
the professional middle class. Some of his ideas persist here,
and, I hope, some trace of his clear and logical approach to
things. David Bazelon, who thought up the "new class" long
before John and I ever did, donated many hours to this project,
along with ideas which turned out to be crucial to the plot.
Frances Fox Piven and Richard A. Cloward have enriched and
emboldened my thinking in many ways, and some of their
thoughts, too, have found their way into the pages ahead.

Jonathan Cobb and Allen Hunter provided painstaking comments on several chapters, and their suggestions, where
heeded, have no doubt saved me from considerable embarrassment. Jane O'Reilly, Donna Gaines, and Charlie Russell read
drafts and provided essential moral support. Ruth Russell
helped in countless ways—for which no amount of thanks will
ever quite suffice. Phil Steinberg, my brilliant and utterly reliable research assistant, also contributed much good judgment.
I am especially indebted to Sara Bershtel, my friend and editor
at Pantheon, who drove me—at times relentlessly—to pull it
all together.

Nothing like this gets done without some form of "welfare," which, in this case, I was proud to accept from the John Simon Guggenheim Foundation. I am also endebted to that familiar beachhead of socialism, the public library system, and to the patient employees of the Nassau County system.

My family has provided much more than loving support. I thank my father, Ben Howes Alexander, for his fine-honed scorn of class pretensions, as well for the years of effort that helped lift me into the middle class. My children, Rosa and Benjamin Ehrenreich, provided many insights and thoughtful suggestions. My husband, Gary Stevenson, was a steady source of information, ideas, and, above all, moral perspective.

*To Gary—and the old-fashioned struggle against class injustice that he so ably serves.*

# FEAR OF FALLING

# INTRODUCTION

## THE CLASS IN
## THE MIDDLE

THIS BOOK IS ABOUT the middle class—more specifically, the *professional* middle class—and its journey—intellectual, political, and moral—from the sixties to the eighties. Even the names of these decades seem to tell a story, one that begins with a mood of generosity and optimism and ends with cynicism and narrowing self-interest. And that, in the largest sense, is the theme of this book: the retreat from liberalism and the rise, in the professional middle class, of a meaner, more selfish outlook, hostile to the aspirations of those less fortunate.

If the focus on one class seems unnecessarily narrow, I would point out that most books, and especially those which make large claims about the American character and culture, are in fact about this class and about it alone. We are told, periodically, that "Americans" are becoming more self-involved, materialistic, spineless, or whatever, when actually only a subgroup of Americans is meant: people who are more likely to be white-collar professionals—lawyers, middle managers, or social workers, for example—than machinists or sales clerks. Usually, this limitation goes without mention; for, in our culture, the professional, and largely white, middle class is taken as a social norm—a bland and neutral mainstream—from which every other group or class is ultimately a kind of deviation.

Consider one of the great popular sociological endeavors of the last three decades, *The Lonely Crowd.* In this wonderfully imaginative, wide-ranging book, David Riesman purported to demonstrate a deep change in the American character—a decline, one might say, of inner discipline and will. Only well into the book does the reader discover that many millions of Americans—the members of the blue-collar working class—are exempt from this characterological change, or "immune," as the author puts it. No one seems to have thought this omission strange; though, clearly, Riesman's crowd was far lonelier than it needed to have been.

Many other familiar and important books about the American experience and character turn out to be entries into the swelling biography of the middle class. *The Feminine Mystique,* for all its role in inspiring the feminist revival, was not about "women," but about college-educated, suburban women married to doctors, executives, psychiatrists. *The Greening of America* depicted only the greening of the white-collar crowd and their student young—the blue-collar working class again being "immune" or, in this case, past saving. *Habits of the Heart,* a chronicle of moral numbness and declining public spirit, is again, and by the authors' honest admission, about the habits of middle-class hearts.

These books only reflect a larger tendency to see the middle class as a universal class, a class which is everywhere represented as representing everyone. Television typically displays only a narrow spectrum of American experience and opinion. The pundits who dominate the talk shows are, to a man and an occasional woman, all members of this relatively privileged group—well fed, well educated, and employed in physically restful occupations such as journalism or college teaching. When we see a man in work clothes on the screen, we anticipate some grievance or, at best, information of a highly local or anecdotal nature. On matters of general interest or national importance, waitresses, forklift operators, steamfitters—that is, most "ordinary" Americans—are not invited to opine.

Much, though certainly not all, contemporary fiction shows a similar narrowness of focus. A typical "quality" novel of recent vintage will explore the relationships and reveries of people who live in large houses and employ at least one servant to manage all those details of daily living that are extraneous to the plot. E. L. Doctorow has observed that when a novel featuring poor or working-class people does come along, it is usually judged to be "political" in intent, meaning that it does not qualify as art.

The cultural ubiquity of the professional middle class may seem to make it an easy subject for a writer. There is no need to travel to offbeat settings or conduct extensive interviews to find out what is on its mind. One does not have to consult specialists—sociologists or anthropologists—to discover how people in this class order the details of their daily lives. Their lifestyles, habits, tastes, and attitudes are everywhere, and inescapably before us.

But the very ubiquity of the professional middle class makes it vexingly difficult to write about *as a distinct class*—and a class which, far from representing everyone, is also a distinct minority. Who can presume to step "outside" of it? Its ideas and assumptions are everywhere, and not least in our own minds. Even those of us who come from very different social settings often find it hard to distinguish middle-class views from what we think we *ought* to think. And for those of us who are inside this class, as most professional writers are by definition, if not also by virtue of shared tastes and habits of mind, the effort can be overwhelming.

There is even a problem of what to call this class. One measure of its status as an implicit mainstream and a presumably neutral vantage point is that it has no proper and familiar name. *Middle class* is hardly satisfactory, standing as it often does for almost everyone except the extremes of wealth and poverty. *New Class* is favored by intellectuals, but assumes some awareness of the "old" classes—the bourgeoisie and the proletariat—and has hence remained exotic. *Intelligentsia* is occasionally used but is far too narrow and, I think, unduly flattering. *Professional-managerial class* comes closest to describing the special status of this class, and *professional middle class*—which I will employ here—is close enough. But since that term is cumbersome to read or say, I will fall back, at times, on *middle class.*

But the very things that make this class so hard to talk about also make it urgent that such talk begin. Nameless, and camouflaged by a culture in which it both stars and writes the scripts, this class plays an overweening role in defining "America": its moods, political direction, and moral tone. If we hope to see ourselves with any clarity, we have to begin to make the effort to step back and see the middle class as one class among others, and as a class with its own peculiar assumptions and anxieties. Because it is through the eyes of this class—and often also in its image—that we have, for so long, been content to see America.

My own interest in the professional middle class stems from a long habit of writing about ideas: what might be called "mainstream" ideas, of the kind that are found every day in the media or the ambient culture generally. Much of my time has been spent on *bad* ideas—notions that eventually get shelved as myths, such as the huge edifice of beliefs undergirding the historically unequal relationship between men and women. At some point one is bound to ask, or be called on to explain, just *whose* ideas these were, and why such notions ever arose and took the form they did.

Any honest answer must begin by pointing out that most ideas that find their way into the cultural mainstream originate within a rather narrow social base. They are crafted by a relative elite: people who are well educated, reasonably well paid, and who overlap, socially and through family ties, with at least the middling levels of the business community—in short, the professional middle class.

Such an answer is not, of course, the same as an *explanation* for any particular idea or belief. The professional middle class is not to be imagined as a cabal, or even a very homogeneous lot. Ideas are simply part of the business of this class, or at least the business of its more vocal members—journalists, academics, writers, and commentators. These people are paid to provide the "spin," the verbal wrap that gives coherence to events or serves to justify arrangements we might otherwise be inclined to question. Sometimes members of this class are even paid to do the questioning.

But it can be illuminating to trace ideas to the social milieu from which they arise. For example, many of our traditional ideas about the proper role of women were articulated by physicians and psychiatrists—men of a class (again, the professional middle class) in which it has not usually been necessary, in an economic sense, for women to work outside the home. Similarly, the dilemma we so often read about today, over whether women can combine careers with childraising, is freighted with implicit class assumptions: that women have careers, as opposed to mere jobs, and that they have the wherewithal to abandon these careers without condemning their children to penury.

The ideas that set me off on this project were ideas about another kind of inequality, one shared by men as well as women—the economic inequality of class. While ideas about gender, and even race, have moved, however haltingly, in the direction of greater tolerance and inclusivity, ideas about class remain mired in prejudice and mythology. "Enlightened" people, who might flinch at a racial slur, have no trouble listing the character defects of an ill-defined "underclass," defects which routinely include ignorance, promiscuity, and sloth. There is, if anything, even less inhibition about caricaturing the white or "ethnic" working class: Its tastes are "tacky"; its habits unhealthful; and its views are hopelessly bigoted and parochial.

These stereotypes are hurtful in many ways, not least because they imply that nothing can be done. Efforts to help the poor would only increase their fecklessness and childlike dependence; and the working class, as stereotyped, would be hostile to such efforts anyway.

The prospects for easing economic inequality once seemed much brighter. In the 1960s, equality—at least of opportunity—was a respectable social goal, endorsed by presidents and embraced by leading intellectuals. Today we seldom hear the word. In the sixties, liberalism—as defined by the intention to achieve a more egalitarian society—was an affiliation worn with pride. Today that term has degenerated into a slur, coyly designated as the "L-word." In the early sixties, the big debate was about how best to mobilize the War on Poverty; today such an undertaking would likely be seen as misguided and possibly detrimental to the poor themselves.

It is not that the problems have gone away, or no longer justify our concern. An unseemly proportion of the population still lives in poverty: as much as 20 percent, if we leave aside the federal government's stone-hearted definition for a more realistic measure. Millions more, in the working-class majority, still labor at mind-dulling, repetitive tasks, and count themselves lucky to have a job at all. Meanwhile, the gap between the haves and the have-nots—not only between the rich and poor but between the middle class and the working class—is wider than it has been at any time since the end of World War II, so that America's income distribution is now almost as perilously skewed as that of India.

If the reality has not improved, then ideas have changed for other reasons. We simply care less, or we find the have-nots less worthy of our concern. But why?

I started out with the seemingly straightforward plan of tracing mainstream ideas about the "lower" classes—the poor and the working class—over the past three decades. In mainstream American culture the lower classes had dropped from view in the fifties, vanishing so completely that they had to be "discovered." There was the discovery of poverty in the early sixties and the equally dramatic, though less well-remembered, discovery of the working class at the end of that decade. Each of these events was accompanied by much fanfare—cover stories, television specials, scholarly analyses, even Hollywood attention—and it seemed to me that by mining this material I might gain some insights into our attitudes toward the less-well-off and why these views have seemed to sour.

But in this project, more than any other I had undertaken, the question of *whose* ideas was inescapable. If the poor and the working class had to be discovered, from whose vantage point were they once hidden? And what *we* is implicit in any statement about *our* attitudes? Gradually, and with some initial apprehension, I realized that *our* ideas could not be traced or even understood without clarifying that evasive *we* and introducing the middle class as an actor in the story. What happened, in the life of this class, to cause the retreat from liberalism?

The conventional explanation, such as it is, focuses on events external to this class: In the sixties, as the conventional wisdom goes, rising crime rates led to disillusionment with the black poor and the disadvantaged generally. Liberalism, to paraphrase a conservative aphorism, was mugged. Next came the "blue-collar backlash," which showed that most Americans —at least most white "Middle Americans"—were deeply conservative anyway. Finally there was the economic crunch of the seventies, which awakened any remaining liberals of the middle class to their own material self-interest. They retreated into their careers and private lives, secure in the belief that the "have-nots" were not worth helping anyway.

There is more than a grain of truth to this account. The problem is that it leaves out the element of consciousness—of thought and interpretation. Events do not just hit us on the head, provoking reactions as if by reflex; they come to us already thickly swathed in layers of judgment and interpretation. Sometimes there is very little underneath these layers: The "event" itself represents an act of imagination. For example, as we shall see, the blue-collar backlash which figures so prominently in conventional explanations of American politics was hardly a clear-cut movement or event. It was a highly biased and selective interpretation of the mood of working-class Americans at a certain time. We might raise similar questions about the response to crime, or to the economic downturn. Why does a particular interpretation take hold? Why one way of seeing things and not another?

If external events do not tell the story, or at least not the whole story, then we have to turn to what we might call the "inner life" of the middle class. My straightforward plan, then, of tracing ideas about class and inequality had to be expanded to a more daunting project: an attempt to understand the retreat from liberalism as an episode in the life of the middle class, a change of mind, a shift in consciousness. And the key shift, the one which began to seem most closely linked to the decline of liberalism, was in the middle-class perception of *itself:* from the naïve mid-century idea that the middle class *was* America, and included everyone, to a growing awareness that the middle class was only one class among others, and an isolated, privileged one at that.

The discoveries of the poor and the working class were, of course, essential to this self-awareness. So was something I had not originally figured on: the student rebellion of the sixties, whose impact on middle-class opinion will be explored in the pages ahead. All of these discoveries and events combined to convince an influential minority of the professional middle class that their class was, in fact, a very special group, an elite above the majority of "ordinary" people. It was in this new and emerging self-consciousness *as an elite* that the middle class, or significant segments of it, turned right.

Conventional, or, I should say in this case, conservative, wisdom might argue the reverse. Liberalism, we often hear, is the property of an elite—the so-called liberal elite that has been denounced by Republicans from Spiro Agnew to George Bush. Conservativism—on economic as well as social issues— is, on the other hand, often thought to be native to the common folk, the "average Joe."

Yet historically, and for obvious reasons, elites are seldom the champions of equality and social justice. The youthful members of a social elite may embrace the cause of the down-trodden; scattered individuals may follow their conscience to some course of action beyond mere charity. But on the whole, an elite that is conscious of its status will defend that status, even if this means abandoning, in all but rhetoric, such stated values as democracy and fairness.

In fact, as we shall see, the notion of the professional middle class as a powerful elite finds its most forceful expression among those who are, or who have moved, the farthest from liberal ideals. It is a notion that is central to contemporary right-wing thought, from "neoconservatives" to New Rightists.

It has become, although in a peculiarly disingenuous way, almost the defining obsession of the right.

This book is about what could be called the _class-consciousness_ of the professional middle class, and how this consciousness has developed over the past three decades. In the pages ahead we will follow the emerging middle-class awareness of being a class among others and, ultimately, of being an elite _above_ others. Throughout, we will be concerned with the ways in which this emerging self-image has led to—and sometimes helped to justify—the adoption of the kind of political outlook appropriate to an elite, which is a conservative outlook, and ultimately indifferent to the nonelite majority. Finally, moving up to the present, we will look at the attempt by a significant minority of the professional middle class—briefly known as yuppies—to live as if they actually _were_ an elite of wealth and power.

This is not, on the whole, a pretty story, but one marred by prejudice, delusion, and even, at a deeper level, self-loathing. For this reason alone I owe the reader some qualifications— more, perhaps, than I am prepared to make. First, a class, of course, is never of one mind. Here we will be following a particular stream of thought and imagery, expressed by various intellectuals, scholars, media people, and opinion-makers, and found also in familiar settings such as movies, newsmagazines, and television. Other, less mainstream currents of middle-class opinion, particularly of the left, receive scant scrutiny here; though, to be honest, the left is already represented here— however inadequately—by my point of view.

Second, statements about consciousness and perceptions are not of course amenable to proof. This book is necessarily an interpretative, even rashly speculative, venture. I have tried to connect a great many themes and subjects—from, for example, middle-class anxieties about affluence and status to ideas about poverty and public policy. I have tried to place sweeping ideas about politics and morality in the context of more "mundane" middle-class concerns, for example, about lifestyle and consumption, childraising and the role of women. And I have tried to put all of this into a more or less coherent story. The risk, in this, is of being *too* coherent, too selective, and of imposing a pattern that history, in its willfulness, cannot sustain. I leave it to the more cautious and more scholarly to correct any excesses and propose, if possible, a better pattern.

Before this story can be told, I must first introduce its central character, the professional middle class. This class can be defined, somewhat abstractly, as all those people whose economic and social status is based on education, rather than on the ownership of capital or property. Most professionals are included, and so are white-collar managers, whose positions require at least a college degree, and increasingly also a graduate degree. Not all white-collar people are included, though; some of these are entrepreneurs and some are better classified as "workers." But the professional middle class is still extremely broad, and includes such diverse types as schoolteachers, anchorpersons, engineers, professors, government bureaucrats, corporate executives (at least up through the middle levels of management), scientists, advertising people, therapists, financial managers, architects, and, I should add, myself.

The two major subgroups within the class—professionals and managers—are not as disparate as they sometimes seem. Professionals usually have administrative responsibilities that make them part of management, just as managers and executives may have professional skills and training. Individuals pass easily between one category and the other, and both categories of individuals tend to live in the same neighborhoods, move in the same social circles, and intermarry.

So defined, the professional middle class is a distinct minority, composing no more than about 20 percent of the population. At the lower end there are hard-to-classify occupations like schoolteaching, which is certainly based on education, but which, despite its aspirations, falls short of the kind of income and prestige awarded to professions traditionally dominated by men. At the much more thinly populated upper end there are executives whose wealth, decision-making power, and ownership of stock surely place them in a higher class—the corporate elite that serves as an American ruling class.

If this definition seems insufficiently precise, all I can say, without getting into arcane arguments, is that class is a notion that is inherently fuzzy at the edges. When we talk about class, we are making a generalization about large groups of people, and about how they live and make their livings. Since there are so many borderline situations, and since people do move up and down between classes, a description like middle class may mean very little when applied to a particular individual. But it should tell us something about the broad terrain of inequality, and about how people are clustered, very roughly, at different levels of comfort, status, and control over their lives.

How much it tells us depends on how much the people whom we are lumping together as a class have in common, and whether they share enough experiences to help define some common outlook on the world. Here, in shorthand form, are some points of commonality that define the professional middle class and make this broad group a class.

*Occupation:* Unlike those fortunate enough to find themselves in the upper class, members of the professional middle class must work for a living. A minority, including many physicians, lawyers, therapists, etc., are self-employed, but the trend over the years has been for professionals to be absorbed into the work force of large bureaucratic organizations, like corporations, hospitals, or law firms. Most are salaried employees, sometimes even union members. But there is a key difference between middle-class professionals and their fellow wage earners in the working class. Today, both may wear white (or pink) collars and participate in what might loosely be called "mental work." The difference is that the professional or manager is granted far more autonomy in his or her work and is expected to be fairly self-directing much of the time. In fact, his or her job is often to define the work of others: to conceptualize—and command.

*Defining experiences:* The professional and managerial occupations have a guildlike quality. They are open, for the most part, only to people who have completed a lengthy education and attained certain credentials. The period of study and apprenticeship—which may extend nearly to mid-life—is essential to the social cohesion of the middle class. It is in college or

13

graduate school that the young often find their future spouses and lifelong friends. Much more than an extended childhood, however, this long training period requires the discipline and self-direction that are essential to the adult occupational life of the class.

*Income:* For the most part, members of the professional middle class earn "upper-middle" incomes, though these may range from a non–Ivy League professor's $30,000 to six-figure salaries for a "star" professor or big-city attorney. Typically, middle-class couples earn enough for home ownership in a neighborhood inhabited by other members of their class; college educations for the children; and such enriching experiences as vacation trips, psychotherapy, fitness training, summer camp, and the consumption of "culture" in various forms.

*Lifestyle and tastes:* All of the above shape a rough commonality of lifestyle and consumer tastes. In general, the middle class uses consumption to establish its status, especially relative to the working class. Typically, this has meant an emphasis on things "authentic," "natural," and frequently imported. Such tastes provide the class cues by which middle-class people recognize each other outside of their occupational settings, and help guarantee that a lawyer, for example, does not unwittingly fall into the company of some lower-status person, such as an off-duty plumber or postal worker. Marriage within the group is important to members of the middle class, and helps give this class, like the other classes in American society, a certain castelike quality.

How much these commonalities of income, occupation, and so forth, tend to create a common awareness, psychology, or class-consciousness is of course a question for the chapters ahead. But here we might briefly attempt to answer the somewhat more "objective" question of whether the professional middle class is *really* an elite. For if it is not, then this book only charts a tragic delusion, leading unnecessarily to meanness and to isolation from the American majority.

In some ways, of course, the professional middle class *is* an elite. Compared to the poor and the working class, it certainly is. The difference is not only a matter of money but of authority, influence, and power. Yet the professional middle class is still only a *middle* class, located well below the ultimate elite of wealth and power. Its only "capital" is knowledge and skill, or at least the credentials imputing skill and knowledge. And unlike real capital, these cannot be hoarded against hard times, preserved beyond the lifetime of an individual, or, of course, bequeathed. The "capital" belonging to the middle class is far more evanescent than wealth, and must be renewed in each individual through fresh effort and commitment. In this class, no one escapes the requirements of self-discipline and self-directed labor; they are visited, in each generation, upon the young as they were upon the parents.

If this is an elite, then, it is an insecure and deeply anxious one. It is afraid, like any class below the most securely wealthy, of misfortunes that might lead to a downward slide. But in the middle class there is another anxiety: a fear of inner weakness, of growing soft, of failing to strive, of losing discipline and will. Even the affluence that is so often the goal of all this striving becomes a threat, for it holds out the possibility of hedonism and self-indulgence. Whether the middle class looks down toward the realm of less, or up toward the realm of more, there is the fear, always, of falling.

So there is not, ultimately, an objective answer to the question of whether the middle class is an elite or something less exalted—an extension, perhaps, of the working class. And hence there is no easy answer to the much harder question of whether it is "naturally" inclined to the left or to the right. Is the middle class, by nature, generous or selfish? Overindulged or aggrieved? Committed to equality or defensive of privilege? These are not only possible answers, but *choices* to be made.

## CHAPTER ONE

# AFFLUENCE, DREAD, AND THE DISCOVERY OF POVERTY

THE "DISCOVERY" OF POVERTY at the beginning of the 1960s was something like the "discovery" of America almost five hundred years earlier. In the case of each of these exotic terrains, plenty of people were on the site before the discoverers ever arrived. The fact that they had to be found reveals less about them than it does about the delusions that guided their discoverers. Columbus's discovery, for example, tells us something about the vantage point of fifteenth-century Europeans: Believing that the world was small and conveniently arranged for commerce in spice and gold, they misjudged the size of the earth by at least two continents and an ocean.

So, too, the discovery of poverty tells us something about the peculiarly limited vision of middle-class Americans at the middle of the twentieth century. Living in what they took to be the final stage of material affluence—defined by cars, television, and backyard barbecue pits—they believed that this *was* America. Looking out through their picture windows, they saw only an endless suburb, with no horizon, no frontier, in sight. They believed, almost, that America had stepped outside of history, and that the only changes to come would be the predictable improvements brought by technological progress:

17

automation, space travel, a cure for cancer, more fidelitous hi-fi equipment.

From this vantage point the jagged edges of inequality seemed to have disappeared, smoothed out by the affluence that had come to encase American society like middle-aged girth. There were no distinct social classes—only one vast middle class with no known boundaries. As Vance Packard, one of the few dissenters from the dogma of American class-lessness, wryly reported in 1959:

> A number of influential voices have been advising us that whatever social classes we ever had are now indeed wither-ing away. . . . Some months ago, a national periodical pro-claimed that the United States had recently achieved the "most truly classless society in history." A few weeks later, a publisher hailed the disappearance of the class system as "the biggest news of our era."

Unfortunately, even Packard quickly turned from class, with its implications of persistent injustice, to the more entertaining subject of status—as expressed, for example, by one's sofa:

> The lower-class people preferred a sofa with tassels hanging from the arms and fringe around the bottom. The high-status people preferred a sofa with simple, severe, right-angled lines.

Yet, despite the intricate hierarchy of tastes documented by Packard and others, there was a general sense that America had finally been homogenized into a level mass. Blue-collar workers were reported to be buying houses in Levittown and sending their children to college; union leaders, as C. Wright Mills had shown, were becoming gray-flanneled executives like their corporate antagonists. "Negroes" were on the march, of course, but only for the apparently unobjectionable goal of sitting down at the same lunch counters and consuming the same good things available to white Americans. Wherever one looked, America seemed to have risen above the hurts and injustices that kept less-favored nations febrile and restless. Nothing much would change because no important social group had a stake in making change. They were all happily joining the universal middle class.

## THE PROBLEM OF PROBLEMLESSNESS

If this was the best of times, there was still, inevitably, a flaw. Popular wisdom held that any utopia was bound to be disappointing because "there would be nothing to do," no challenges and no excitement. As evidence, people liked to cite the high suicide rate of the Swedes, who were supposedly enervated by their overprotective welfare state. Now it was as if America had also stumbled into utopia only to confront the ultimate human problem—problemlessness—and with it, the threat of a wasting ennui. "What can we write about?" a college newspaper editor demanded querulously in 1957. "All the problems are solved. All that's left are problems of technical adjustments."

America's best-known intellectuals—who were themselves, almost to a man, members of the professional middle class— agreed. "The fundamental political problems of the industrial revolution have been solved," pronounced Seymour Martin Lipset in 1960. There was nothing to do, and certainly nothing worth doing with enthusiasm. After surveying the American scene in 1955, David Riesman and Nathan Glazer taxed their minds to discover an issue that might engage the reform-minded. "One could raise the floor under wages," they considered briefly, or "press for socialized medicine," but most people, they concluded, were too comfortable to care. "To be sure," they mused, "there are enclaves where the underprivileged still can be found, as in the Southern Alleghenies or the rural Deep South." But this problem of "underprivilege" was so marginal, so geographically isolated, that it would hardly take a full day's work. "There are still pools of poverty to be mopped up," Arthur Schlesinger, Jr., noted, but then we would be right back to the more vexing problems posed by "an economy of abundance."

It was the "end of ideology," Daniel Bell announced in

1960, and if no one missed it, this was because no one, perhaps including Bell, seemed to remember what ideology was. Searching for a definition, he kept falling back on the hot word *passion:* "A total ideology is . . . a set of beliefs infused with passion. . . . What gives ideology its force is its passion." But the waning of passion was hardly worth mourning, for passionate beliefs about society could flower, apparently, only in the harsh ground of inequality, in circumstances where social position was scripted from birth. In "modern" society, occupation and hence status were determined by "technical skill," a purely neutral attribute that anyone could pick up along the way. In this situation, Bell asked rhetorically, "What then is the meaning of class?" Not much, the reader, numbed by ideology's slow death in the author's hands, would have to agree. If there were no deep injustices and only an occasional matter for "technical adjustment," there were surely no inequalities worth getting passionate about.

This still left problemlessness, "the search for a cause," as Bell put it. The search itself had a certain urgency, for without a cause to engage, at least briefly, the young, America would become soft and stupid. Schlesinger described Americans in the fifties as gripped by "torpor," "weary and drained." Bell subtitled his book "The *Exhaustion* of Political Ideas in the Fifties." America needed some bracing challenge, and President Dwight Eisenhower appointed a high-level commission to come up with some "goals for Americans." The results were disappointing. "The paramount goal of the United States," the commission reported in 1960, "is to guard the rights of the individual, and to enlarge his opportunity." This goal was depressingly similar to the "ultimate purpose" of the American economy, as defined by the chairman of Eisenhower's Council of Economic Advisers: "to produce more consumer goods. This is the goal. This is the object of everything we are working at; to produce things for consumers."

Individualism, as critics pointed out, was what Americans were already pursuing through their choices in home furnishings and frozen foods; it was not a goal capable of inspiring the nation with collective zeal. The commission had detected a few genuine problems, such as race relations, but these were only the "last stubborn barriers" to the condition of perfection that America was rapidly approaching.

Even America's most liberal intellectuals were at a loss for a genuine problem. In 1963, Schlesinger made a list of "concrete issues" that might rouse the educated public. By today's standards, the list is enviably tame: no nuclear war, epidemic disease, environmental disaster, hunger and homelessness, race hatred—although most of these horrors shadowed American life then as they do now. The only truly burning issue on his list was equal rights for blacks, but also prominent were such limp suggestions as "the refinement of our mass media and the elevation of our popular culture."

In a society that was almost without problems, the state of liberalism was necessarily "dull." In fact, there was little on the American political scene that was recognizably "liberal" by the standards of the mid-sixties and the seventies. Liberals were, then as now, more concerned about civil rights and civil liberties than were those to their right, and more willing to use the power of government to defend them. They also prided themselves in a populist tradition inherited from Franklin Roosevelt and Harry Truman, and, when populist rhetoric was called for, could claim to be the defenders of the "little man" against the plutocratic interests unabashedly represented by Eisenhower's Republican Party.

But, lacking any urgent problems to define it, the liberalism of the late fifties bore a strong resemblance to conservatism. Like conservatives, liberals believed that economic growth was the key to domestic well-being and that military strength was the guarantor of peace—only liberals wanted more of both. As Alan Wolfe has written, "A liberal was one who believed that growth should happen rapidly and a conservative, one who believed that growth should happen in a more tempered fashion." Reforms like national health insurance were still high on the liberal agenda; but, ultimately, liberal Democrats, like conservative Republicans, trusted in endlessly rising indices of production to guarantee prosperity and employment. And in foreign policy, liberals were the "hawks," berating their political antagonists for their lack of enterprise in the contest with world communism. An aggressive, interventionist foreign policy and the swollen bureaucracy that pursues it were, in Wolfe's words, "basically liberal inventions."

When Arthur Schlesinger, Jr., undertook to differentiate John Kennedy from Richard Nixon in the 1960 campaign, he found no compelling clash of issues. Both men had been compromised in Joseph McCarthy's crusade against domestic communism; both wanted a tougher stance against communism; both had hazy views on domestic policy. The harshest thing Schlesinger could find to say about Nixon was not that he was illiberal relative to Kennedy but that he was an "other-directed" man, of the spineless, conformist type Riesman had decried in *The Lonely Crowd*. The other-directed man, such as Nixon, "has no inner ideals to violate" and is driven only by his "effort to be in harmony with the crowd," Schlesinger wrote in *Kennedy or Nixon: Does It Make Any Difference?* and the issues-oriented reader might well conclude that it did not.

Schlesinger himself was acutely aware of the futility of liberalism in an age of problemlessness. As he wrote in *The Politics of Hope*, "Contemporary American liberalism has no overpowering mystique. It lacks a rhapsodic sense. It has jettisoned many illusions. Its temper is realistic, even skeptical. Its objectives are limited." It was, in short, no less committed to the general outlines of the status quo than conservatism was. And this was entirely appropriate if there were indeed no problems left to solve, but it left liberals—at least the relatively complacent liberals of the middle class—in search of a defining "mystique."

## SOCIOLOGY AND THE SPECTER OF CLASS

There was one problem, visible at least in the tabloids and movies, if not on the lists of scholars: juvenile delinquency. Juvenile delinquency gripped the public imagination in the fifties much as the inverse problem, child abuse, did in the eighties. The reported rate of juvenile crime had risen sharply since the forties, but, as with child abuse more recently, public alarm rose faster than the statistics and no doubt served to inflate them. In retrospect, the juvenile delinquent, or at least the stereotyped JD seen in so many B movies, should have served as a vivid reminder of the persistence of class, and ethnic, differences. With his duck-tail haircut, black leather jacket, and distinctive slang, he was certainly not middle class. In fact, the stereotype was indistinguishable from the style affected, to one degree or another, by lower-class youth in general, including the noncriminal majority. It was a rude, macho look, deliberately defiant of the clean-cut Tab Hunter style adopted by the college-bound.

But precisely because the JD was a delinquent, and a youthful one at that, he did not inspire widespread soul-searching on the subject of class inequality. It was too easy to explain him in other ways. J. Edgar Hoover blamed juvenile delinquency on an absence of adequate religious training, and Bishop Fulton J. Sheen blamed the "3 D's"—parents who were "doting, drinking, and discordant." Most experts agreed that juvenile delinquency was the result of family pathology that could arise in the best of neighborhoods—broken homes, working mothers, erratic or (as in *Rebel Without a Cause*) effeminate fathers. The juvenile delinquent was, in sociological terms, not a possibly well-adjusted member of a class ground down by low wages and menial labor but a "deviant," someone who had failed to adjust to the larger (middle-class) scheme of things, and classifiable in the same general category as the mentally ill and the willfully unemployed.

Simultaneously, the JD raised the issue of class and provided a comforting distraction from it. If there were other classes, other ways of life than that known by the white middle class, they could be seen as "deviations" from the white middle-class standard. And since the JD was, after all, a juvenile, the potential menace of these lower classes took on, from a middle-class perspective, the diminished stature of a child. The notion that the lower classes are children compared to their "betters" is, of course, an ancient and reassuring one.

23

It was possible, then, to grow up in mid-century, middle-class America without the vaguest suspicion that human beings might be lumped, quite involuntarily, into a few large groupings defined by income, opportunity, and lifestyle. Not that Americans lacked firsthand insight into the existence of social classes; the mainstream vocabulary simply lacked a word for this phenomenon. In fact, the era of official classlessness was also an era of intense preoccupation with the innumerable little cues distinguishing one layer of taste and achievement from another: Did one drink martinis (a status item) or rye and ginger ale? Eat beef stroganoff or meat loaf and macaroni? Dwell in an enclave named Executive Manors or in an untitled housing development?

The public high schools provided a comprehensive education in the nuances of class recognition. Just as today there are "preppies" and "dirtbags," there were "nice" boys and "hoods," "nice" girls and "cheap" ones—the latter distinguished by their tight skirts, eye-liner, and cigarettes. Further, it almost went without saying that the "hoods" and "cheap" girls, along with their mousier siblings, would end up taking typing and shop while their "nicer" classmates studied French and biology. With a little more probing, the pattern enlarged to reveal that the fathers of "nice" kids tended to be white-collar men, while the fathers of the future waitresses and mechanics went to work in flannel shirts and denim. But all this could be taken for coincidence. If there was some causal connection between a child's future occupation, manner of dress, and father's occupation, no one in the middle class seemed to know what it was.

The one place a middle-class youth might have been expected to find some enlightenment on the subject of class was in a college sociology course. American sociology had a stake in the notion of class. Important studies had shown that the members of medium-sized communities could be sorted into as many as five or six social classes, with names such as "Class I," "Class II," and so forth. In addition, there was a venerable sociological tradition of studying the behavior—almost invariably "deviant"—of the lower classes, as represented for example by street gangs.

But the anticommunism of the fifties had thrown an embarrassing light on the sociological fascination with inequality, or "stratification" as it was more genteelly termed. The full-blooded, old-fashioned notion of class—as in *class struggle*—was now suspect and un-American, part of a left-wing heritage that mainstream intellectuals were fast repudiating. Classlessness had become part of America's official ideology, and those who believed otherwise risked being driven from their teaching posts and rejected by publishers. Ironically, our patriotic denial of class was one of the few ideological notions we shared with the communist nations. They saw any honest talk about class as an affront to communism; Americans were likely to see it as an affront to democracy—and possibly inspired by communism.

The myth of classlessness left American sociology in a bind. It was impossible to deny the existence of inequality, which was part of the central lore of the discipline. But it was equally impossible, or unwise, to address the issue forcefully and directly. So sociology texts approached it with a sickly mixture of bad faith, muddled thinking, and outright evasion. Some books argued that classes did not exist in American society; others argued that they did exist, but only in a ghostly and ambiguous form; and still others argued that they did exist but were not such a bad thing after all. A number of texts argued all of these things at once.

One of the most common arguments was that classes had been replaced by individually held "roles." For example, in the widely cited 1965 text *Social Psychology*, Roger Brown concluded flatly that "classes are not functionally real." Why? Because the only "real social categories" are "roles," such as male and female, husband and wife, child and adult, doctor and nurse (the list may strike the feminist reader as more than a little redundant). One's occupation was a "role," so that the fact that some men are janitors and others bank presidents could be taken as reflecting nothing more than their preferences in the matter of careers.

But most introductory sociology texts from the fifties and well into the sixties were more ambivalent about the existence of classes. The 1964 text *Sociology,* by William F. Ogburn and

Meyer F. Nimkoff, introduces the notion of class in a tone that is both dogmatic and otherworldly:

> In addition to the age and sex categories in which he is placed, every individual is at birth assigned to a particular social class. By a social class we mean one of two or more broad groups of individuals who are ranked by the members of the community in socially superior or inferior positions.

This is an alarming proposition. In addition to being "placed" in a sex, male or female, everyone had been assigned a rank, superior or inferior. Why and by whom? The passive voice gives no clue, leaving the student to wonder whether the ranking was done by that same Unseen Hand that assigns people's sex. No sooner have we absorbed this vast injustice than we are reassured, in boldface, that "*in rapidly changing modern urban America*, traditional social classes are nonexistent or imperfectly developed." Turn the page, and class has sprung to life again, with the authors cataloging all the known differences between the classes ("upper, middle, and lower") of American society.

Another approach was to concede that classes may once have existed but had now been washed out in the warm solvent bath of affluence. According to Arnold W. Green's *Sociology*, "the major shift to a 'classless society' comes not with Marxist dogma but when the capitalist market is attuned to the big numbers. . . . Privilege becomes a series of minute gradations when GM offers cars for every pocketbook, cars that are similarly styled." Yet, having reduced class to a matter of the options on one's automobile, *Sociology* is seized by ambivalence and goes on to dismiss the "American myth of ideological equalitarianism." Although "there is a widespread belief in the United States that class lines are not drawn so sharply in America as in England or Europe," the text reveals that "there is no significant difference in rates of social mobility among industrial countries."

But no matter how great their ambivalence about the existence of classes—or fear, perhaps, of being seen as subscribers to a "Marxist" ideology—the sociologists were not about to abandon class as a useful way of categorizing the American population. Having fudged the existence of classes, most sociology texts moved on—without missing a beat—to describe the major classes of American society. And they did so in terms that were invariably flattering to the middle class in which sociologists themselves could claim membership.

The lower class, a category which until the end of the sixties still indiscriminately harbored everyone from drifters and marginally employed slum dwellers to blue-collar union members, was characterized by a lack of discipline and perspective. At worst, the lower-class person "sedulously avoids work, responsibility, and the consequences of tomorrow. His life is drunkenness, momentary hedonism, sexual license, violence and street scenes." In contrast, the 1957 text *Society and Culture* informs us, "The superego (conscience) tends to be stronger in the middle class," where one found "good character integration," "less delinquency and overt conflict with society," "more inhibition of impulses," and "less conscious discontent."

If the "lower class" suffered from actual want, this sad fact was rarely mentioned, unless to illustrate the sedulous avoidance of work. Green's textbook offers a full-page photo of a beggar—an old woman playing the accordion on a busy street —but reassures us with the caption: "An atypical confrontation that is by now as outmoded as a Hogarth print." In fact, it would be easy for any middle-class sociology student to conclude that the major problem of the lower-class person was stupidity. "His perspective is limited," Green tells us, "and so is his ability to understand the world around him." Furthermore, "matters of good taste and refinement, the knowledge that the most imposing piece of furniture or the flashiest automobile is not universally regarded as the best, for the most part are unknown to members of this class."

There was, of course, a radical tradition in sociology represented by Alice and Robert Lynd, among others, which understood that matters of taste were in fact matters of class preference, and that middle-class preferences were not absolute standards of aesthetic judgment. But most beginning sociology textbooks, which were all the average college student was likely to read, presented a self-contained world of middle-class judgments, tastes, and prejudices. The very characteristics of the lower class—lack of "perspective," etc.—excluded it from the sociological project of labeling, sorting, and judging the groups that make up American society. According to *Society and Culture*, members of the lower class (interchangeably called working class) were so "inarticulate" they were not even worth listening to. To engage the working-class person in conversation was to risk being seriously bored, since he was "comparatively insensitive to differences in perspective between himself and the listener, and often fails to realize that his story is neither understandable nor interesting to the other person."

Such cloddish people, one might reasonably conclude, *deserved* to be in something called the lower class. In fact, this was the hidden bias of many mid-century sociologists; that if there were classes in American society, they were there for a good reason—they were *functional*. In the dominant sociological theory of Talcott Parsons, society was like a living organism in which each part (class, sex, occupational group) contributed to the smooth and orderly functioning of the whole. Social classes were functional insofar as they guided people into roles appropriate to their ability. You could not have just anyone aspiring to be a corporate executive, a physician, or, for that matter, a sociologist. As Green explained:

> Our complex division of labor requires *some* inequality of opportunity. . . . Particularly do positions of high trust and responsibility require that training be started, literally, in infancy. It is in so-called middle and upper-class families that youngsters receive the training appropriate for the positions they will later assume.

The 1954 text *Sociology* expressed the same sentiment as a theoretical principle:

> Social organization consists of the interaction of different functional classes. The more readily recognized each class

28

is, the more readily will each class perform the functions expected of it.

In fact, in the Parsonian worldview expressed by this text-book, even sociology was functional, in that it helped people find their place in the scheme of things. Under the heading "Why Study Sociology?" we are told that "the scientific method of adjusting ourselves to the physical world"—that is, the sociological approach—shows

> *how* things happen and how we can do something about it, if anything can be done. This saves us from nervous wear and tear . . . that may result in unhappiness or even mental breakdown. In short, science [meaning sociology] can serve as a sort of mental hygiene to the individual, enabling him to come to terms with many of his problems.

## THE BLIGHT OF AFFLUENCE

In a society that appeared to have no social classes—or at least none of the sting of class injustice—there was still a reason for nervous stress, if not outright alarm. Affluence, the very condition that was credited with dissolving class distinctions, had become a looming problem in itself. On the eve of the discovery of poverty, middle-class commentators (and hardly any commentators, then as now, were not at least middle class) were beginning to see America's material affluence as a hideous, smothering weight, a pall upon the collective spirit. "The steady pressure to consume, absorb, participate, receive, by eye, ear, mouth, and mail," wrote essayist Herbert Gold, only half-jokingly, "involves a cruelty to intestines, blood pressure, and psyche unparalleled in history. We are being killed with kindness. We are being stifled with cultural and material joys."

In fact, when the War on Poverty was launched in early 1964, many intellectuals worried, not that it would fail, but that it would only lead to more of the same problem, affluence. Eric

Goldman, "intellectual adviser" to President Lyndon Johnson, polled a number of intellectuals for their views on what "general thrust" the new administration should take. Norman Podhoretz, the editor of *Commentary,* wanted a "spiritual revolution . . . in order to cope with affluence and automation." Barbara Tuchman called for a shift of emphasis from "the material to the moral." Robert Heilbroner denounced "the climate of relentless and ceaseless exhortation to eat, smoke, ride, dress, and live in the manner glorified by television advertising 'dramas.' " And Richard Rovere decried the "production, distribution and consumption of trashy things . . . trashy houses and landscapes . . . trashy education and ideas," and warned that defeating poverty might only "spread the blight of mediocrity and impoverished imaginations into the distressed areas of our country." One might almost conclude that it would be more merciful to leave the poor in their "natural" state.

Affluence was an appealing target for indignation, as Todd Gitlin has pointed out, in part because it offered a way of talking about wealth without talking about class. If the problem had been described as wealth, one would have had to specify *whose* wealth. Wealth is property, it belongs to someone. Affluence was seen as a general condition, attached to no particular persons or groups. It hung over the entire landscape like a bright, numbing haze, a kind of smog with no known source or cure. Since it had no proprietors and perpetrators, affluence could be attacked without seeming to question the priorities of a business-dominated economy. It was a politically innocuous target—and a comfortably snobbish one. "The loudest complaints about tailfins," historian Stephan Thernstrom observed, were "voiced by people whose own Spartan mode of transportation was a Porsche."

But the revulsion against affluence was by no means confined to a few well-fed intellectuals in search of a cause or, what often amounts to the same thing, a subject for an essay. By the late fifties, there were signs of widespread anxiety and discontent among the broad class of people who now had "everything"—house, cars, children, dozens of gleaming, purring appliances. White-collar men were reading (or reading about) William H. Whyte's book *The Organization Man,* and they were questioning the "rat race" and the corporate demand for conformity, right down to the drinks one ordered (martini, very dry) and suits one wore (gray flannel). Housewives, in national surveys, were beginning to complain of the tedium and isolation of life in their well-furnished, all-electric ranch homes. In suburban Pacific Palisades, where I lived as a teenager in 1959, one neighboring housewife took to hand-looming colorful wall hangings and listening to folk music. Another, who had spent much of her adult life studying cookbooks and Sears catalogs, was reading Thoreau.

The only people to clearly *act* on their revulsion against mass culture were the Beats—men, for the most part, who had dropped out of college or various undistinguished occupations to live in barren apartments and devote themselves to poetry, good fellowship, and the search for ecstatic insight. The Beats were the true radicals of the fifties, not in any conventional political sense but for the depth of their critique of America's desperate materialism. There may have been no more than a thousand genuine Beats, in a Kerouacian sense, scattered between the low-rent districts of Manhattan, San Francisco, and Los Angeles, but they fascinated Americans almost as much as if they had been a mass movement. In 1958 and 1959 they were featured in *Life, Time,* and *Playboy.* No one could miss the fact that here at last were a group of rebels who dared refuse "the general demand that they consume production and therefore have to work for the privilege of consuming, all that crap they didn't really want anyway such as refrigerators, TV sets, cars, at least fancy new cars, [everyone] imprisoned in a system of work, produce, consume, work, produce, consume."

Most middle-class Americans expressed their anxieties over affluence in a far less articulate, or even conscious, fashion: They sought to change their bodies. If affluence was a weight on the human spirit, expressed in the mass of things a suburban family now required for comfort and status, it was also manifested in the literal weight of the human body. According to historian Hillel Schwartz, the number of people who believed they were overweight and those who were actually di-

31

eting shot up rapidly in the fifties. Diet foods became big business in 1959, when Mead Johnson and Company launched the first major advertising campaign for its diet formula Metrecal. The first group diet program, TOPS (for Take Off Pounds Sensibly), had started in 1948. It was followed in 1960 with Overeaters Anonymous and in 1961 with Weight Watchers. Not everyone, especially not those who knew hunger as a daily hazard rather than as an omen of future slimness, was swept up by the diet craze. The typical dieter, then as now, was affluent and well educated. Schwartz quoted a 1962 report by Vance Packard that even men who were merely "plump" were getting "harder to find in the larger executive suites."

The ostensible reasons for dieting were of course beauty and health. At the time, no one questioned the equation between excruciating thinness and longevity or the efficacy of dieting as a way to achieve them. But dieting, as we know now from the pathological extremes of anorexia and bulimia (both of which existed in the late fifties but were not yet recognized as "diseases"), can become a compulsion detached from conscious goals. The woman, or sometimes the man, who routinely ate a half grapefruit for breakfast, cottage cheese for lunch, and a skinned chicken breast for dinner was, in some unacknowledged sense, a defiant holdout against a commercial culture that exhorted one to consume, consume, to the point of satiety and well beyond. Dieting was an exercise in control, an assertion of dignity in the face of powerful external forces. As Schwartz suggests:

> Americans of the Depression and the Cold War projected onto fat men and women their own basic fears of abundance, their own confusions about how to handle themselves in a world that seemed to offer so much and yet guaranteed so little.

The anxious middle class was obsessed with not only how much they ate but also what they ate. The early sixties was the period of maximum alarm over coronary heart disease, which was mistakenly believed to be a disease of the middle class, and especially of successful executives. Many factors were implicated—smoking, stress, lack of exercise—but the one that excited the most concern was dietary fat, especially "saturated fat." Wives were warned to reduce the saturated fat in their husbands' dinners or risk widowhood. Executive dining rooms began to feature low-calorie, low-fat lunch specials. Cooking oils were proudly advertised as "polyunsaturated." It was as if affluence had congealed into the form of a single substance, saturated fat, that is, a fat which was itself surfeited to the point of disgust. Once inside the body, saturated fat created cholesterol, the inner residue of affluence, a greasy pollution that clogged the arteries and finally starved the heart.

Anxiety about affluence intersected with other worries, such as communism. At one level, affluence seemed to be the ultimate rebuttal to the Soviets, as Nixon made clear to Nikita Khrushchev in their famous kitchen debate. *Life* frequently underscored the point with pictures of dumpy, lipstick-less Russian women sweeping streets. Forced to live without private cars, home freezers, or drip-dry clothes, the Russians appeared pathetic, practically serfs. But their very lack of consumer goods was also disquieting. It raised the suspicion that Americans had been treacherously softened by affluence, while the Russians were still strong enough to cope with deprivation on a daily basis. In 1957, Sputnik confirmed the suspicion that the Russians were striving in a disciplined, purposeful way, while Americans had been "meandering along in a stupor of fat." "Russia," Schlesinger observed sternly in 1960, "more than makes up for its smaller annual output by its harder sense of national purpose."

Nor could we expect to compete with the Russians in the realm of values. If they represented "godless materialism," America, as Schlesinger pointed out, had only substituted a "godly materialism." "With the supermarket as our temple and the singing commercial as our litany," Adlai Stevenson had warned, "are we likely to fire the world with an irresistible vision of America's exalted purposes and inspiring way of life?"

Affluence could also be blamed in part for the masculinity crisis that gripped middle-class men in the late fifties. "The consumer culture—in which leisure is a menace to be met by anxious and continual consuming—devours both the masculinity of men and the femininity of women," complained essayist Herbert Gold. He gave as examples the fact that men were buying cologne and women were buying men's shirts, but the problem went deeper than the occasional androgynous purchase. For a generation of men who had fought in World War II and worked their way up from blue-collar backgrounds, affluence was unexpectedly emasculating. Shopping and buying were women's traditional domain; and as consumption loomed larger in the life of the family, so did women. Men might earn money (although in dull white-collar jobs that were emasculating in their own way), but women determined how most of it would be spent, and it was to women that advertisers directed their pitches for the big-ticket items like houses, refrigerators, and living-room sets. In the temple of consumption which was the suburban home, women were priestesses and men mere altar boys.

But neither the masculinity crisis nor the cold war could plausibly be said to have caused the middle-class revulsion against affluence. Men would no doubt have felt themselves far more emasculated by inadequate salaries than by rising ones. And the Russians would have been all the more threatening if they had had, in addition to tanks and satellites, toaster ovens and hi-fis. Something else was happening, something that defies the usual assumptions about "economic man"—that heartless abstraction (and cornerstone of economic theory) who desires only more. It had to do with fears about what affluence would do to the affluent themselves, but it also had to do with the actual things—the cornucopia of commodities— that defined affluence in mid-century America.

## THE SOURCES OF DREAD

As they never tired of telling their children, many affluent young adults had grown up in far sterner circumstances than those they confronted in the fifties. There had been the

Depression, then the deprivations of the war years. And the backdrop for both these catastrophes was an America still relatively innocent of commercial penetration, where one could, for example, drive for hundreds of miles without being distracted by any human message more seductive than a Burma Shave sign.

Historians differ on when the consumer culture came to dominate American culture. Some say it was in the twenties, when advertising became a major industry and the middle class bought radios to hear the ads and cars to get to the stores. Some say it was in the late nineteenth century, when the first department stores appeared in American cities and a class of wealthy, idle women arose to shop in them. But there is no question that the consumer culture had begun to crowd out all other cultural possibilities by the years following World War II. The growth of the highway system promoted suburbanization; suburbanization necessitated a more expensive way of life than people had known in modest urban apartments; television told people what they needed to buy; and in the empty leisure left by equally empty work, buying itself became a way of life.

For many, the means to buy things seemed to have come a little too quickly and easily. The devastation of Germany, Japan, and the Soviet Union guaranteed American industrial preeminence and, with it, rising incomes for blue-collar union men as well as the growing army of white-collar executives and professionals. Big government helped too: building the highways that led to the suburbs, financing home purchases and, for veterans, college educations. For those who had grown up when discretionary spending meant a beer after work or an ice cream on Saturdays, the suddenness of affluence was itself unnerving. "In the late forties and the fifties, it was hard to know economic struggle and want," declared Herbert Gold, "and it was hard for the skilled and the trained not to know success."

At the same time, businessmen were consciously trying to wean Americans from the old habits of thrift and self-reliance. William H. Whyte quoted a "motivation researcher's" advice to businessmen:

We are now confronted with the problem of permitting the average American to feel moral . . . even when he is spending, even when he is not saving, even when he is taking two vacations a year and buying a second or third car. One of the basic problems of prosperity, then, is to demonstrate that the hedonistic approach to his life is a moral, not an immoral one.

Historian David M. Potter observed with some alarm that, in 1951, the amount spent on advertising was $199 per American family, compared to $152 per family for public education. "Certainly it marks a profound social change," he observed, that such vast expenditures should be directed not "to the inculcation of beliefs or attitudes [that] are held to be of social value, but rather to the stimulation or even exploitation of materialistic drives and emulative anxieties."

So it was not uncommon for Americans to express the vague feeling that they had been "suckered" into something: buying things they did not clearly need, and paying for them with jobs they did not wholly like. Moreover, the ensemble of commodities that defined a middle-class lifestyle did not exactly promise "hedonism." The washing machine, the double-door refrigerator, the matched furniture sets—these may have saved labor and enhanced status, but they were not fun. Even the car, marketed as a ticket to adventure and guarantor of sex appeal, quickly settled into its functional role, like any other appliance. Economist Albert O. Hirschman argues that consumer goods "are likely to generate a great deal of vaguely felt disappointment, particularly at the time of their first massive diffusion in a society." Durable goods are especially disappointing because they persist as reminders "that these possessions have failed to bring the hoped-for private happiness." Anyone who believed that his or her life would be qualitatively transformed by a walnut television console or wall-to-wall carpeting, as the advertisements insisted, would have to confront the failure of these objects every day. They were the dead residue of ambition, hope, effort, hardened into lame, unloving objects.

A certain malaise afflicted even the cheerleaders of consumerism—the ad men. On Madison Avenue there was worried talk about "the creative problem." Advertising had become, in the words of historian Stephen Fox, "safe and dull, without flair or distinction." A cigarette ad might show a lonely pack, with only a disembodied hand nearby to suggest their use. Appliance ads starred the appliances themselves, sometimes accompanied by a sprightly model housewife. One Admiral TV ad from the early sixties featured three stolid TV sets suspended against a black background, their gray screens staring vacantly out from the page. If there was a creative triumph in the early sixties it was the Hathaway man, his eye patch suggesting adventures unavailable to those merely wearing shirts. Part of the problem, an executive with the BBDO advertising agency suggested, was that the ad men themselves had been mellowed by the ambient affluence:

> The creative man has lost the chip on his shoulder, the fire in his eye. Success has made him courteous, obedient, cautious. . . . He has moved to the suburbs, bought a boat, which he is careful not to rock!

But it may be, too, that the ad men were simply not inspired by the erotic possibilities inherent in, say, a pack of Tareytons or a new electric range.

No group was more disappointed in the commodities that defined affluence than the intellectuals of the middle class, a group that includes all the sociologists, commentators, and generic thinkers quoted above. For one thing, they sensed uneasily that the general affluence was eroding their traditional status vis-à-vis lower-level white-collar men and even the blue-collar working class. In reality, the earning gap between professional or managerial men and blue-collar workers did not change much at all during the fifties. Yet one of the great boasts of the time was that developments like Levittown allowed a blue-collar worker to live next door to a professor—and no one, comparing their houses, lawns, or cars, would ever know the difference. This was democracy or, depending on one's point of view, the nadir of conformity.

How, in fact, could one signal a crucial status difference in a world where so many people had access to the same vast display of consumer goods? As social historian and *Harper's* editor Russell Lynes suggested in a satirical essay, you could "have rather more than the usual number of books, some drawings and probably a painting or two . . . and possibly a mobile." You might ostentatiously display the *New Yorker* on the coffee table, move the TV from the living room to the den, serve wine with meals, join the Book-of-the-Month Club. But the possibilities were limited. As the sociologists said, in a society dominated by mass-produced goods, "privilege becomes a series of minute gradations." There was not yet a broadly accessible upscale market offering special goods—custom-made furniture, distinctive brands of appliances—to consumers who wanted their possessions to make a clearer statement about their status. At mid-century, about the only statement the average middle-class family's possessions were capable of uttering was, "Me too!"—leaving those who felt somehow better also feeling sadly voiceless.

## FEMINISM AND "PROGRESSIVE DEMORALIZATION"

For thinking members of the middle class, the worst feature of affluence was not the things (often "trashy") that had become so abundant, but the effects of that abundance on the mind itself. Professional and managerial people, whose livelihoods depend on some combination of intellect and drive, feared not only the leveling effects of affluence but its possible psychological impact: One would get soft, one would cease striving, and in occupations that depended on at least the appearance of striving, softness could be fatal. In the fifties, one writer after another had warned of the dangers of affluence not only to society in general, but to the middle class in particular. "When a group is either satisfied or exhausted," warned Riesman and Glazer in 1955, "when for whatever reason it no longer makes demands, then it has lost the élan which can attract new forces."

But the harshest indictment of the effects of affluence on the middle class was a book that is seldom associated with class at all, Betty Friedan's *Feminine Mystique*. Critics within the women's movement have often dismissed Friedan's work for being limited to middle-class women. If this concentration weakened *The Feminine Mystique* as a feminist manifesto, though, it gave the book another dimension—as a class-conscious call to arms that only happens to be about women.

"All social classes," Russell Lynes observed, "are divided down the middle by a line which, however classless we may think we are, maintains a state of social tension. On one side of the line are men; on the other, women." This was somewhat less true for the blue-collar working class, where both boys and girls were trained for a life of manual (or at least fairly menial) labor. Men held jobs as craftsmen or laborers; women worked in low-level, often clerical, jobs or as housewives. Neither was expected to innovate or command the labor of others, but, rather, to test themselves against a world of objects, whether it was screws and wrenches or dirty dishes and vacuum cleaners.

Within the professional middle class, however, Lynes's barrier might have been the Berlin Wall. The young of both sexes were pushed into an educational track that was designed to lead to the professions or higher management. Increasingly, middle-class girls were even going to, and finishing, college along with the boys. But then, in adulthood, a vast divide opened up. Middle-class men became the professionals or managers they were trained to be; middle-class women for the most part became housewives—just like lower-class women.

The absence, or unpopularity, of domestic servants heightened the almost classlike difference between middle-class men and women. Since early in the century, the employment of servants had declined, in part because poor women preferred the relative freedom of factory jobs and in part because middle-class women had embraced a domestic ethic that upheld housework and childraising as labor too important, too challenging, to be left to a member of the lower classes. But no matter how vigorously promoted by the *Ladies' Home Journal*, the ideology that claimed homemaking as a kind of profession could not upgrade the actual tasks: wiping counters, folding laundry, searching for missing socks, cleaning toilets. The middle-class male spent his working day telling other people what to do (type this, move that, build this); his wife spent her working day doing the kind of tasks he would never have been aware of, in his place of work, unless the janitorial staff had been on strike. There is a reason why America produced the most vigorous feminist movement in the world: We were one of the only countries in which the middle class (which is wealthy by world standards) customarily employed its own women as domestic servants.

This arrangement was, in some ways, supremely wasteful. For one thing, it is far more expensive to maintain a wife at a middle-class standard of living than to pay an actual servant wages commensurate with her social class. The fact that so many men could afford to do so reflected the genuine affluence of the middle class at mid-century, when one (male) income still sufficed to support a family at a middling level of comfort. And, from a social perspective, to have nearly 60 percent of the nation's college-educated young women tossing aside their French lit and organic chemistry for a life of diaper-changing and counter-wiping was dangerously extravagant. Commentators on the "woman problem" were haunted by the image of Russian women applying their talents to such endeavors as "building . . . [a] huge dam and hydroelectric works at Bratsk" —a far cry from polishing an end table in Westchester. One possibility, discussed until well into the sixties, was to stop wasting higher education on girls—acknowledge that their adult occupations would be more like those of lower-class women than middle-class men, and train them accordingly.

Friedan argued, of course, that women should be admitted into the middle class on the same terms as men. If they were educated to take up the "burden of the battle with the world," let them do so. Housework could be left to actual servants who did not have educations to waste, since, in her view, it required no great intelligence and was "particularly suited to the capacities of feeble-minded girls." In Friedan's analysis, the only real economic function of the middle-class housewife was to consume. This was not a "traditional" role but a requirement of the voracious consumer culture, which demanded that one-half the adult population specialize, not in any useful profession, but in shopping. Friedan asked:

> Why is it never said that the really crucial function, the really important role that women serve as housewives is *to buy things for the house* . . . ? Somehow, somewhere, someone must have figured out that women will buy more things if they are kept in the underused, nameless-yearning, energy-to-get-rid-of state of being housewives.

The argument for pushing women into productive lives (and Friedan did not talk about "freeing" women, only putting them to work) was, first, that they were miserable. The educated housewives she surveyed were withdrawing into tranquilizer abuse, suffering from a dozen vague complaints the baffled doctors called "housewives' syndrome," and courting serious depression in middle age. But the argument did not end with women. The future of the entire middle class was at stake; and Friedan charted the "progressive demoralization" that was spreading from underemployed women to their over-protected children, who were displaying a "frightening passivity, softness, boredom," "a new vacant sleepwalking," even "muscular deterioration." How could the children of these "in-fantilized" mothers ever match the achievements of their hard-working, successful fathers?

Evidently, they could not. Friedan had gone beyond Ries-man's analysis of the "other-directed" middle-class personality into the family that was the core of middle-class life, and she found it rotting. The home, that sinkhole of consumerism, had become a "comfortable concentration camp," producing children capable only of an inmate's muffled existence. A class that was half working professionals and half domestics, half strivers and half shoppers, could not reproduce itself. Affluence, abetted by the ancient tradition of gender inequality, was reducing the middle class to a race of sleepwalkers.

41

## POVERTY DISCOVERED

The discovery of poverty took almost three years, as if a condition so far removed from the general affluence had to be verified with extreme caution. First there was John F. Kennedy's 1960 tour of Appalachia, which impressed on him that at least some Americans—sober, white ones at that—lived in rags and with uncertain prospects for the next meal. (He was not impressed enough, however, to alter his basically conservative economic philosophy.) Next came the 1962 publication of Michael Harrington's book *The Other America.* But for all its eloquence and urgency, the book sold only scantily until Dwight Macdonald reviewed it for the *New Yorker* in 1963, along with several other books and reports on poverty. *The Other America* then became a best-seller, and hundreds of thousands of members of the reading public, including President Kennedy himself, discovered poverty as a widespread condition. Finally, in his 1964 State of the Union address, President Johnson announced an "unconditional war on poverty," and poverty was at last discovered on every newsstand and television screen in America.

Poverty was, of course, the last problem that anyone searching for an issue might have expected to find. In his 1958 book *The Affluent Society,* John Kenneth Galbraith had mentioned the persistence of poverty, but he had seen it not as a "massive affliction" but "more nearly an afterthought." Even former Trotskyist Macdonald found it "difficult to believe" the evidence in *The Other America* that up to fifty million Americans were poor even by the most stringent definitions. "We seem to have suddenly awakened," he wrote, "rubbing our eyes like Rip Van Winkle," to the conditions of life experienced by as many as one-quarter of the American population.

If the poor had to be "found," how had they been "lost" in the first place? Poverty had been undeniable in the thirties and remained a vivid fact of life in the forties. But suburbanization, probably more than any other single factor, hid the poor from view. Between 1950 and 1960, in one of the largest internal migrations of the century, millions of middle-class Americans moved from cities to the suburbs. In the cities, the poor might live only blocks away, and share the same sidewalks and public spaces. But in the monochromatic world of the suburbs, where everyone was at least a homeowner, it was easy to believe there were no classes. Suburbanization nourished the solipsism of the middle class, which had looked around its new environment and concluded, shortsightedly, that it was alone in America.

The discovery of poverty was less unsettling than it might have been, thanks largely to the persistence—even in the face of poverty—of the myth of universal affluence. As every major magazine reassured its readers, "our" poor were wealthy by world standards, eager consumers like everyone else. In depressed Harlan County, *Newsweek* reported, "88 percent of the families have TV sets, 42 percent have telephones, and 59 percent own cars," while on New York's Lower East Side, "a Puerto Rican family living on relief is paying for a stereo phonograph set." *U.S. News and World Report* was so impressed by the relative wealth of America's poor that it insisted on calling their condition "poverty" (in quotation marks) while noting smugly that the poverty line in the United States ($3,000 a year for a family of four) was higher than the median family income in Russia. (The article also complained that the $3,000 income that marked the U.S. poverty line did not take into account non-cash income such as "free rent and home-produced food," yet it failed to consider the many non-cash benefits Russians received from their more generous welfare state.)

The unique and reassuring thing about American poverty, however, was that it was so imminently curable. American affluence seemed to guarantee that no matter how numerous the poor, or how needy, there would be enough to go around. In fact, as *Fortune* suggested, poverty probably wouldn't have been discovered at all if it was still an "ineradicable condition of human life" rather than "something that can be solved." Poverty seemed marginal, aberrant—as if it had only to be seen to be corrected. "Suddenly," enthused Herman Miller of the U.S. Census Bureau, "we seem to have it within our means to eliminate it completely."

*Time* even took a moment to "wonder what society might be like without the poor," as if "society" had not already gotten by quite handily for more than a decade without being aware of their existence. "Would they be missed?" the editors mused. "After all, the poor provide often beneficial political ferment and a useful troubling of the sluggish conscience." Fortunately, they concluded, the poor would always be with us in at least a relative sense, and some future president was bound to "deplore 'one-third of a nation ill-wined, ill-minked and ill-mansioned.' "

For the most part, though, America's opinion-makers felt roused to the challenge of this "painful paradox," this anomaly that had been uncovered in a world of affluence. At the very beginning of the sixties, Arthur Schlesinger, Jr., had written tremulously:

> Certainly the goal of adding to our material comforts and our leisure time has not filled our lives. Are we not beginning to yearn for something beyond ourselves? We are uncertain but expectant, dismayed but hopeful, troubled but sanguine. It is an odd and baffled moment in our history—a moment of doubt and suspense and anticipation. It is as if increasing numbers of Americans were waiting for a trumpet to sound.

Here at last was the trumpet call, a problem worthy of the smothered energies of the middle class. This was not the first time, as economist Albert O. Hirschman reminds us, that an affluent people had suddenly roused themselves from the stupor of materialism to face what appeared to be a higher challenge. The long period of peace and prosperity before World War I, he writes, left the European middle and upper classes with a "feeling of revulsion against bourgeois order, security, acquisitiveness, and pettiness. For these groups, the war came as a release from boredom and emptiness . . . and as an overdue return to heroic action and sacrifice."

The discovery of poverty gave middle-class liberalism the

grit and definition it had been seeking. The "old" New Deal liberalism of the trade unions and their working-class constituency had seemed to offer no new challenges. But with the discovery of poverty, the liberal agenda could be expanded beyond such innocuous postwar goals as "growth." Henceforth, middle-class liberalism had a mission, and a "middle-class liberal" would be defined as someone who—however vaguely or remotely—"cared about" the poor and their condition.

It was in heroic terms—soaring to mystic transport—that President Johnson's leading antipoverty official, Sargent Shriver, presented the War on Poverty to middle-class America. The "ultimate dimension" of the battle, he told Congress, was "the spiritual dimension." It was to be a "movement of conscience—a national act of expiation, of humbling and prostrating ourselves before our Creator." Sometimes, in Shriver's rhetoric, the objective problem of poverty almost got lost in the uplifting challenge of ending it. A man from a comfortable background who had married into the plutocratic Kennedy family, Shriver had no personal experience of the problem he was assigned to eliminate, and had once confided to an aide, "I just can't hold on to money. I just can't think of it as having any real value."

Perhaps because he was so indifferent to the one factor that clearly distinguishes the poor from everyone else, he was the perfect person to pitch the War on Poverty to the middle class. The "real test," he announced to an audience at Georgetown University, would not simply be what the War on Poverty did for the poor but whether it provided "interaction, dedication and fulfillment" to the nonpoor majority. It was this "interaction," he promised, that would "transmute" the slums and "give us all a new wealth of spirit that dwarfs even our national affluence."

There was very little that most middle-class people could actually do to advance the war against poverty—especially since no one was proposing the perfect "act of expiation," which would have been for the more fortunate to share some of their wealth with the underprivileged. Yet the discovery of poverty produced a bracing sense that at least there was something to do, something worthy of energy and commitment. College students in particular were invited to "commit themselves" to waging the War on Poverty by volunteering to go into the slums to tutor children, organize sports programs, or help out in community organizations and settlement houses. Thousands of them did, and even those who did not gained a new standard for the value of human effort: Whatever one did should be "relevant," meaning, above all, relevant to the lives of the poor and excluded. For my own generation of students, coming of age in the early sixties, the poor may have been a remote backdrop to our studies, but their presence passed a silent judgment on our lives: Would we find a way to use our skills on their behalf, or would we merely repeat the evidently futile, self-absorbed existence of our parents' generation?

Still, it was reasonable to ask, as a few voices in the media did at the time, why poverty? There were other problems, such as the bomb or pollution or racial segregation, all of which were beginning to inspire genuine movements. And however appalling the current statistics, poverty had actually been declining since the forties. Certainly, the poor as a group—and as a group the poor are an extremely diverse lot—had done nothing to signal their own existence.

The legendary explanation, and one that is still favored by many today, is that the focus on poverty grew out of Michael Harrington's book *The Other America*. The book fell into the hands of an intellectual young president, and the idea took hold in the nation left grieving by Kennedy's assassination. Now, the importance of Harrington's book cannot be underestimated. Engagingly written and passionately argued, it was, for many middle-class readers, the first glimpse of a world outside their own. But from a middle-class point of view, the legendary explanation is also an intensely self-serving one: a view of history in which there are no actors other than a handful of educated men, and no actions more significant than the publication, or reviewing, of their books.

In fact, by 1960 there was plenty of action on the American scene. The civil rights movement, which had seemed so peripheral to intellectuals in search of a problem, was mobilizing black Americans in an acute challenge to white supremacy. Here were people who had not been passively selected by news photographers, like the exemplars of poverty featured in magazine stories, but who were actively forcing themselves on the national conscience: challenging segregation on buses and at lunch counters, organizing boycotts and picket lines, and, by 1961 and 1962, attacking employment and housing discrimination in the North. Many were poor people by any standard. They were also intelligent, courageous, and inspired. If there had been no civil rights movement there would have been no discovery of poverty, or at least not much more than a ripple of intellectual concern. The movement dramatized poverty for white, middle-class Americans; and the War on Poverty was, above all, their response to this movement.

It was, at best, an oblique response. After all, the poor were, as they are now, mostly white; and the civil rights movement did not represent only the poor. Poverty may ultimately be a more challenging problem than racial injustice, as Martin Luther King, Jr., for one, was eventually to conclude; but in the early sixties it did not seem so. The focus on poverty was a way, almost, of changing the subject. Kennedy had been notoriously disappointing on civil rights. He had beaten Nixon by only a hair, and could not afford to offend the segregationists in the Democratic Party. Yet, as the movement grew, he could not afford to keep brushing off the civil rights leaders, who increasingly were gaining the power to sway black (and white liberal) voters. The focus on poverty, Frances Fox Piven and Richard Cloward have argued, was Kennedy's way out, allowing him "to evade civil rights demands while maintaining black support."

In the media, the contrast was striking: The black insurgency was vivid and real; "the poor," as a category, had been assembled by a magazine editor. Consider the representatives of poverty gathered together by *Newsweek* under a reminder that "the impoverished are people too." Here was a retired white couple scraping along on Social Security, a single mother of six in Spanish Harlem, a destitute black family in rural Georgia ("when de wages went up, de mills just shet down," in *Newsweek*'s irritating rendition), a laid-off warehouse worker in Detroit, a hobo on Los Angeles's skid row, and a slightly retarded, almost certainly unemployable young man from Des Moines. All of these people were indeed poor, and perhaps had the potential for coming together as a political constituency with common demands, but at the time they were "discovered" they had little more in common than a shortage of assets and their shared space in the pages of a national magazine.

Perhaps, ultimately, the poor were less threatening to white, middle-class sensibilities than the swelling black movement. Black pride was in the air, but poverty was not an identity anyone proudly claimed. As Sargent Shriver admitted, it was hard to get the poor involved in their own uplift:

> If you just enlist a person and put him or her on the committee and say, "You are the poor representative". . . what do they do? They get off the committee. Why? Obviously, they don't want to be labeled as poor.

## INFANTILIZING THE POOR

Yet the very diversity that made the poor such a politically vacuous category was the first thing poverty experts forgot when they attempted to characterize the poor. The result was that the middle-class conception of the poor bore little resemblance to any actual group of people—certainly not the insurgent black poor, and not even the sad collections of case studies lumped together by the newsmagazines. The invented poor were a reflection of middle-class needs and a projection of middle-class anxieties. They were, first of all, "others," aliens inhabiting a world of their own that might as well have lain outside the national boundaries. Michael Harrington, who was certainly one of the most committed advocates of the poor, set the tone when he wrote:

48

There is, in short, a language of the poor, a psychology of the poor, a world view of the poor. To be impoverished is to be an internal alien, to grow up in a culture that is radically different from the one that dominates society.

That culture was the "culture of poverty," and no matter how diverse the actual poor might be—senior citizens, share-croppers, bohemians, laid-off blue-collar workers—most middle-class poverty experts believed they were all citizens of a single invisible nation, the culture of poverty.

In fact, the poor are not even a class in any meaningful sense. Poverty is a condition shared by people who come from many different starting points. For many it is a temporary condition, set to rights when a plant starts rehiring, a sickness passes, or a spouse returns. A University of Michigan study completed in the eighties found that, in the ten-year period of the study, one out of four Americans experienced poverty severe enough to qualify them for welfare. Others, of course, remain in poverty for life, working intermittently—or steadily—at low-wage jobs. Strictly speaking, the great majority of the poor are members of what we usually call the working class—its least fortunate members, among whom blacks, Hispanics, and women of all races are disproportionately represented.

The notion of a distinct culture of poverty was in part simply an extension of the prejudices against the lower classes that could be found in any sociology text. The phrase came from anthropologist Oscar Lewis's 1959 study of impoverished Mexican families, which he found lacking in drive, depressed, and apathetic. As he defined it, the culture of poverty was a mind-set characterized by feelings of "fatalism, helplessness, dependence and inferiority." Or, in psychiatric terms,

a high incidence of weak ego structure, orality and confusion of sexual identification, all reflecting maternal deprivation; a strong present-time orientation with relatively little disposition to defer gratification and plan for the future, with a high tolerance for psychopathology of all kinds.

Lewis thought of this as a "technical" definition which probably applied to no more than 20 percent of the poor, and was somewhat chagrined to find that by 1965 the culture of poverty had become coterminous with poverty itself.

The idea that the poor were victims of some shared character defect seemed to be supported by a number of studies in the late fifties and early sixties that found more actual, diagnosable mental illness among the poor than among the more comfortable classes. As psychiatrist Robert Coles observed glumly, "Those pockets of poverty whose existence is increasingly acknowledged are also pockets of many kinds of psychopathology, mostly untreated."

But the studies did not find that all the poor were mentally ill, or that all the poor who were mentally ill suffered from the same syndrome. The poor had a variety of mental disorders, as did the middle class, only the poor had more, just as they had more, and more serious, physical ailments. One reason is that people who become ill, physically or mentally, tend also to lose their jobs and become poor. The other, numerically more significant, explanation is that poverty is unbearably stressful: To live in poverty is to live with constant uncertainty, to accept galling indignities, and to expect harassment by the police, welfare officials, and employers, as well as by others who are poor and desperate.

Yet in the theorizing that accompanied the discovery of poverty, the causality was often reversed: The poor lacked money because they suffered from a collective disorder which had been identified as the "culture of poverty." In fact, it was hard for the antipoverty experts to know what to deal with first, poverty or its culture, an economic condition or a mental illness.

The peculiar psychopathology, or "culture," of the poor was (and still is) thought to be defined by two related traits: "present-time orientation" and an insufficiently developed "deferred gratification pattern" (or "DGP," as some sociologists put it handily). In simpler words, the poor person lived for the moment, unable to think ahead, to save or plan for the future. These were the very opposite of the traits the middle class liked to ascribe to itself—self-discipline, a strong super-ego, an ability to plan ahead to meet self-imposed goals, and so forth. From a middle-class point of view, the culture of poverty even had a certain kind of charm. "Living in the present," Oscar Lewis observed, one "may develop a capacity for spontaneity, for the enjoyment of the sensual, which is often blunted in middle-class, future-oriented man."

Leaving aside the psychiatric jargon, a person who lives entirely in the present, unable to wait for the next anticipated pleasure, is, of course, a child. The conceit of the poor as children has an ancient, aristocratic lineage. In mid-century America, it was bolstered by the perception of poverty as a vestigial condition, something "left over" that did not really belong in the affluent, modern world. Mass poverty seemed to belong in the historical past; along with the Depression, sweatshops, dirt farms, labor struggles. And what belongs in the historical past is easy to confuse with the personal past—which is, for all of us, childhood. The invented poor, the inhabitants of the culture of poverty, were not so much "present-oriented" as trapped in the past, unable or unwilling to "grow up," as the middle class had, into the ever-available, up-to-date affluence.

The poor person as half child, half psychopath, was of course related to the familiar figure of the juvenile delinquent, and it was not entirely an accident that Washington's War on Poverty evolved out of an earlier project to abolish delinquency. Before there was poverty, there had been only juvenile delinquency to stand as a faint reminder of class inequality, and much of what was known about the "psychopathology" of poverty had come from the study of juvenile delinquents. As a category in which to place society's outsiders, poverty was an improvement because it did not imply delinquency—only psychic immaturity.

But the invented poor were not only children. They had come to represent what the middle class feared most in itself: softening of character, a lack of firm internal values. Two contemporary critics of the "culture of poverty" notion, S. M. Miller and Frank Riessman, pointed out that the self-image the middle-class derived from its reflections on the poor was unduly flattering to the middle class and probably out of date. In contrast to the poor, they wrote, the middle class liked to characterize itself as "delighting in hard work . . . abjuring debt, and constantly forgoing the indulgence of present gain in order to reap future rewards." But these were exactly the traits the middle class feared it was losing and—from the point of view of the purveyors of consumer goods—could not lose fast enough. As Miller and Riessman observed, "It is hard to recognize this 'Protestant Ethic' pattern in the new middle classes possessed by 'other-direction' and pursuing the consumption euphoria of today."

What the middle class saw in the poor—or, more accurately, projected onto the poor—was the dreaded effects of affluence on the middle class. The poor did not participate in affluence themselves, but, strangely, they came to represent its worst effects on the human character. What kind of personality developed in the culture of poverty if not that of the ideal consumer? Historian Donald Meyer has described the consumer personality as it emerged in the early twentieth century as "passive,"

> weaned from saving and hoarding so that he [the consumer] might spend, weaned from piling up possessions in order to expedite planned obsolescence, weaned from ascetic discipline so that he might respond to every innovation, weaned from work-identities so that he might have the time for consumption.

The ideal consumer, like the denizen of the culture of poverty, is hedonistic, impulsive, self-indulgent. Nothing could better serve the consumer-goods industries than for everyone to abandon their "capacity for deferred gratification" and become as suggestible and addicted to sensation as the poor were said to be. These were the traits that marketing men hoped to inculcate in all Americans, and especially those who had money to spend. And they were the same traits, more or less, that intellectuals such as David Riesman and Betty Friedan found spreading throughout the middle class. With the discov-

52

ery of poverty, the threat could be externalized: Someone else had succumbed to the softening effects of the consumer culture, someone so alien, so aberrant, as to dwell outside of affluence itself.

The experts and policy-makers who promoted the notion of the culture of poverty had generous enough intentions. They simply wanted to underscore the psychic damage inflicted by poverty. Poverty *is* damaging, but the picture they ended up painting of the poor lent itself readily to reactionary interpretations. If the poor were at best permanent children, moving from one easy gratification to the next, they were at worst a criminal menace, lacking any of the inhibitions required for civilized existence. One could easily conclude, as the *New Republic* did in a 1964 editorial, that the goal was not so much to eliminate poverty as to eliminate the poor:

> The poor have become in our affluent society a sealed-off community with its own crippled values, liable to erupt into crime and psychopathic violence. They form pockets of misery in city slums throughout the land as well as in remote rural areas, and they have to go if society is not to be poisoned.

Whatever happened, one might wonder, to the abstemious pensioners, the sad-eyed children, the laid-off blue-collar workers, who had appeared in every major cover story on poverty? Fortunately for them, the *New Republic* hoped to get rid of the poor nonviolently, by absorbing them "back into society as human beings."

In one form or another, this became the predominant conservative interpretation of the discovery of poverty: It was not poverty that had to be cured, only the culture of poverty. Before the poor could be made affluent, they had to be made "human beings." Many examples could be given, but perhaps the first fully developed brief against the poor themselves was Harvard urbanologist Edward C. Banfield's 1968 book, *The Unheavenly City*. It is interesting not only as a remarkably unselfconscious expression of middle-class prejudice but also as a forerunner of what would come to be, by the 1980s, mainstream views on poverty and how to cure it. In quick, vivid strokes, he summarized the culture of poverty:

> The lower-class individual lives from moment to moment. . . . Impulse governs his behavior. . . . He is therefore radically improvident: whatever he cannot consume immediately he considers valueless. His bodily needs (especially for sex) and his taste for "action" take precedence over everything else. . . . [He] has a feeble, attenuated sense of self.

If this is the lower class, it hardly needs to be said that the vantage point of the author is that of a "higher" class, but he says it anyway: "In the chapters that follow, the term *normal* will be used to refer to class culture that is not lower-class."

The problem, then, is to make the lower class more normal —that is, not less poor but less present-oriented. Poverty itself is not an issue, since "the lower-class forms of all problems are at bottom a single problem: the existence of an outlook and style of life which [are] radically present-oriented." After dismissing the possibility that the lower class will simply die off ("Improvements in public sanitation and in medical and hospital care . . . keep many lower-class people alive, often in spite of themselves"), Banfield considers a number of possible solutions to "present-orientedness." Psychotherapy must be rejected because the poor are too inarticulate to benefit from it. Besides, "there are not nearly enough therapists to treat the insane, let alone the present-oriented." Another possibility is that lower-class children could be taken away from their parents "at a very early age and brought up by people whose culture is normal." "As a matter of logic," the simplest way to accomplish this "would be to permit the sale of infants and children to qualified bidders both private and public." Unfortunately, there are problems with this approach too, not least of which is that—unless threatened with sterilization—the poor might overcome their present-orientedness enough to start bearing babies for profit.

Finally there is the possibility of institutionalization, at least for the "hardest cases":

Such persons could be cared for in what might be called semi-institutions [where] . . . they might agree to receive most of their income in kind rather than in cash, to forgo ownership of automobiles, to have no more than two or three children, and to accept a certain amount of surveillance and supervision from a semi-social-worker–semi-policeman.

But alas, even this relatively restrained approach must be rejected, since " 'being lower class' is not a crime or committable condition and is not at all likely to be made one." Banfield was left with a few pallid but, he hoped, more feasible proposals, such as tighter law enforcement, more aggressive population control, and a lower minimum wage. (This last is a perennial conservative favorite. If wages could be lowered, the argument goes, employers would create more jobs. Of course, low-paid jobs do not lift people out of poverty.)

Views like Banfield's would not dominate public policy until the eighties. But even in what we now think of as the liberal sixties, the notion that the poor were alien members of a "culture of poverty" had a profound effect on how middle-class people viewed the poor and plotted solutions to their distress. Some antipoverty warriors saw the culture of poverty as an excuse for a middle-class-dominated, technocratic approach to ending poverty: If the poor were so shiftless and disorganized, they could not be expected to help themselves. As Shriver noted in one of his more down-to-earth moments, the War on Poverty could be thought of as "a set of production goals, a series of specific target goals and production quotas." In such an effort, the poor themselves could expect to figure chiefly as numbers in the federal ledger, not as leaders.

Others, however, used the culture of poverty to argue for a more activist and populist approach: If the poor were so deeply damaged by their condition, they needed government encouragement to organize their communities and stand up for themselves, almost as a kind of collective therapy. Either way, the middle-class view of the poor guaranteed that, whatever else they got—multiservice centers, area-redevelopment programs, community-action projects—they would not get money. In fact, the one clear policy implication of the "culture of poverty" was that the poor could not be trusted with money. And as the view of people who had money—enough in fact to have been disturbed by affluence—there could hardly have been a more brazen defense of the status quo.

Thus the middle class discovered it was not alone. There were "others" in America, people who were unfortunate, downtrodden, needing help. But it was the further misfortune of the poor to be discovered by a middle class that was tormented by the prospect of its own decline. In all the debate and discussion that surrounded the beginning of the War on Poverty—and later, in the endless evaluations of it—the poor had no voice. In fact, their principal virtue, as opposed to the black insurgency, was that they were so agreeably silent. The poor—the invented poor—came to serve as a mirror for the middle class, reflecting its own dread submission to the imperatives of consumption, the tyranny of affluence. More than that, the poor became the scapegoats for an affluence they alone were fully excluded from and fully innocent of. And so they have remained, even though, as we shall see next, the middle class soon found its worst fears realized—in its own children.

## CHAPTER TWO

# THE MIDDLE CLASS
# ON THE DEFENSIVE

THE MIDDLE-CLASS INTELLECTUALS who hoped the sixties would provide some challenge worthy of their talents had not expected literal danger. Yet by the middle of the decade many of them came to feel that their jobs, and possibly even their professions, were about to be lost, blown away in a violent, unforeseen cataclysm. An account by Diana Trilling, writer and wife of the famous Columbia University professor Lionel Trilling, conveys the terror felt by many of her age and station: In the spring of 1968, she experienced something so harrowing that she could only compare it to a hurricane she had once witnessed on the Connecticut shore:

> Sleep was impossible for everyone in the vicinity—the most decorous of us had no hesitation in phoning each other at whatever hour of the night, two o'clock, four o'clock, when the lonely waiting got to be more than we could bear.

Trilling described the vicinity in question—the Columbia campus and its environs—as "a constantly shrinking white island," and no one could sleep because they were lying awake listening for "the tramp or rush or scuffle of invasion."

The danger arose from the student rebellion at Columbia, which was terrifying enough to Trilling and her beleaguered comrades but also suggested the "potential horror" of an uprising in nearby Harlem. Already the students had demonstrated what Trilling saw as a "capacity for hatred and violence," reportedly shouting at an old couple crossing the campus, "Go home and die, you old people!" and gratuitously punching a law professor in the stomach. Worse, the student rebels routinely used words calculated to distress the decorous, like *bullshit* and *motherfucker*. For Trilling, Columbia had become a war zone:

> A faculty wife became short-order chef at any hour of the day or night for her husband and his exhausted colleagues, working without rest to protect, not the abstract idea of a university . . . but the living University which must be sustained against a saner day.

For a significant number of America's best-known intellectuals, the student uprising was ultimately a more grievous threat than the black insurgency because it struck so close to home. The university is, after all, the core institution of the professional middle class—employer of its intellectual elite and producer of the next generation of middle-class, professional personnel. Attack the university and you attack the heart —and surely the womb—of the class itself.

In response to this unprecedented threat, erstwhile liberals like Trilling began to think of their place in American society in a new way. Once, they had seen themselves as part of a universal middle class, set off only by the superior education and "good taste" that entitled them to mild reservations about affluence and mass culture. The discovery of poverty had shown that the middle class was not universal, that America was not yet perfect. But this discovery had in no way dampened the confidence of middle-class liberals that poverty could be eliminated, at no apparent cost to anyone; and middle-class people—activists and intellectuals—would lead the way.

The student movement prompted a grim reassessment. Middle-class intellectuals, many of them liberal on matters of race and poverty, began to think of themselves as part of a social group that might indeed have something to lose if others were to gain. Looking at the student movement, they foresaw cherished institutions in flames, and beyond that the threat of a radically egalitarian future in which education and intellect would be valued no more than, say, the skills of a mechanic or the insights of the downtrodden. They began to think of themselves, however dimly, as members not of a formless, all-inclusive middle class but of an *elite*. And a self-conscious elite, no matter how inclined to noblesse oblige, has a stake in maintaining the inequalities that define the status quo.

Worse still, the student movement seemed to signal the moral failure of the middle class. It was not the young who had failed, for the young are seldom taken seriously as moral agents for either good or evil, but the adults—parents, professors, and professionals generally—who represent authority. Whatever else the student rebellion meant, it meant that this authority had failed. In the eyes of the student rebels, adult authority had failed because it was discredited by its complicity in war and domestic injustice. But in the eyes of many intellectuals, middle-class adults had simply grown too lax, too soft, or—in the word that came to dominate the middle-class reassessment —too *permissive*.

An elite can still be liberal in its attitudes toward those who are less favored. But an elite that feels beleaguered and, beyond that, doubts the firmness of its own will is not likely to remain liberal for long. We think of the sixties as the high-water mark of middle-class liberalism. But they were also, for an influential minority, the point of departure for a much harsher, more cynical and self-interested view of the world.

## THE THREAT OF THE LEFT

Trilling's anxiety aside, the only people in danger on Manhattan's Upper West Side in April 1968 were the approximately one thousand students who occupied the campus to protest Columbia's involvement in military research and its arrogant behavior toward the neighboring community of Harlem. They were, for the most part, children of the affluent, idealists who took seriously their parents' concerns about poverty and racial injustice. Their movement—our movement, for I was a part of it—began at Berkeley in 1963 when the university administration barred civil rights organizations from soliciting funds on campus. Actions like that revealed the limits of liberalism, while the war in Vietnam seemed to reveal its violent excesses. By 1968, tens of thousands of students had marched, petitioned, organized, sat in, taught in, and demonstrated against the draft, against racism, and above all against the war. They took their protests to the Pentagon and the White House, and they brought them home to the universities where they lived and studied. Few universities were as arguably complicit in militarism and racism as Columbia, but by 1968, almost every university seemed to represent the moral failure of the adult "establishment": its commitment to America's imperialist mission in the world, its tolerance of racial intolerance, its elitist "irrelevance" to the oppressed and excluded.

For their efforts, the student occupiers at Columbia were hauled out of the occupied buildings and beaten with appalling viciousness by the New York City police, who had been summoned by the Columbia administration. The bust produced one of the most striking photographic images of the movement: a sweet-faced, blond young man making the peace sign with one hand while blood streams down his face. The other great photographic icon of the student movement is from Kent State in 1970: a stunned girl crouching over the body of a friend, shot dead by the National Guard. I mention these dramatic images only because so many accounts have located the violence on the protesters' side. Trilling, for example, had scant sympathy for the hundreds of students who were beaten bloody, but reported plaintively:

The personal, moral, and intellectual offense suffered by the Columbia faculty in the uprising was indeed momentous. It is to be thought of only with pain. . . . There were emotional breakdowns among the faculty due to the uprising, and several car accidents attributed to exhaustion.

The story of the student left has been well told elsewhere, and here I would only mention that, contrary to the views of its critics, the movement was not all dramatic confrontations and spontaneous defiance. For every media-worthy protest there were hundreds of hours of patient organizing—talking, reasoning, persuading others to join in. The uprising at Columbia, for example, came about after years of more courteous attempts to influence the university administration. And for every project that culminated in a media-worthy protest there were scores of projects with quieter goals, such as winning much-needed services for poor communities.

But this movement was unlike anything its critics might have remembered from their own student days in the thirties or forties. There had been a sizable student left then, but it limited its concerns to conventional left-wing issues: support for the Spanish Loyalists, for racial integration, for radical economic measures to alleviate unemployment. It produced no "generation gap," no attack on academia, no cultural shocks or outrages to middle-class decorum.

In contrast, the student movement of the sixties rode along on a huge, anarchic current of rebellion that had no precise analogue in American history. The counterculture, as it came to be called, was a youth rebellion for the sake of youth, an upsurge that was not so much apolitical as opposed to all conventional versions of politics, with their hierarchies, deals, formalistic procedures. To join the counterculture one had only to drop out (actually or in spirit) and pursue one's chosen path to liberation, which might be through drugs, sex, spirituality, communal living, subsistence farming, music, or any combination of these possibilities. A student left was at least comprehensible, but everything about the counterculture—the easy nudity, the drugs, the disdain for careers, the casual approach to dress and personal hygiene—was an affront to middle-class values.

Yet the counterculture was also a continuation and logical climax of the distinctly middle-class critique of affluence. The staid critics of mass commercial culture had found it squalid and deadening, yet they saw no way out, except possibly through a gradual upgrading of popular tastes: classical music, perhaps more Modigliani on living-room walls and *Masterpiece Theatre* on public television. Hippies and other counterculture types went much further. They rejected the consumer culture, not because it was mindless and enervating but because it was not even pleasurable. It promised only the cramped hedonism of what Herbert Marcuse called "repressive desublimation" (as in, "buy this and feel sexier, freer, etc."). And the price of even that small pleasure was years of numb obedience at school or work. As left leader and countercultural exemplar Jerry Rubin wrote:

> Dad looked at his house and car and manicured lawn, and he was proud. All of his material possessions justified his life.
> He tried to teach his kids: he told us not to do anything that would lead us from the path of Success.
> work don't play
> study don't loaf
> obey don't ask questions
> fit in don't stand out
> be sober don't take drugs
> make money don't make waves
> We were conditioned in self-denial:
> We were taught that fucking was bad because it was immoral . . . We were warned that masturbation caused insanity and pimples.
> And we were confused. We didn't dig why we needed to work toward owning bigger houses? bigger cars? bigger manicured lawns?
> We went crazy. We couldn't hold it back anymore.

The student left and the counterculture were not the same thing, although few adult critics bothered to make the distinction. On what might be called the hard left, plenty of white students, as well as groups like the Black Panthers, disdained what they saw as the frivolity of the counterculture.

And in the counterculture there were plenty of self-absorbed souls who regarded any effort to change the world (as opposed to one's own perceptions) as a "bummer." Yet as historian Winni Breines writes, the overlap was vast and important:

> In the period until 1968 there was great continuity between the hippie and political wings of the movement. Student demonstrations, occupations, and other rebellions against the university and federal government, as well as life style changes embodied in the counter-culture, were groping attempts to create a more meaningful, free and moral existence. The student movement was anti-war and anti-authoritarian as well, an expression of "rejection and revolt," a search for a democratic community.

In the intersection of the left and the counterculture, a new kind of political ideology emerged. It was definitely of the left, in its hatred of corporate power and the military-industrial complex, but too wary of government to be socialist. It was altruistic in its commitment to the downtrodden, but too invested in a vision of personal liberation to be dour and self-sacrificing. It was egalitarian, but in a way that went far beyond the reach of law or Supreme Court rulings—demanding and envisioning nothing less than the abolition of all hierarchy—whites over blacks, teachers over students, parents over children, and (by the late sixties) men over women. It was, of course, utopian, contemptuous of mere reform, and committed to a startling, total transformation that would bring human social arrangements into line with human needs and desires.

The same themes were echoed in the antiauthoritarianism of the German student left, the leveling spirit of the Chinese Red Guards, and the anarchic ebullience of the French student movement, which demanded no less than "All Power to the Imagination!" At the most general level, the worldwide student movement of the sixties represented the aspirations of the first generation to come of age after a half century of world war, genocide, and global depression: to put aside the gloom of history and live, at last, in full freedom and genuine equality.

## THE INTELLECTUAL BACKLASH

Our concern here is with a somewhat more inglorious side of the sixties: the intellectuals' backlash against the student left. *Backlash* is a word usually associated with hard-hats and rednecks, but it was the intellectual leadership of the middle class that first rejected, and reacted against, the student movement. Throughout the sixties, hundreds, perhaps thousands, of professors suffered the kind of terror—or more accurately, hurt feelings—experienced by the Trillings and their circle of friends in New York. Some of them had had unpleasant encounters with the student left: They had been shouted down in their classrooms, insulted (though probably not "punched in the stomach," even at Columbia), and, in far more cases, simply ignored. Others no doubt resented having their role as genteel social critics preempted so suddenly, and by a movement that never bothered to be genteel. Most of them depended for their livelihoods on the universities that now seemed to be teetering toward anarchy. As Trilling wrote, "Touch a university with hostile hands and the blood you draw is prompt, copious, and real."

There were, of course, exceptions: well-known professors and intellectuals who supported and even inspired the student left, just as there were many more who simply held their breath and waited for it to go away. But even those intellectuals who did not depend directly on the university for their income and prestige had reason to fear this new left that respected no hierarchies, not even those based on "objective knowledge" and expertise. To all of them, professors and pundits, the student movement demanded, in so many words (and sometimes in these very words): Why should we listen to you? What do you know about American society compared to a black woman on welfare, a Southern sharecropper, or, for that matter, a Vietnamese peasant whose village has just been devastated by American firepower? What is your vaunted objectivity but a mask for privilege, your expertise but an excuse for power?

The breadth and fury of the backlash were startling. Psychiatrist Bruno Bettelheim likened the student rebels to Nazis. Then-liberal professor John Silber (later the conservative president of Boston University) called them "the new Fascisti." Nathan Glazer compared them not only to Hitler but to Lenin and Stalin. Daniel Bell described the students at Columbia as "impelled not to innovation, but to destruction." Irving Kristol, not yet a conservative, called them "rebels without a cause—and without a hope of accomplishing anything except mischief and ruin."

Nor did the howls of outrage come only from the liberal center of the political spectrum. Marxist Eugene Genovese attacked the "nihilist perversions" of the student left. Socialist Irving Howe dismissed the student movement as "romantic primitivism," motivated by a "quasi-religious impulse." Philosopher and former Marxist Sidney Hook organized faculty members on ninety-seven campuses into a Coordinating Center for Democratic Opinion, to combat the student insurgency. And leftist William Appleman Williams, whose critiques of U.S. foreign policy were deeply influential within the New Left, had this to say of the movement that included so many of his young fans: "They are the most selfish people I know. They just terrify me. They are acting out a society I'd like to live in as an orangutan."

What had gone wrong? As recently as 1960, the major complaint about American students was that they were too stupid, too besotted with affluence, to play any worthwhile role in life, such as taking up their fathers' occupations. Now, a half-dozen years later, they seemed to have become revolutionary zealots, bent on destroying the very institutions that nurtured them. The least that intellectuals can do is to explain things, and the very least is to explain things to themselves. So, while the student movement spread and grew, its elders brooded, analyzed, and scolded in prolix dismay.

All speculations on the sources of the rebellion had this in common: They completely discounted the explanations the radicals themselves gave, readily enough and in innumerable forums. To the theorists of the backlash, the substance of the students' protests was as irrelevant as, say, the stated object of a three-year-old's tantrum. For example, in his testimony to Congress on student unrest, Bettelheim drew parallels between contemporary American students and Nazi students in Germany, only to admit midway that "of course, the German student rebels embraced politically the extreme right, while here they are of the extreme left." And, of course, the German students were also racists, "while here the radical students intend to help a discriminated [sic] minority." But these "differences" were quickly brushed aside as Bettelheim continued to develop his morbid parallels. The same thing happened when other intellectuals took up their pens against the student left. They departed from America as it was in the mid-sixties—with its persistent racial inequality, its vicious and indefensible war in Southeast Asia—and entered a timeless world of psychological generalizations and mythic archetypes.

There were two basic theories of the student rebellion, neither of them flattering to the rebels. One, the generational-conflict theory, posited some unconscious drive to overthrow "the father" as represented, for example, by professors and university administrators. The other theory, and the one that eventually won out, traced the student rebellion to the corrupting power of affluence, which now took the more personalized, almost palpable, form of "permissiveness." According to this line of reasoning, the students were simply engaging in the kind of behavior to be expected of spoiled children anywhere.

The two theories contained rather opposite images of the student radicals: In the generational-conflict account, they were deluded but potent warriors against patriarchy, like the members of Freud's parricidal "primal horde." In the permissiveness theory, they were squalling, ineffectual infants. But this obvious discordance did not prevent the two theories from being seen as complementary views of the same reality. Nor did the lack of supporting evidence—and the presence of much contradictory evidence—deter the proponents of either view.

The fullest account of the generational-conflict theory came from sociologist Lewis Feuer, who was well positioned to attack the student left by virtue of his prior studies of student movements elsewhere and in the past. Something of his bias is revealed in a 1964 paper that described, as he later put it, "the traits of elitism, suicidalism, populism, filiarchy, and juvenocracy which one found in all student movements." In Feuer's account, student rebels had no conscious understanding of what they were up to. They were driven by a primal, Oedipal urge to destroy "the father." But since their actual fathers were not around, or were not inspiring targets, they turned on the university instead. In their deluded rage, the students came to see the faculty and administration as "the Cruel, Heartless, Impersonal Father who aimed to destroy his sons." And since this was only a substitute, the students were bound to rage on without ever achieving satisfaction: "Their fruitless rebellions never reached to the unconscious cause within themselves, the inner, inaccessible Being who tyrannized over and emasculated them."

For an argument advanced in the interests of "rationality," Feuer's was remarkably uninhibited by logic. There is nothing wrong with finding a pattern in student revolts at different historical times and places, but, for Feuer, the pattern became the explanation for, and even the cause of, student behavior. Thus he found that what he called "the hallucinogenic phase" of the American student movement was "rooted" not in the specific circumstances of the sixties but in "the self-destructive ingredient characteristic of [all] such movements." Nor is there anything wrong with advancing a psychological theory for political behavior, so long as you are willing to make occasional concessions to facts. One small but obstinate detail was that Berkeley student leader Mario Savio, whom Feuer singled out for individual analysis, was extremely close to his own actual father. But Feuer nimbly explains that this "apparent family equilibrium" was possible only because Savio and his comrades had deflected their Oedipal rage toward the university, thus sparing their biological fathers. It is hard to refute such ingenious logic, and when students at Berkeley scoffed at Feuer's theories, he only took this as further confirmation, observing smugly, "Their indignation had all the earmarks of the 'resistance' phenomenon [in psychoanalysis]."

## "PERMISSIVENESS" ENTERS POLITICS

The permissiveness theory was launched, or at least introduced to the mass media, by a man quite sympathetic to the student movement and, in fact, not much older than most of its participants. In a March 1968 issue of the *New York Times Magazine,* Christopher Jencks argued that the student rebellion was symptomatic of a deeper tension in American society: Middle-class children were raised to ask questions and think for themselves, yet most of the institutions of adult society rewarded conformity and obedience over innovation and independence. Nowhere did he suggest that permissiveness in childraising was a bad thing, or that the student movement was a symptom of psychological impairment; in fact, he thought that the man most commonly associated with permissive childraising, Dr. Benjamin Spock, had done "for the young what the Wagner Act had done a few years earlier for the labor movement." If anything needed changing, it was the bureaucratic institutions, not the children. Yet the *Times* titled the article "Is It All Dr. Spock's Fault?" and would have preferred, if Jencks had not objected, to title it more affirmatively "It's All Dr. Spock's Fault."

Within months, almost every critic of the student movement had seized upon the permissiveness theory with punitive zeal. David Truman, the administrator who had unleashed the police on the Columbia students, blamed the rebellion on "the permissive doctrines of Dr. Benjamin Spock." Rabbi Emmanuel Rackman told the congregation at his Fifth Avenue temple that they themselves were to blame for the "unrelenting and excessive permissiveness" that led to the "revolt of youth." Among the academics, Edward Shils described the students as "a uniquely indulged generation," led astray by "parents who were . . . persuaded of the merits of hedonism." And, looking back from the seventies, sociologist Robert Nisbet fulsomely indicted the

> massive doses of affection, adulation, devotion, permissive-
> ness, incessant and instant recognition of youthful "bright-
> ness" by parents, a constantly relaxing curriculum in the
> schools under the administrations of those who claimed, but
> did not understand, John Dewey as a prophet, a whole na-
> tional mood not only of indulgence but of almost awed, per-
> haps, guilt-ridden adoration of the young.

Bruno Bettelheim added the weight of medical respectabil-
ity to the outcry against permissiveness. Ironically, he was
himself under fire from other psychiatrists for his "ultrapermis-
sive" approach to the treatment of autistic children, which had
earned him the dubious title of "Dr. Yes." Many of his early
comments on the student movement stressed generational conflict: Rebellious youth wanted not only to overthrow the father
but to find a better one, which turned out to be Hitler in the
case of Nazi youth, Mao Zedong or Ho Chi Minh in the case of
the American radicals. By 1969, however, he had moved on to
permissiveness, citing as evidence:

> I have known mothers of extreme campus activists who,
> when the children were infants, fed them goodies against
> inner resistance because that is what good mothers were
> supposed to do.

The image of a baby being force-fed "goodies" neatly summarized middle-class anxieties about affluence. At least adults
still had some "inner resistance." They could, if necessary,
protect themselves by dieting. But the child has no way of
resisting. If its mother cannot save it from the onslaught of
goodies, if she in fact feels she is supposed to offer them, the
child will spiritually fatten, grow soft, and embark on the prolonged tantrum of "extreme" campus activism.

The emphasis on permissiveness transformed the student
rebels from an active menace into a problem of passivity. If
they were "acting out" it was only because they had been

acted upon—in the wrong way—by their indulgent parents. They were permanent babies, and perhaps the most worrisome thing about them was not what they were doing, which was bad enough, but what they seemed incapable of doing: that is, submitting to the long, arduous course of preparation required for membership in the middle-class professions. Decrying "the belief in the possibility and validity of total permissiveness," former State Department official George F. Kennan warned Swarthmore students that "it is only through effort, through doing, through action—never through passive experience— that man grows creatively." According to backlash stereotypes, the student radical had lost what Robert Nisbet called "the motivation toward hard intellectual pursuits, which require unremitting discipline, constantly invoked criteria of excellence, and even (so hateful a word in the fifties and sixties) conformity."

Bettelheim put it more succinctly: Students had lost that indispensable middle-class virtue, the capacity for deferred gratification. Pampered as babies, they now had no "inner controls" and readily resorted to "violence" to get their way. They were missing something essential: "Call it the teaching of a middle-class morality; in psychoanalysis we call it the 'reality principle.'" They had become, in other words, like those permanent children who lived beyond affluence and normality, the poor. The solution—surprisingly, from a man known for his humanistic approach to the problems of childhood—was that "children must learn to fear," if not in the home, then in the schools.

The men who pinpointed permissiveness as the cause of the student rebellion were, for the most part, liberal in their political sympathies. Yet the notion of permissiveness, with its intimations of a culture grown soft and tolerant, was irresistible to conservatives. Spiro Agnew made permissiveness the major theme of his 1968 campaign for vice-president, and the image he crafted for his candidacy was that of the "strong father" the protesters so obviously lacked. Giving credit to backlash theorists Bruno Bettelheim, Sidney Hook, and Irving Kristol, Agnew explained to his audiences on the campaign trail that "the true responsibility" for the student movement "rests . . . with those who so miserably failed to guide them," that is, the "affluent, permissive, upper-middle-class parents who learned their Dr. Spock and threw discipline out the window."

But those were by far the most temperate words he had to say on the subject. More characteristically, Agnew went after the student radicals as "spoiled brats who have never had a good spanking," warning the nation's parents that "a society which comes to fear its children is effete. A sniveling, hand-wringing power structure deserves the violent rebellion it encourages."

Before going any further, we should briefly defer to the "reality principle" that Bettelheim and others were so strongly urging upon the student left. Whether or not middle-class parents were as permissive as the backlash theorists claimed is a question we will take up a little later; but there is no evidence that permissive childraising, to whatever extent it was practiced, was a causative factor in the student movement. For one thing, as at least some adult observers had the wit to point out, the student insurgency of the sixties was global in scope. Whatever permissiveness had to do with American student politics, it could hardly explain the simultaneous radicalism of Chinese, Czechoslovakian, Italian, Mexican, or Filipino youth.

Furthermore, sociologist Richard Flacks's surveys of the American radicals found that they had not come from excessively permissive homes, nor from homes torn by generational conflict. The factor most clearly associated with student radicalism at the time of his research in the mid-sixties was the parents' political views: Liberal parents tended to produce activist students. No occult psychoanalytic mechanism was necessary to explain this, only the normal transmission of values that all parents hope to achieve.

To give the theorists of the backlash their due, the permissiveness theory made sense, intuitively, when applied to the more countercultural aspects of the youth revolt. Like the spoiled children who bedeviled Bettelheim, the counterculture rejected the very notion of deferred gratification. Why work and save and wait for the faint pleasure of material ownership when real pleasure—in fact, the ecstasy of self-loss in drugs and rock 'n' roll—is available *now*? But the critics seldom noticed how much the hedonism of the counterculture mirrored and amplified the hedonistic promise of their own, perfectly respectable, consumer culture. The difference, a cynic might say, was in the products: marijuana vs. gin, love beads vs. rhinestones, the hard-driving motion of rock 'n' roll vs. the advertised thrill of a car.

Nor did the critics, who never managed to tell the hippies from the radicals, ever notice that the activists who inspired the movement and held it together were far from being the stereotyped products of permissiveness. In fact, they were no doubt among the hardest-working, most disciplined members of their generation. But the critics never acknowledged the long hours of volunteer labor, or met the activists who, at the age of twenty or so, were already suffering from what we would now call burnout. They saw only the psychedelic colors, the illicit drugs, the sometimes naïve impatience for change, and perhaps ultimately judged the radicals "spoiled" for refusing to wait for decades of orderly democratic process to stop the war in Vietnam.

But for all its empirical shortcomings, the permissiveness theory held a grim appeal for many middle-class adults. For one thing, it crystallized the middle class's longstanding anxiety about affluence. Affluence was, after all, only a vague ambience; permissiveness appeared to be the actual mechanism by which it left its mark on the human personality. How it was that affluence led to permissiveness was not a question most backlash theorists bothered to explore; what mattered was that the human product was so much worse than anyone had anticipated. David Riesman's other-directed man had at least been a harmless, genial fellow. In the eyes of their critics, the student rebels were vipers, or, in Agnew's words, "a social criminal class," as if juvenile delinquency had now become a majority undertaking. The permissiveness theory not only affirmed the middle-class uneasiness about affluence; it seemed to confirm the ultimate fear that the middle class was sliding into its final decline.

At the same time, the permissiveness theory relocated the

"problem" of radicalism from a specific generation to a specific class. Blaming permissive childraising for youthful radicalism did not excuse the young, but it did shift the burden of responsibility to the adults who had somehow failed them. And now these adults could see that they had something more in common than "affluence," which, presumably, almost all Americans shared in anyway. They had bad children; and they had bad children because they had, each in their own homes, made the terrible mistake that now seemed characteristic of their class: they had been too indulgent, too yielding, too lenient.

One of the best examples of the negative and illiberal class-consciousness provoked by the student movement is Midge Decter's 1975 book *Liberal Parents, Radical Children.* "I am," she introduced herself with strained self-consciousness, "a member of what must be called America's professional, or enlightened, liberal middle class." What defines this class is its children, or rather, the problem of its children. In a chapter titled "A Letter to the Young," Decter writes, "You indeed, and our common property in you, are the primary means by which we make known our connection to one another." But this system of recognition is not just a matter of putting Harvard and Yale decals on the rear window of one's car. "From one end of this country to another," she writes, "in each of the comfortable suburbs and fashionable neighborhoods that have been settled by members of the 'new class,' are to be found people of my age huddling together from time to time . . . asking one another [what] has gone wrong with the children?"

The answer by this time is inevitable: Their upbringing was too permissive. Decter's generation had hoped to give their children a life with "no pain," "no heartache," but this really meant that

> We refused to assume . . . one of the central obligations of parenthood: to make ourselves the final authority on good and bad, right and wrong. . . . The truth is that we neglected you.

Underneath Decter's concern lay a hard edge of class-conscious ambition. These children had not been raised simply to be happy or good. They were meant to inherit their parents' positions within what Decter clearly describes not as a universal middle class but as a social elite. Addressing the errant young, she writes:

> As children of this peculiar enlightened class, you were expected one day to be manning a more than proportional share of the positions of power and prestige in this society. It was at least partly to this end that we brought you up.

And what a disappointment these "radical children" turned out to be! "You are more than usually incapable of facing, tolerating, or withstanding difficulty of any kind," Decter scolds, invoking the problem of the "capacity for deferred gratification," already familiar from studies of the poor. The danger was that the student rebels would fail to attain the "positions of power and prestige" that they had been so carefully prepared for. Decter introduces as examples a number of cases drawn, presumably, from her own circle of acquaintances. One former radical is in a mental hospital; one "has taken up photography"; one is living with a divorced man; one has set off after her third ("or is it her fourth?") postgraduate degree.

What dreadful pattern, one might wonder, are these cases meant to illustrate? A few pages later the answer emerges: The radical children have not joined their own class; they have sunk into such occupations as "pushcart vendors, taxi drivers, keepers of small neighborhood shops that deal in such commodities as dirty comic books and handmade candles . . . housepainters, housecleaners, and movers of furniture." A parent might be justified in fearing that these occupations would pay inadequately, or would pall after a few years. But Decter has another concern. The problem with these pursuits, she writes, with a snobbery that is this time wholly unselfconscious, is that they are "free of all that patient overcoming and hard-won new attainment that attend the conquest of a professional career." They are mere occupations, not professions—suitable for the undisciplined members of the lower classes but unworthy of the elite that composed the "enlightened" middle class.

## THE YOUTH REVOLT AS CLASS TREASON

Decter's fears were not entirely silly. At any point in this century, a middle-class parent might reasonably worry about whether his or her children would end up in respected professions or in mere jobs, like house painting or taxi driving. The reason has less to do with the fecklessness of youth than with a problem inherent to the middle-class condition: In other classes, membership is transmitted by simple inheritance. If you are born into the upper class, you can expect to remain there for life. Sadly, too, most of those born into the lower classes can expect to remain where they started out. Extraordinary circumstances can plunge a few of the wealthy into poverty or propel a few of the poor into wealth, but for most people at the extremes of the social spectrum, class position is inherited along with money or the lack of it. Not so for the middle class, where birth alone is no guarantee of eventual class position. As Margaret Mead observed in the forties:

> The member of the upper class rests upon his birth; born a gentleman, only his own act can take from him something that birth and breeding have given him. The member of the lower class rests in a sense on his birth also; born to a certain way of life and without the education which would give him an ambition to change it for the better, he conducts himself in that state of life to which it has pleased God to call him. But the true member of the middle class denies this fixity to which both upper and lower are committed. Life depends, not upon birth and status, not upon breeding or beauty, but upon effort.

Mead was wrong only in implying that this expenditure of effort is a matter of individual choice, or, as she seems to suggest, class pride. Aside from the very recent surge in entry-level salaries for graduates of the elite business and law schools, most would-be holders of middle-class occupations must expect to undergo six or more years of higher education, followed by an apprenticeship period, before earning "adult" levels of income or respect. The highest-status professions—medicine, law, and the academic disciplines—require a four-year college degree, followed by several years of graduate education, followed usually by several more years of relatively low-paid apprenticeship—the residency in medicine, the assistant professorship in academia, the associate position in law. Lower-status professions, such as dentistry and social work, are only slightly less demanding; and management, which fancies itself a profession also, requires not only four years of college but increasingly a master's degree as well. We may be born into the middle class, but we are expected to spend almost thirty years of our lives establishing ourselves as members of that class in good standing.

In the sixties, the pressures on youthful aspirants to the middle class were rising. Graduate degrees were replacing mere college degrees as the ticket to white-collar professional employment. Even the elite colleges were coming to regard themselves less as playgrounds for the children of the rich and more as serious training grounds for future professionals. As Kenneth Keniston observed in a 1966 essay:

> There is less energy or interest left for fraternities, hazing, and the tribal rites of student culture; there is less room for experimentation, risk-taking, making mistakes, and taking false tacks. . . . [Most students] must work far harder in college than their parents ever thought of working.

It is an understatement to say that this arrangement contains the potential for "generational conflict"—not so much between parents and children, or mythic fathers and sons, but between the young and the established. The middle class is the only class that routinely cannibalizes its young—denies them an adult-level income till near middle age, exploits their labor, and ignores or appropriates their creative contributions. Underpaid and overworked medical residents care for the patients of overpaid, grown-up attending physicians. Impecunious graduate students carry the teaching load for full professors; they also do research that established investigators can, if they are so minded, take the credit for. Fledgling lawyers, paid at about the same rate as legal secretaries, do the detailed preparation for the cases their superiors will argue in court. In any of these fields, to be young and an aspirant to middle-class status is to be a servant to those who have already achieved it.

Put another way, the requirement of lengthy education and apprenticeship makes the youth of the middle class into a sort of internal lower class. As Seymour Martin Lipset and Gerald M. Schaflander acknowledged, somewhat ambiguously, "There is much in the professor-student relationship which produces 'class' ideology and resentment, almost without regard to variation in objective condition." At least part of the anger of the student rebellion stemmed from this classlike tension within the middle class, expressed in Jerry Farber's hyperbolically titled book *The Student as Nigger*:

> Schools exploit you because they tap your power and use it to perpetuate society's trip, while they teach you not to respect your own. . . . Schools petrify society because their method, characterized by coercion from the top down, works against any substantial social change. Students are coerced by teachers, who take orders from administrators, who do the bidding of those stalwarts of the status quo on the board of education or the board of trustees. Schools petrify society because students, through them, learn to adjust unquestioningly to institutions.

And at least part of the horror that suffused the intellectuals' backlash stemmed from the fact that students no longer seemed to know their place. As Edward Shils wrote indignantly of the student radicals:

> The idea that there is a measure of inequality which is constitutive in the university's transmission of knowledge from those who possess more of it in particular spheres to those who possess less of it in those spheres is alien to their conception of the right order of life.

But there was far more at stake than the docility of the "apprentice class." The spokespersons for the backlash understood that if students could challenge the wisdom of professors

—and beyond that, the moral legitimacy of the university— then the professions themselves were in jeopardy. And if the professionals' claims to authority were not respected, then what Midge Decter saw as the "power and prestige" that made the middle class a social elite would be lost. Physicians and attorneys, sociologists and scientists would have no more standing in the world than mechanics or secretaries.

Many spokespersons for the backlash hinted at this frightful possibility, but Robert Brustein, professor of drama at Yale, confronted it squarely in an attack on the student movement titled "The Case for Professionalism." If students and professors were to be "coequal," as the students seemed to want, then all respect for an "inherited body of knowledge" would be gone, and professionals would find themselves with no more authority (or importance) than "amateurs." The result, he warned, would be a "bleak future . . . of monochromatic amateurism in which everyone has opinions, few have facts, nobody has an idea."

## THE PROFESSIONS AS CLASS FORTRESS

To step back for a moment from the immediate fray: The professions are indeed the unique occupational "space" possessed by the middle class. The period in which the professions arose, about 1870 to 1920, was also the period in which the middle class itself appeared in its present form on the American scene. In every field, professionalization was presented as a reform, a bold new measure aimed at replacing guesswork and tradition with science and rationality. But it was also an economic strategy, linked, as historian Samuel Haber has written, with "the 'art of rising in life,' with upward mobility." Through professionalization, the middle class sought to carve out an occupational niche that would be closed both to the poor and to those who were merely rich.

Our modern middle class is the descendant of an older gentry composed of independent farmers, small businessmen, self-employed lawyers, doctors, and ministers. In the fifty years surrounding the turn of the twentieth century, that gentry—the "old" middle class—found itself squeezed between an insurgent lower class and a powerful new capitalist class. As the monopolies tightened their grip on the economy, small business became risky business. At the same time, the old, unregulated professions of medicine and law, which almost anyone could enter simply by hanging out a shingle, were becoming "overpopulated" with upstarts from less genteel backgrounds.

Professionalization was, above all, a way to restrict entry to existing occupations. In medicine, for example, alarm over an oversupply of doctors ultimately convinced the American Medical Association of the value of "scientific" reforms limiting the practice of medicine to those who had completed a college education and four additional years of standardized medical training. At a time when less than 5 percent of the college-age population actually attended college, these reforms guaranteed that medicine would henceforth be limited to "gentlemen" and closed, as reformer Abraham Flexner explained, to the "crude boy or jaded clerk." For those already in practice, it was a matter of pulling the ladder up after oneself. As the famed physician and medical professor William Osler quipped to a colleague, "We are lucky to get in [to the medical profession] as professors, for I am sure that neither you nor I could ever get in as students."

Other occupations adopted a similar strategy. Law and social work declared themselves "scientific," instituted steep educational barriers, and succeeded in closing their ranks to any "crude boys" or (in the case of social work) dilettantish volunteers who might seek entry. Academia sorted itself into most of the familiar disciplines (sociology, political science, psychology, and so forth) and established the equally familiar hierarchy of degrees (bachelor's, master's, doctor's). Even management claimed to be "scientific" and sought (unsuccessfully, at the time) to limit entry to the appropriately, and expensively, educated. Each group publicized its professionalization as a major reform in the interests of science, rationality, and public service. And each succeeded, to a greater or lesser degree, in carving out an occupational monopoly restricted to the elite minority who could afford college educations and graduate degrees.

Through professionalization, the middle class gained purchase in an increasingly uncertain world. Henceforth it would be shielded, at least slightly, from the upheavals of the market economy. Its "capital" would be knowledge or, more precisely, expertise. Its security would lie in the monopolization of that expertise through the device of professionalization. Its hallmark would be higher education and, with it, the exclusive license to practice, consult, or teach, in exchange for that more mundane form of capital, money.

To this day, the educational barriers to the professions serve as much to exclude as to educate. Consider the case of medicine, which is usually regarded, at least by sociologists, as the most secure and least assailable of the professions. The critical barrier—the key "weeding out" course for undergraduate premed majors—is organic chemistry. In fact, organic chemistry was the example Brustein seized on, in his defense of professionalism, to refute student demands in the sixties for socially relevant education. "My very simple point was that in order to become a doctor and help the sick of the ghettos," he wrote in response to a critic of his essay, "you must first study 'irrelevant' subjects like comparative anatomy and organic chemistry." But why should organic chemistry be the critical barrier to becoming a doctor? Why not a course in nutrition, or in the social and environmental causes of disease? (Incidentally, these courses are not even part of the premed program and are only recently being added to medical school curricula.)

Of course premed students *should* study organic chemistry —and so, I believe, should drama students if they are so inclined—because it is an intrinsically fascinating subject. But it should be acknowledged that much of the content of a college course in organic chemistry has little or no relevance to the practice of medicine. Despite the scientific aspirations of early twentieth-century medical reformers, medicine has not reached the point where knowledge of the quantum chemistry of covalent bonds is helpful in the treatment of patients. Calculus, another hurdle for the would-be medical student, is even less defensible: A subject of great charm to many, it is of no conceivable value to the practicing physician or, for that matter, the great majority of medical researchers. Most premed students know perfectly well that these requirements are irrelevant to their future careers. They do not enjoy organic chemistry; they get through it, one way or another, and promptly forget it.

But such courses still serve one of their original functions: to screen out students who have not had the benefit of a high-quality, middle-class, secondary education (as well as those who simply cannot afford to go to college). In other areas, such as law and social work, the requirement of a generic college degree serves the same screening function, regardless of whether one earns it in a subject remotely relevant to the practice of these professions. The academic disciplines appear to be on somewhat more solid ground, since they involve no "practice" apart from research—research which can only be judged by those already within the discipline. No one but a sociologist, say, can judge what constitutes sociology and what is relevant for a would-be sociologist to study. But, here too, a screening function is at work, eliminating not only the poor and underprepared but any amateurs—journalists or free-lance intellectuals, for example—who might wish to dignify their efforts as "sociology," "history," or whatever.

So we can begin to understand the fury and spitefulness of the backlash against the student movement. When students challenged the authority of their professors, when they questioned the validity and relevance of the knowledge from which that authority was said to be derived, they struck at the fundamental assumptions of their class. Judged in the context of that class and its interests, they were guilty of nothing less than treason. They had exposed, in however inarticulate a fashion, the conceit on which middle-class privilege rests: We know more, and are therefore entitled to positions of privilege and authority.

In response, the spokespersons for the backlash fell back on every shibboleth of professional ideology: the reality of purely objective knowledge, untainted by self-interest; the sanctity of the university; the unassailable integrity of the "inherited body of knowledge." * What they abandoned, unfortunately, was the middle class's historical claim to be the agent of reform and rationality. The backlash ultimately degenerated into mere conservativism—the defense of hierarchy for its own sake. "There is no blinking the fact that some people are brighter than others," Brustein wrote, ostensibly in defense of a kind of status that is normally achieved only through years of disciplined study, "some more beautiful, some more gifted."

## MIDDLE-CLASS CHILDRAISING: AMBIVALENCE AND ANXIETY

Viewed as a strategy for class advancement, professionalism contains one nearly fatal flaw. The emerging middle class had erected steep barriers around its professional domain for the purpose of excluding intruders from other classes. But, like it or not, the same barriers not only stand in the way of "outsiders"—upstarts from the lower classes and the occasional amateur from the upper class—they also stand in the way of the children of the middle class.

For most children born to the middle class, the barriers are not insurmountable. Unlike those who are poorer, middle-class youths are likely to have the money for tuition and the leisure for an extended education. Beyond that, they have various intangible advantages: contacts, recommendations, prac-

---

* In detail, their defense of professionalism was lamentably weak. Consider Brustein's defense of medicine, the only profession for which he actually ventured a substantive defense of any kind. "It is unlikely," he wrote, "(though anything is possible these days) that medical students will insist on making a diagnosis through majority vote, or that students entering surgery will refuse anaesthesia because they want to participate in decisions that affect their lives and, therefore, demand to choose the surgeon's instruments or tell him where to cut."

But these are not unreasonable demands. First, while diagnostic decisions should not be made by "majority vote," they are—or should be—arrived at through open discussion, preferably involving nurses and technicians as well as

tice in taking tests (which are likely to be biased in favor of the middle class in the first place), and otherwise winning the approval of educated, middle-class adults. In extreme cases rules can be bent, admissions criteria subtly relaxed, and so forth, but not by much, because the professional domain inhabited by the middle class is respected—and tolerated—by the larger public only in the belief that it is impartial and meritocratic.

Thus barriers that the middle class erected to protect itself make it painfully difficult to reproduce itself. It is one thing to have children, and another thing, as Midge Decter realized in the early seventies, to have children who will be disciplined enough to devote the first twenty or thirty years of their lives to scaling the educational obstacles to a middle-class career. Nor is there any obvious, reliable way the older generation can help. All that parents can do is attempt, through careful molding and psychological pressure, to predispose each child to retrace the same long road they themselves once took.

Hence the perennial middle-class preoccupation with the problems of childraising. In *The Lonely Crowd,* David Riesman wrote of the "contagious, highly diffuse anxiety" middle-class adults bring to the business of parenting. Nor, in the middle class, is childraising a matter that can be entrusted to parents alone: "For in their uneasiness as to how to bring up children," Riesman noted, parents "turn increasingly to books, magazines, government pamphlets, and radio programs." Though the day-to-day work of childraising is left largely to women, isolated in their homes, childraising in this class is

---

physicians. Second, most patients do indeed want to "participate in decisions that affect their lives," which is why they seek second opinions and try to find physicians who are willing to answer questions and discuss alternatives. Finally, it should be observed that the example of surgery is often invoked as a last-ditch defense of professional authority. When community groups demanded a voice in the management of Harlem Hospital in the late sixties, lobbying, for example, for more accessible clinic hours, administrators and doctors responded that "next they'll want to tell the surgeon where to cut." This is a standard professional ploy, using expertise in one area ("where to cut") to legitimize authority in other areas (clinic hours). Similarly, Brustein sought to spread the acknowledged authority of the surgeon *at the time of surgery* to all professionals, including, presumably, the professor of drama holding forth in his lecture hall.

also something of a collective endeavor: the province of scores of experts, psychologists, commentators, counselors, each feeding off of parental anxieties, offering new "solutions," raising new alarms.

Middle-class parents face a particular dilemma. On the one hand, they must encourage their children to be innovative and to "express themselves," for these traits are usually valued in the professions. But the child will never gain entry to a profession in the first place without developing a quite different set of traits, centered on self-discipline and control. The challenge of middle-class childraising—almost the entire point of it, in fact—is to inculcate what the reader will recognize as the deferred-gratification pattern. It is this habit of mind that supposedly distinguishes the middle class from the poor; and it is this talent for deferral that a middle-class child actually needs in order to endure his or her long period of education and apprenticeship.

So when the spokespersons for the backlash blamed the student rebellion on permissiveness, they were not—as it seemed to students at the time—changing the subject from politics to a "trivial" domestic issue. Since in this class childraising is of grave professional concern to many people beyond the parents, the blame for permissiveness fell not only on the actual mothers but also on the spiritual "fathers" of the class—the experts and professionals. Permissiveness pointed to some fundamental weakness in the entire class, some breakdown of rationality, will, or, as Bettelheim termed it, "inner resistance."

Is the middle class overly permissive toward its children? The late-sixties anxiety about permissiveness reflected a real change in middle-class childraising practices, but one which was certainly overdue, apparently short-lived (in its extreme form), and, at any rate, highly ambiguous in its consequences. For most of the first half of this century, permissive childraising was unknown, or at least strongly disapproved of, within middle-class homes. It was almost a sociological truism that the "lower" classes were permissive; the middle class was rigid and disciplined. As late as 1957 a sociology textbook reported, for example, that the middle-class child is "subjected earlier and more consistently to the influences which make a child an orderly, conscientious, responsible, and tame person." Some academic observers even hinted that the middle class went too far in its demands on its children:

> The result is the producing of persons who are controlled (sometimes to the point of lack of spontaneity), regulated, diligent, and able to forgo the pleasures of today for the rewards of tomorrow.

The middle class's emphasis on discipline and deferred gratification goes back to its emergence as a class near the turn of the century. One of the many areas of endeavor that middle-class professionals meant to rationalize and reform was child-raising, and what they meant to reform was what they saw as the old habits of indulgence and coddling. In the new scientific age that seemed to be dawning, children would have to grow up to be disciplined and efficient; therefore they would have to be raised in a disciplined and efficient manner. Times for feeding and sleeping had to be rigidly scheduled; impulses squelched; "bad habits" (thumb-sucking, crying, masturbation) swiftly punished. In fact, in turn-of-the-century childraising advice, pleasure of any kind was subversive to the "production" of useful adults:

> Eating a thing because it tastes good, or drinking a thing because it tastes good, is doing a thing that gratifies the sensual! Mothers, if you begin that way . . . what are you going to do fifteen years later when the primordial urge gets into that young person's blood and he looks out at the world and turns to the right and to the left for other forms of sense gratification?

One of America's first generation of professional psychologists, John B. Watson, laid out in the late teens and twenties what became the middle-class childraising dogma for decades: Babies were to be picked up only at scheduled feeding times; other than that they were to cry until they learned the wisdom of self-control. Children were to be seen, but only briefly, and then for the purpose of useful correction. The ideal child, he wrote, is one who

> never cries unless actually stuck by a pin, illustratively speaking . . . who puts on such habits of politeness and neatness and cleanliness that adults are willing to be around him at least part of the day . . . who eats what is set before him— who sleeps and rests when put to bed for sleep and rest . . . who finally enters manhood so bulwarked with stable work and emotional habits that no adversity can quite overwhelm him.

To achieve this ideal, parents were to guard against any reckless display of emotion on their own part. "Never hug and kiss [your children]," Watson warned. "Never let them sit on your lap. If you must, kiss them once on the forehead when they say goodnight. Shake hands with them in the morning."

As Martha Wolfenstein, a colleague of Margaret Mead, observed in her study of government childraising pamphlets issued between 1914 and 1960, babies were originally portrayed as having "strong and dangerous impulses," which it was the business of the parents to suppress with vigor. In the 1914 edition of *Infant Care,* she reports, childish impulses are said to "easily grow beyond control," leaving some children "wrecked for life." Infant pleasure of any kind was described as unwholesome and injurious to the baby's nerves. "The rule that parents should not play with the baby may seem hard," *Infant Care* advised parents, "but it is without doubt a safe one."

It is hard to believe, from the vantage point of the 1980s, that anyone ever followed these Draconian instructions to the letter. But one widely cited study published in 1948 found that middle-class parents were at least trying: They "place their children under a stricter regimen," the study concluded, "with more frustration of impulses than do lower-class parents." Middle-class mothers were more likely to feed their babies only at scheduled times, less likely to breast-feed, and were inclined to begin weaning and toilet training months earlier than were lower-class mothers. In fact, one reason for the decline of household servants among the early twentieth-century middle class was that lower-class women could no longer be trusted with middle-class children. They would spoil them with hugs and sweets, and contaminate them with an easygoing outlook fatal to middle-class achievement.

But sometime in the forties there was a sudden shift in the experts' advice. Middle-class parents were encouraged to take a more relaxed approach, to trust their instincts, and to respect, at least in a limited way, their child's demands. Whether this shift signaled a radical breakdown of parental authority and middle-class self-discipline is, of course, a matter of judgment. In retrospect, it looks more like the inevitable correction of an approach that had bordered on cruelty and neglect.

The new permissiveness, as reflected, for example, in the 1940s editions of the government's *Infant Care* pamphlet, reads today like common sense. Where the baby's impulses had formerly been described as "fierce," they now subsided into "almost complete harmlessness." Masturbation had previously been described as a threat to health and character, which parents were instructed to prevent by tying the baby's hands and feet down to the mattress at night. Now it was portrayed as innocent exploration. Play ceased to be a dangerous form of overstimulation and became the natural, and in fact required, interaction of mother and child. "Play and singing," advised the 1942 edition of *Infant Care*, "make both mother and baby enjoy the routine of life."

Almost as soon as the advice changed, so too, apparently, did the actual behavior of middle-class parents. In fact, the change was so swift and unexpected that it precipitated a period of deep confusion among sociologists and psychologists: Which class was doing what, and which class was right? According to surveys of parents, the middle class had precipitously abandoned its Watsonian regime and embraced the permissiveness that had formerly been observed only among the poor and the working class. In fact, some studies suggested that by the mid-fifties the middle class had actually surpassed the permissiveness of the lower classes, toilet training their children "late" (at a year or older), feeding them on demand, and treating them more or less as reasonable little people with legitimate desires.

The shift in childraising practices reflected a profound change in the conditions of middle-class life. The switch to what was later pejoratively described as "permissiveness" coincided, give or take a few years, with the onset of postwar affluence. Mothers who might otherwise have worked outside the home were devoting themselves full-time to childraising—and, no doubt, expecting a role more satisfying than that of drill sergeant. Furthermore, middle-class homes increasingly gained the space and appliances to cope with messy behavior and prolonged incontinence. It may have been the automatic washing machine, as much as anything, that allowed middle-class parents to overcome their traditional obsession with cleanliness and postpone toilet training into the second year.

There was also, as sociologist David Potter recognized, a subtle psychological relaxation that came with material abundance. "We may think of [permissive childraising] as a result of our 'enlightened' ideas or as a result of 'developments in the specific field of child psychology,' " he wrote. "But the fact is that the authoritarian discipline of the child . . . was but an aspect of the authoritarian social system which was linked with the economy of scarcity."

At a time when businessmen were trying to figure out how to make hedonism seem moral and thrift seem misguided, it made little sense for childraising to be an exercise in mutual deprivation. In the more permissive childraising literature of the postwar period, the baby was even conceived of as a tiny consumer: its impulses were valid, its wants legitimate. If it wanted to wake up at four in the morning, eat nothing but strained apricots, or eschew the potty seat until the age of three, it must, in its infant wisdom, know what it was doing. The good mother did not worry. Indeed, as Dr. Spock advised, she trusted her own maternal impulses to mesh neatly with the baby's infant ones. The ultimate test and measure of the parent-child relationship was pleasure. As *Infant Care* told mothers in the early forties, the baby will "enjoy the new experience better [in this case, solid foods] if you are having a good time." This was the permissive ideal: mother and baby enjoying each other, consuming each other, moving from one tiny gratification—a smile, a meal, a bath—to the next.

But this was only the ideal, and it was the ideal only briefly. Full-blown permissiveness, even as an ideal, lasted for less than a decade. By the early fifties, most experts were renouncing "overpermissiveness" and stressing "the importance of setting limits appropriate ... to the realities of the environmental situation"—meaning, presumably, that toddlers should not pee on the living-room carpet. In the 1951 edition of the government's *Infant Care,* parents were even warned against infant megalomania. The baby, whose needs had been harmless only a few years earlier, could now get the parents "at his mercy by unreasonable demands for attention," and the indulgent mother "may find her baby getting more and more demanding."

Dr. Spock himself was a leading critic of overpermissiveness, observing that it "seems to be *much* commoner here than in any other country." He added that "professional people from other countries ... have had trouble concealing their surprise and irritation at the behavior of certain children they have seen here." So, long before permissiveness became a political slur, it had fallen out of favor and come to be seen as a mistake, an overcorrection perhaps, but still a pitfall for the unwary parent.

More to the point, permissive childraising was not the total betrayal of middle-class values that backlash theorists seemed to think it was. It may ultimately be even more effective than authoritarianism in producing the habits of conformity and discipline that middle-class parents have sought to inculcate throughout this century. Compared to a punitive, authoritarian approach, developmental psychologist Urie Bronfenbrenner has written, "the [relatively permissive] techniques preferred by middle-class parents are more likely to bring about the development of internalized values and controls." The child who is commanded may submit blankly or rebel, but the child who is cajoled and reasoned with internalizes the voice—and the aspirations—of its parents.

In fact, in its extreme form, permissiveness may be far more intrusive and manipulative than mere command. I think of middle-class parents I have known and observed who are in my judgment truly overpermissive, but they are by no means simply lax and yielding in the way that permissive parents of the lower classes were supposed to be. The middle-class permissive relationship becomes a ceaseless, intense dialogue: "Do you want this or that? Now or later? Or maybe something else?"—a dialogue extending, in some cases, right down to which morsels of food on a plate will be eaten and in what order. No statement is ever final ("You can't have that now"); everything can be renegotiated ("Well, maybe you can have it if you're good"). If this is permissiveness, then the secret of it is that "permission" must be won, or at least fought over, minute by minute; and the kind of personality that results is not likely to be easygoing but profoundly insecure and desperate to please.

The child of authoritarian parents can at least withdraw into fantasies of freedom or revenge, but the child of overly permissive parents has little inner space to retreat to. All of its whims have been noted and addressed, even if not always indulged. It has learned to expect from its parents not only security and affection but the pleasure of instant response and approval. By the age of three or four it has, more likely than not, become addicted to approval, or at least to attention, and has no sure sense of itself when the attention is momentarily withdrawn. As the perspicacious social observer Philip Slater has observed, " 'permissiveness' . . . is actually more totalitarian— the child no longer has a private sphere, but has his entire being involved with parental aspirations."

Perhaps what was ultimately most disturbing about the student rebels was that they reflected their parents' aspirations only too well. The problem was that these were, by the 1950s and the 1960s, violently conflicting aspirations. On the one hand, there was the stern, technocratic ambition, nurtured by the middle class since its origins in the Progressive Era, to achieve self-mastery, and in the process, make the world conform to human reason, or at least, to their own version of rationality. And this was represented in the young Jacobins of the left, who sometimes liked to fancy themselves *"professional revolutionaries,"* and whose imaginations were drawn to the third world, in part, as a land of perpetual scarcity and hard-edged moral issues, unblurred by affluence.

On the other hand, there was, in the parents' generation, the languid desire to surrender to affluence, to forget the world and enjoy the moment, or at least the next purchase. And this less noble impulse was vividly parodied by the hippies, freaks, acid heads, and flower children of the counterculture. The fact that the hippie and the Jacobin were often the same person did not make the parallel between the generations any less compelling. Their grown-up critics, the defenders of discipline and professionalism, knew themselves to be no less compromised by the easy life.

Permissiveness became a potent charge because it symbolized that fatal compromise with affluence and self-indulgence. Beginning in the sixties, permissiveness replaced affluence as the focus of middle-class anxiety and class-conscious introspection. In fact, as we shall see, the scope of concerns embraced by the notion of permissiveness quickly expanded beyond childraising to include every possible failing of the middle class. By the end of the sixties, even the limited generosity that had been inspired by the discovery of poverty would be vulnerable to the charge of permissiveness, as if the poor and the young had at last been fused into a single, massive social problem.

## THE REVENGE OF THE LOWER CLASS

*Something* had "gone wrong" with the children who became the sixties rebels, but it was not permissiveness, or much of anything that went on between parent, child, and Dr. Spock in the split-level privacy of the suburbs. What the back-

lash theorists forgot was that in the fifties the home had become a receptacle open to other influences that poured in
through television, radio, phonographs, movies. Most of the
incoming images were bland enough, instructing the public-
as-audience how the middle class lives: Mom behind the
counter in a spotless, motel-like setting; perky kids waving
Dad off to work; teenage romances leading to more of the
same. But another signal was also coming through, an incite-
ment to the young to think of themselves as a distinct social
group, with a rebellious agenda of its own.

One consequence of affluence was that children, and particularly teenagers, had money to spend; they were *consumers.*
Teens had only recently become a clearly demarcated age
group (in the forties, when the word *teenager* came into widespread usage). In the fifties, they became something else: a
market. According to historian J. Ronald Oakley:

> By the mid-fifties, teenagers were buying 43 percent of all
> records, 44 percent of all cameras, 39 percent of all new
> radios, 9 percent of all new cars, and 53 percent of movie
> tickets. By 1959, the amount of money spent on teenagers by
> themselves and by their parents had reached the staggering
> total of $10 billion a year.

When a group becomes a "market" in the U.S. consumer
economy, it inevitably gains a certain self-awareness. American teenagers were still divided by the nearly impassable gulfs
of class and race, but marketing men did their best to encourage the development of a universal teen identity, defined by
teen clothing styles (formerly, one went directly from children's to adult clothes), teen-oriented entertainment, teen
music, teen fads. The products heightened the sense of collective identity; the heightened sense of identity sold more products. So, for reasons that had little to do with either politics or
childraising practices, the generation that came of age in the
sixties was the first such age cohort to think of itself as a distinct group—not young adults or older children, but *the young.*

This group consciousness was an essential foundation for
the student radicalism and youthful counterculture that fol-

lowed in the sixties, not only in the United States but to a
lesser extent in the rest of the noncommunist world. The issues
—the war, civil rights, poverty—were decisive; without them
there would have been no movement. But without youth's new
awareness of itself as something more than pre-adults, the
movement would never have taken the form that it did. The
generation that entered college in the sixties brought with it a
prideful knowledge of its own, a culture impenetrable to most
adults, including those who made up the professoriat. More
than any preceding generation of twentieth-century students,
this one was not prepared to submit without protest to the
lengthy apprenticeship that lay between childhood and full
membership in the middle class. The apprenticeship was too
long and the goal, it sometimes seemed, was hardly worth the
effort.

Worse still, from a grown-up perspective, the teen culture of
the fifties and early sixties contained themes that were hostile
to business and tauntingly subversive of middle-class values.
Recall that at the time of the emergence of the youth market,
the adult-oriented consumer culture, centered on products for
home and family, was becoming too dull to inspire even the
ad men. New images, new products, new excitement were
needed; and in the teen culture of the fifties, these came from
that invisible, repressed side of American culture that sociologists knew as the lower class. No matter how passive and unappealing the lower class appeared in the eyes of academics
and experts on social problems, it held what Richard Rovere,
writing of the fifties, saw as

> the perverse appeal of the bum, the mucker, the Dead End
> kid, the James Jones–Nelson Algren–Jack Kerouac hero to
> a nation uneasy in its growing order and stability and not
> altogether happy about the vast leveling process in which
> everyone appeared to be sliding, from one direction or
> another, into middle-class commonplaceness and respect-
> ability.

Fused with youth, the lower class became a reservoir of
powerful, erotically charged imagery: Brando in *The Wild One,*
James Dean in *Rebel Without a Cause,* the young hoods in

*Blackboard Jungle.* All of these films delivered impeccable middle-class messages: Crime doesn't pay; authority figures are usually right; you can get ahead by studying. But it is not Brando being chastised by the sheriff that anyone remembers from *The Wild One*—it is Brando tearing into town on his motorcycle, terrorizing the citizenry. And it is not Sidney Poitier's conversion to middle-class values that incited the teen audiences of *Blackboard Jungle* to riot—it was the spectacle of those other teens, those unrepentant juvenile delinquents, rioting on the screen.

Most of all it was rock 'n' roll that forged the new teen culture. Rock was a potent commodity itself; it was also the theme that linked other commodities—clothes, movies, cars—to create a common teen style. Rock gave *Blackboard Jungle* (the first movie with a rock sound track) its insurrectionary power, and it was rock music that swept white middle-class audiences, along with the greasers and the gang members, to their feet, stomping and shouting. It was the music of the movement, the beat of insurrection, just as folk songs were the music of the student left in the 1930s. The difference was that folk songs were for singing along to; rock was for "fighting in the street," cutting loose, getting stoned, screaming with hysteria, merging with a thousand other young people in all-night, three-chord communion. It was the sound, to youthful ears, of freedom and defiance, just as it was also, especially in the fifties and early sixties, the "jungle beat" in which adults could hear the coming downfall of civilization.

But rock 'n' roll was not the invention of the young; it was the invention of the poor. I heard a rock beat for the first time on the radio of a black cleaning lady working in a friend's house, and I remember being shocked that this apparent nonentity, this invisible woman, was privy to such a wonder, while people like her employers, and myself, had to make do with Patti Page. Rock came up from what we would now call the black underclass. It was brought to white audiences by a truck driver from Mississippi. It went to England and bounced back on the creative energies of four working-class boys from Liverpool. If there was a "culture of poverty," this was its sound.

And it was saying something to middle-class youth that they had not heard before. The message was not, to say the least, about discipline, achievement, and careers. It was not even about love, although that is what the lyrics usually spoke of. Love is one of the only ways we have, in a secular, commercial culture, of talking about transcendent experience. And rock said that transcendent experience was available, possible, now: not just pleasure or comfort or pride of ownership, but ecstasy. Rock (and of course drugs) took ecstasy out of the private realms of mysticism and sexual obsession and put it back into the public sphere as a social good—the point, in fact, of human community.

To say that rock 'n' roll was antagonistic to middle-class values is, of course, to understate the case. If theories of the "culture of poverty" were the middle-class critique of the poor, rock was a critique of the middle class, bubbling up from America's invisible "others." It mocked work ("Get a Job"), study ("Don't know much 'bout his-to-ry"), authority ("Charlie Brown, you're a clown"). It held out no professions, no career except that of the reckless "Love Man," not even a certainty of adulthood ("Teen Angel"). Its idea of time ("Rock Around the Clock") had nothing to do with a scheduled ordered of achievements. In serious moments it told of a world in which hard work went unrewarded, just as love so often went unrequited, where the good died young and the proud trampled on the humble. Over time, the lyrics grew more overtly political and topical, but for many of us in the student left in the summer of 1965, Bob Dylan's mocking, elusive "Like a Rolling Stone" already seemed to say all that needed to be said about middle-class arrogance and the futility of the professional paths middle-class young people were programmed to follow.

Rock 'n' roll, whether sung by a middle-class youth like Dylan or a vulgar-looking greaser like Elvis, was the revenge of the lower class. And if there is an explanation for the student revolt that goes deeper than politics and public events, it was in the vibrant new consumer culture addressed to the young and fortified with the repressed defiance of the poor. This was the Pied Piper that led middle-class youth off the path of professional achievement and seduced them into betraying the ideals of their own class. This was the true source of "permissiveness," or at least of a true permissiveness unqualified by parental ambition and manipulation. Such is the ingenuity of capitalism: It had taken the anger and yearning of the poor and sold them to the restless youth of the middle class.

But the backlash theorists would not blame the consumer economy and were still too liberal to blame the poor. In identifying the problem as their own permissiveness, they had foolishly blamed themselves. In so doing, they laid the foundations for a far more vicious kind of conservativism, one which would attempt to discredit the professional middle class altogether. With the middle class in turmoil, someone else would have to be found to represent its traditional values—hard work and self-denial—against the tide of anarchy and hedonism. By the end of the sixties that "someone" would be found in an unlikely place—the all-but-forgotten working class.

## CHAPTER THREE

# THE DISCOVERY
# OF THE WORKING CLASS

THE STUDENT REBELLION awakened middle-class adults to the uneasy awareness that they were, in some sense, an elite. But an elite relative to whom? Except for the extremes of wealth and poverty, everyone was still part of a monolithic "middle class." Commentators and professors still spoke sonorously of a *we* that included themselves and the majority of Americans, from auto workers to ad men. Radical students at Columbia or Harvard still fancied themselves representatives of "youth." No one felt disqualified—by virtue of wealth, education, or occupation—from speaking for "the common man."

Then came what Nora Sayre has described as the "huge, crude astonishment" at the discovery of the "working/forgotten/average man." Here was the missing part of the picture: a vast segment of the population that was not middle class, and relative to whom the professional middle class was indeed an elite: paid better, and privileged to sit while others stood or moved about, to speak while others listened.

The commentators, professors, and Ivy League radicals awoke with a rude jolt to the idea that they were no longer the authentic voice of the American people but something more like a special-interest group, a minority, or, as some were eventually to decide, a "new class" unto themselves. "Most of us in what is called the communications field are not rooted in the great mass of ordinary Americans," confessed columnist Joseph Kraft at the very dawn of the discovery, in the summer of 1968, but represent only "the outlook of upper-income whites."

Working-class whites, unlike the amorphous category of the poor in the early sixties, *had* done something to signal their existence. They showed scattered signs of discontent that became, in the media, a full-scale backlash: against the civil rights movement, the antiwar movement, and apparently against middle-class liberalism in general. More specifically, *some* members of the traditionally Democratic, white working class, in some parts of the country, were suddenly rallying to public figures who appealed to racist sentiments: Louise Day Hicks, the leading opponent of school integration in Boston; Charles Stenvig, policeman-turned-politician in Minneapolis; Anthony Imperiale, organizer of neighborhood vigilante squads in Newark; Mario Proccacino, the law-and-order challenger to New York's upper-class, liberal mayor, John Lindsay; and above all, George Wallace, the Alabama segregationist who, having been beaten in the 1958 gubernatorial primary by a Ku Klux Klan member, had vowed never to be "out-niggered" again.

According to British journalist Godfrey Hodgson, the moment of awakening to the existence of this irascible new social class occurred in the summer of '68, in the aftermath of the violence that surrounded, and virtually swallowed up, the Democratic convention. Tens of thousands of youthful radicals had converged in Chicago to protest the war and the front-running Democratic candidate, liberal but pro-war Hubert Humphrey. Mayor Richard Daley's police attacked, mercilessly and indiscriminately. Not only did the yippies, pacifists, radicals, and sundry countercultural types fall under the billy clubs; so did stray convention delegates, bystanders, and, most importantly, reporters and camera crews. Even the maverick publisher Hugh Hefner had his moment of confrontation. Stepping out in a rare excursion from the Playboy Mansion (then located in Chicago), he was struck by a policeman's club and instantly retreated back inside, an angrier and, one must imagine, wiser man. In a rare moment of collective courage, the editors of all the nation's major newspapers telegrammed a strong protest to Mayor Daley. Chet Huntley told the nation on the evening news that "the news profession in this city is now under assault by the Chicago police."

Then came a sobering message from the viewing public. Polls taken immediately after the convention showed that the majority of Americans—56 percent—sympathized with the police, not with the bloodied demonstrators or the press. Indeed, what one could see of the action on television did not resemble dignified protest but the anarchic breakdown of a great city (if only because, once the police began to rampage, dignity was out of the question). Overnight the press abandoned its protest. The collapse was abrupt and craven. As bumper stickers began to appear saying "We support Mayor Daley and his Chicago police," the national media awoke to the disturbing possibility that they had grown estranged from a sizable segment of the public. "I was stunned by the public reaction to Chicago," said NBC's documentary producer Shad Northshield. "We all were. I was stunned, astonished, *hurt*. It's the key thing that opened my eyes to the cleavage between newsmen and the majority."

Media leaders moved quickly to correct what they now came to see as their "bias." They now felt they had been too sympathetic to militant minorities (a judgment the minorities might well have contested). Henceforth they would focus on the enigmatic—and in Richard Nixon's famous phrase—silent, majority. The switch was announced in the trade journal *Editor and Publisher* and, on the same day, September 27, 1969, in *TV Guide*, in an article that quoted one penitent network official after another: "We didn't know it [the white, adult majority] was *there!*" one admitted. "The world doesn't end at the Hudson," another claimed to have discovered. To NBC's Fred Freed the fault lay in the peculiar parochialism of the men who dominated the media:

The blue- and white-collar people who are in revolt now do have cause for complaint against us. We've ignored their point of view. . . . It's bad to pretend they don't exist. We did this because we tend to be upper-middle-class liberals.

Sooner or later the producers of ideas and images would inevitably have discovered the "forgotten" or "troubled" majority, if just for a change of pace. Former Housing and Urban Development undersecretary Robert Wood, who had been one of the first to point out the existence of the (largely white) working class as early as 1966, suggested that the discovery might just be a matter of "the liberal academic and interpreter getting tired of the minority kick and looking for a new folk hero, who happens to be white."

But it was not only the search for novelty that sent media people and intellectuals in search of "a new folk hero." Godfrey Hodgson suggests that the media's discovery of the "middle Americans" was prompted by something darker: the "fear [that] haunts all elites . . . the fear of being out of touch with the majority." Indeed, they had been out of touch. In a nation where one-quarter of the citizenry were poor by any reasonable definition, America's intellectuals and media people had not known poverty existed until Michael Harrington pointed it out to them. And in a nation where the great majority of people are not newsmen or media executives or professors, they had been too caught up in their own world—blinded, perhaps, by their success and affluence—to notice that the majority was, somehow, different from themselves.

There were reasons, then, for the wave of contrition that swept through the professional middle class at the end of the sixties. They had presumed to speak for everyone, and now "everyone" turned out to be a social group almost as baffling and exotic as the poor had been at the time of their discovery. For the next few years media people, intellectuals, and others of their class would work overtime to make up for their embarrassing neglect of this new social "other." They would examine, fearfully and almost reverently, that curious segment of America: the majority. And within it, they would find that supposedly extinct—or at least thoroughly assimilated—category, the working class.

Like the poor before it, the working class *as discovered* was the imaginative product of middle-class anxiety and prejudice. This discovery occurred at what was for many middle-class intellectuals a time of waning confidence and emerging conservatism. Professional authority was under attack; permissiveness seemed already to have ruined at least one generation of middle-class youth. And so, in turning to the working class, middle-class observers tended to seek legitimation for their own more conservative impulses. They did not discover the working class that was—in the late sixties and early seventies —caught up in the greatest wave of labor militancy since World War II. They discovered a working class more suited to their mood: dumb, reactionary, and bigoted.

## "MIDDLE AMERICANS" IN THE MEDIA

Beginning in the fall of 1969, the networks geared up to show "what's right with America," offering soothing new dramas such as *Country Preacher* and *Small Town Judge*. Then, in 1970, came the ambiguous caricature represented by Archie Bunker in *All in the Family*. Almost simultaneously, academia, foundations, and policy-makers discovered the "forgotten majority." The Nixon administration commissioned a task force on "The Problem of the Blue-Collar Worker." The Lindsay administration in New York (for which I worked as "program-planning analyst" for several months in 1968–69) almost overnight began to search for white neighborhoods to reward with new municipal services, even though none of them were anywhere near as needy as the city's black and Puerto Rican communities. The Ford Foundation, which had been generously funding black community activism, suddenly switched its attention to white ethnic groups and devoted a January 1970 staff conference to "the blue-collar problem." Writers and academics moved quickly to fill in the general ignorance with books and studies, some of them—such as *The White Majority, Middle Class Rage, The Radical Center,* and *The Troubled American*—quite thoughtful and sensitive. And in the fall and winter of 1969, every major newsmagazine ran a cover story on the "middle Americans," the "troubled Americans," or the "forgotten Americans."

The newsmagazines were strangely unembarrassed to announce their discovery. It was one thing to discover the poor, most of whom cannot afford to subscribe to newsmagazines anyway. But it was quite another thing, one might have thought, for a magazine to "discover" a majority that overlapped with its readership. "Now the pendulum of public attention is in the midst of one of those great swings that profoundly change the way the nation thinks about itself," *Newsweek* announced, not bothering to explain that it, and the media generally, were the ones pushing the pendulum. *Time* was more honest, explaining that the "Middle Americans" were " 'discovered' first by politicians and the press," and attributing this belated discovery to a "pervasive discontent" and, mysteriously, to "the character and achievements of the astronauts." *U.S. News and World Report* merely observed that "the common man is beginning to look like a Very Important Person indeed," leaving the reader to wonder about the elite perspective from which the "common man" must have looked, until just now, so insignificant.

The Middle Americans that the media discovered were, of course, a far larger category than the blue-collar working class. In fact, in their haste to get away from the no-longer-newsworthy blacks, hippies, radicals, and poor people, most media analysts were content to define Middle Americans as almost anybody but the members of those disturbing groups. In a Gallup poll commissioned by *Newsweek*, for example, Middle Americans were defined more or less as white people. Although the poll claimed to be presenting a sketch of "the little guy," 28 percent of the people polled were in families dependent on wage-earners in business and professional occupations. For its definition of Middle America, *Time* felt it could exclude only "the nation's intellectuals, its liberals, its professors, its surgeons," and, naturally, its blacks. This left quite a large chunk of the population, which the magazine struggled to shape into a meaningful social category:

> The Middle Americans tend to be grouped in the nation's heartland more than on its coasts. But they live in Queens, N.Y., and Van Nuys, Calif., as well as in Skokie or Chilli-cothe. . . . They are defined as much by what they are not as by what they are. As a rule, they are not the poor or the rich. Still, many wealthy business executives are Middle Americans. . . . They are both Republicans and Democrats.

"Above all," *Time* concluded, apparently exhausted by this effort at definition, "Middle America is a state of mind."

Defining that state of mind, though, was almost as difficult as defining the social group that shared it. The "pervasive discontent" *Time* and *Newsweek* discovered ranged through almost every possible issue. Predictably, Middle Americans complained about drugs and crime and what they saw as the violent tactics of black and student activists. They complained about antiwar demonstrators and about the war itself; about high taxes and welfare expenditures and also about government inaction in the face of pressing social problems, such as poverty. "They spend $50 million to send a f—— monkey around the moon and there are people starving at home," a Milwaukee garage man "growl[ed]" to *Newsweek*. They complained about being poor themselves: "Why, I can't even afford a color-TV set!" a Los Angeles plumber "explod[ed]" in the same cover story. They complained about environmental pollution and the breakdown of community. In fact, if a Middle American complained about anything at all, the media were now eager to record it, as in this case from *Time*'s cover story:

> Mrs. Dorothy King, 47, a mother of three and wife of an Atlanta manufacturer's representative, reads a book a week —a somewhat un—Middle American habit in a television age —but finds fewer and fewer books to her taste: "I read one book about a brother and sister living together. 'This is sick,' I told myself."

If there was any kind of journalistic core to the otherwise empty notion of Middle America, it was the blue-collar working class. "The essence of the 'silent majority,'" *U.S. News and World Report* asserted, "turns up most strongly among the blue-collar workers of America." *Newsweek* told its readers:

> The disgruntlement of Middle America finds its cutting edge in the nation's traditional working class—families whose breadwinners have at most a high-school education, hold blue-collar jobs and bring home incomes of $5,000 to $10,000 a year. . . . It is in this group that troubled discontent shades closest to angry violence.

On most of the key "backlash" issues, as defined by the media, it was hard to distinguish the blue-collar people singled out by the newsmagazines from the rest of the Middle Americans. In the Gallup poll commissioned by *Newsweek*, blue-collar respondents stood out in two respects: They were more likely to be pessimistic about the future than white-collarites and less likely to be sympathetic to black economic demands.* However, some of the most viciously racist statements collected by the pollsters came not from blue-collar workers but from brokers, finance managers, businessmen, and even one unnamed MIT professor, who opined that successful Negroes are "almost all light-colored." And it was an "investment ad-

---

* Seventy-nine percent of blue-collar respondents felt blacks "could have done something" about living conditions in the slums (compared to 69 percent of the white-collar respondents), and 49 percent felt that blacks actually had a better chance of getting a job than they did. But as Richard Lemon explained in his book *The Troubled American*, based on the *Newsweek*/Gallup poll, even the racist blue-collar respondents were by no means consistently hostile to government action on behalf of black Americans:

> *Of the blue-collar workers who said the Negro could have improved his own slums, the largest number, 48 percent, also would use a [federal budget] surplus to improve conditions, and 34 percent favored spending more on housing for the poor, while only 16 percent were opposed. Of those who said that the Negro already had a better chance at a good job than they themselves did, 54 percent also favored job training for the unemployed. Nor did their answers suggest that they wanted such programs for themselves. Sixty-one percent of them said that the country had changed for the better in providing opportunities for themselves.*

visor" who, when asked how he would define "law and order," responded, "Get the niggers. Nothing else." But, as the news media presented it, a blue-collar vanguard was leading Middle America in its shift to the right.

There were, on the sidelines, a few dissenters. The *Nation* observed that the Middle American category was "ambiguous ... assembled for the most part by intellectuals whose knowledge of the people alleged to constitute the group is no more than marginal." These "intellectuals" (a perhaps overly flattering description of the media people in question) were guilty of reporting "loosely and inaccurately" on social groups they saw only remotely as "anthropological subjects." Other critics from the left, such as the authors of *The American Melodrama*, objected to the media's singling out of working-class Americans as the vanguard of reaction:

> By repeating the rather comforting doctrine that racial hostility was to be found among the working class and particularly among ... "the ethnics," rather than among "people of substantial place and means," the media were spreading an unproven simplification and one that was in danger of being self-verifying.

But the mainstream media's very distance from blue-collar America made it an attractive place to locate the "essence" and "cutting edge" of Middle American reaction. From the vantage point, for example, of the contrite network executives quoted in *TV Guide*, blue-collar Americans were genuinely exotic folk. People like Mrs. King, the anomalous book-reader, and the male white-collar representatives of Middle America had the kind of faces you might see on any page of a national magazine in any week. Average people, selected for their averageness, do not add much to a magazine page, especially because they look so deceptively like actual newsmakers—statesmen, business leaders, authors. Blue-collar people add much more visual interest precisely because neither they nor anyone who looks like them are usually seen as newsmakers. *Newsweek's* most arresting photographs were of hard-faced, beer-bellied men standing in bleachers and pudgy women in beehives and miniskirts. If indeed some affinity for the novel and striking had once led the media to overemphasize hippies, black militants, and white radicals, that same affinity now drove them to select blue-collar people—out of all the possible Middle Americans—as the vanguard of the backlash.

Besides, the blue-collar people expressed themselves in ways not usually found in the national media, providing titillating opportunities to print such well-known one-letter words as *f*—— and *s*——. The most ominous, and colorful, backlash sentiments *Newsweek* reported came from two middle-aged men, an auto mechanic and a house repairer:

> "Paint your face black and you can get a new Cadillac and the county will come in and feed your family ..." says [Frank] Reis.... "There's only one way to solve this, and that's gonna be with a revolution. I'm for fighting it out between us," [David] Pedroza says angrily.... "What do you call dragging the American flag on the ground and burning draft cards and all that s——?" asks Reis.... "We should have a Hitler here to get rid of the troublemakers the way they did with the Jews in Germany."

In addition to their vivid language, there was another way that the blue-collar (or "lower-middle-class") people featured in the magazines differed from the mass of Middle Americans. If they were relatively unsympathetic to blacks, they were actively hostile to the professional middle class. *Newsweek* saw this hostility as a spillover from working-class racism, warning, "The hunt for scapegoats goes beyond the blacks to their allies: the liberal white elite." And the press, which after Chicago believed it epitomized that elite, had to admit that the hostility went both ways. *U.S. News and World Report*, which could at least not be accused of liberalism, was perhaps the most direct:

> Affluent "liberals" are inclined to deplore such [conservative, "silent majority"] views. Intellectuals look down their

noses. Young radicals say it figures: *"Squares! Racists! Pigs!"*

An ugly incident underscored the tensions between the working class and the professional middle class, and seemed to confirm the image of the blue-collar male as a violent reactionary. On May 8, 1970, hundreds of helmeted construction workers attacked a peaceful student antiwar demonstration in Manhattan's Wall Street district, leaving seventy students and bystanders injured. It was a terrifying event—not only to the student protesters but to the normal denizens of Wall Street. One of the injured was a young Wall Street lawyer, who, one may safely assume, was unprovocatively attired in short hair and a business suit.

But the attack, which quickly became emblematic of blue-collar sentiments, was neither spontaneous nor representative of blue-collar union men. At the time of the incident, some of the nation's largest unions, including the thoroughly blue-collar Teamsters, United Auto Workers, and Oil, Chemical, and Atomic Workers, had taken official stands against the war in Vietnam. Peter Brennan, president of New York City's Building Trades Council, had not; he was a hawk and a Nixon supporter. A few members of Brennan's union disclosed to the press that the workers' attack had been planned and announced through the union in advance. Bystanders reported that the attack had been directed by teams of gray-suited men. Nevertheless, the rampaging construction workers were widely taken to be representative of their class and race. In no time at all, the term *hardhat* replaced *redneck* as the epithet for a lower-class bigot.

## THE BLUE-COLLAR STEREOTYPE

In *An Introduction to Sociology*, a textbook published in 1976, well after the discovery of the working class, there is a photograph captioned "Stereotypical Image of the Blue-

Collar Worker." In it, an overweight, middle-aged man wearing overalls, T-shirt, and a workman's cap stares dully into the middle distance, apparently at some point just above the Rheingold beer can set in front of him on the table. Next to him, a thin, bright-eyed woman, who has no Rheingold can to consider, stares inquisitively at him, this "worker" who is perhaps her husband. She may be wondering the same thing the reader is: Is this an accurate stereotype, in which case the caption should have read "Typical Blue-Collar Worker"? Or are the distancing words *stereotypical* and *image* meant to warn us that he is a representative of a widely held prejudice, rather than of blue-collar men in general? Despite the heading on the same page, "Life Styles and Class Values," the text offers no enlightenment. The message to the student seems to be: "This is what we, the authors, think blue-collar men are like, though we do not have any way of supporting our view. But at least this picture may help you to identify them, should you encounter any."

One more point, before we set aside this intriguing illustration: It is clear from the focus of the woman's attention that it is the man who is both the "worker" and the "image." Her questioning gaze locates her on the side of the sociologists, examining, as it were, a sociological specimen. In other words, *she* is not the problem. And, in general, middle-class fascination with the working class in the years immediately following its discovery was fascination with the working-class male—in particular, the white working-class male. Poverty, as discovered, had a feminine cast: its victims were portrayed as passive, aimless, beaten down. In the mid-sixties, poor black women even became objects of special concern and study in their own right—thanks to their supposedly prodigious fecundity and matriarchal power over men.

But the working class, from the moment of its discovery, was conceived in masculine terms. In part, this was because work, and especially manual labor, was still considered a masculine activity. Also, sociologists and other commentators believed that working-class women were more middle-class in their values and attitudes, partly because they were more enmeshed than their husbands in the consumer culture. Certainly, as we observed in the first chapter, the daily lives of homemakers—shopping, cleaning, caring for children—still did not vary as radically from class to class as the daily lives of men. Furthermore, the major outside occupations of working-class women —clerical and sales work—demanded at least the appearance of middle-class gentility. The working-class woman might be unstylishly overweight, unfashionably dressed, and, by middle-class standards, tastelessly made-up, but she was not a social alien, not a *threat*.

The working class, as discovered, was also white. In reality, the American working class—defined broadly and crudely as people who work for hourly wages, rather than salaries—was becoming increasingly female, black, and Hispanic. Middle-class expectations also dictated that workers were white, just as poor people who were not Appalachians were commonly envisioned as black. All the working-class stereotypes we will consider are images of white males—a group that is sometimes imagined to be exempt from the burden of prejudice.

At the time of the discovery, there were few available images of the working-class male (or female) to draw on. As we have seen, sociologists tended either to toss the working class in with the poor as one vast lower class, or, more optimistically, to absorb it into the catchall middle class. Popular culture was not much help. Fifties movies provided only two outstanding working-class characters, Marty, and Terry Malloy in *On the Waterfront*. Both were dumb, likable, and mistakenly loyal to their working-class comrades—a fault overcome by marriage in Marty's case, and by the betrayal of his comrades in Terry's case. And unless one counts cowboys and the occasional anachronistic juvenile delinquent, the working class had been banished from the screen in the sixties.

Recent social science offered one major reflection on the character of the working class, Seymour Martin Lipset's 1959 essay "Working-Class Authoritarianism." Fascism had put authoritarianism, understood as a personality trait, on the sociological agenda. Anticommunism kept it alive as an issue in the fifties, especially for scholars like Lipset who saw fascism and communism as two manifestations of the same slavish predilection on the part of the masses. In his analysis, the working class was responsible for totalitarianism of all varieties, at all times, because working-class people were inherently narrow-minded, intolerant, and most of all, "authoritarian." The paradoxical—and, one might say, self-serving—implication was that the only people with any talent for democracy were the members of privileged elites. In Lipset's words, "Acceptance of the norms of democracy requires a high level of sophistication," an indefinable quality possessed only by the professional middle class and well-read members of the aristocracy of wealth.

Lipset's description of the working-class personality, which, even at the time, at least some sociologists rejected as fanciful, has since been painstakingly refuted. Thanks to the work of historian Richard F. Hamilton, we know now, for example, that Nazism was not a movement of the "masses"—the lower middle class or working class—but received its strongest backing from wealthy urbanites and the rural gentry. Similarly, Hamilton has shown that other notorious outbreaks of "authoritarianism" and intolerance, such as lynchings in the American South or McCarthyism in the 1950s, tended to be initiated by the wealthy and only later embraced by the lower classes. In an exhaustive analysis of American survey and voting data from the late forties through the sixties, he found *no* significant or consistent evidence for any inherent working-class authoritarianism, intolerance, or hostility to democratic norms.

Lipset's study is still valuable, however, as a summary of middle-class prejudices. The "lower-class individual," Lipset wrote—using *lower-class* and *working-class* interchangeably, as was the custom in the fifties—is a bundle of "deep-rooted hostilities expressed by ethnic prejudice, political authoritarianism, and chiliastic transvaluational religion." The blame for these exotic-sounding personality defects lay less with the individual himself than with the company he kept—namely, other working-class individuals. His parents had exposed him to "punishment, lack of love, and a general atmosphere of tension and aggression." In school, his associations with "others of similar background" canceled the efforts of his teachers. At work, the bad influences continued: "He is surrounded on the job by others with a similarly restricted cultural, educational, and family background."

The working class, in short, is bad company. Lipset quoted the 1926 book *Social Differentiation* to establish that the working-class social environment operates to "limit the source of information, to retard the development of efficiency in judgment and reasoning abilities, and to confine the attention to more trivial interests in life." For Lipset, the limited intellect of the working-class individual—especially "trivial interests," "an impatience with talk," and "a desire for immediate action" —accounted for the class's historic predilection for left-wing (or otherwise "extremist") political movements. There was a catch, however, which Lipset readily acknowledged: Left-wing working-class movements, both in Europe and America, have historically fought not only for "trivial" bread-and-butter goals but for political freedoms, such as suffrage and freedom of speech and association, which were often bitterly resisted by the more "sophisticated" elites. For this apparent anomaly, Lipset offered two explanations. First, that the *leaders* of working-class movements were usually better educated and more middle class in their values than their followers. Second, that the witless rank and file did not understand what they were fighting for anyway: "The fact that the movement's ideology is democratic does not mean that its supporters actually understand the implications."

Alas, the members of this benighted class could do nothing right! If they supported "extremist" movements, it was because they were more or less impelled to by their "authoritarian personalities." If they supported liberal, civil-libertarian causes, it was because they didn't know what they were doing. And when they had the right attitude, according to the middle-class fashion of the day, it was for the wrong reason. Thus in the 1981 edition of *Political Man*, Lipset had to confront a recent study showing that the American working class had been more opposed to the Korean and Vietnamese wars than the middle class. The explanation? Working-class opposition reflected not pacifist feelings but archaic and conservative "isolationist sentiments." Presumably, the relatively pro-war stance of the middle class was an expression of a healthy, concerned interventionism, or something to that effect.

Lipset's explanation of why the working class was historically too left-wing lent itself readily to the sociological concern in the late sixties and early seventies that the working class had now become too right-wing. Introductory sociology textbooks published in the seventies solemnly repeated the prejudices Lipset had dignified as political science: Blue-collar people are "more enthnocentric, more authoritarian, and more isolationist than people at higher levels," instructed *Sociology*. In another introductory text we find that the "lower-blue-collar" person is "reluctant to meet new people and new situations, to form new social relationships, and above all, to initiate contact with strangers. On the contrary, he values and seeks out, more than anybody else, the routine, the familiar, the predictable."

By the seventies, the Middle American blue-collar backlash began to introduce an uneasy element of self-consciousness into the sociological generalizations. It was clear that, though the blue-collar person might be authoritarian, one kind of authority he did *not* respect was that of the middle-class expert, including perhaps even the sociologist. Thus we find, in a 1976 introductory text, the somewhat bad-tempered observation that the working-class person (here still labeled *lower-class*)

> appears reluctant to accept new ideas and practices and is suspicious of the innovators. . . . Their limited education, reading habits, and associations isolate the lower class from a knowledge of the reasons for these changes, and this ignorance together with their class position makes them suspicious of the middle- and upper-class "experts" and "do-gooders" who promote the changes.

The next step would have been to acknowledge that some sort of Heisenberg-like Uncertainty Principle applied to the sociology of social classes: that observations made by the middle-class experts were no doubt routinely distorted by the hostility of the lower classes for these experts—not to mention the hostility of the experts for the lower-class objects of their study.

One text, published in 1972, went so far as to suggest that the official stereotypes might have their own real existence in the eye of the sociological observer. First, the student is given the familiar summary of lower- or working-class traits: "He usually has little ability to take another person's point of view" (as opposed, of course, to the middle-class author). "His perspective is limited, and so is his ability to understand the world around him." He is "traditionalistic, 'old-fashioned' . . . patriarchal." In fact, "not many of these people are given to 'listening to reason.' " In the copy of this text that I read, these passages had been copiously underlined by some anxious undergraduate. Unmarked, and possibly unread, was the thoughtful footnote on the same page:

AUTHOR'S NOTE: Some sociologists and psychologists have been guilty of distorting evidence in this general area to serve their own moral purposes. . . . In the literature, terms applied to this "class" are often pejorative: why is "authoritarian" consistently used instead of, for example, "respectful of authority"?

As Richard F. Hamilton observed in *Class and Politics in the United States,* also published in 1972, the myth of working-class intolerance and authoritarianism is one of the most cherished beliefs of American sociologists. Even when confronted with directly contradictory evidence, they will simply assert their class-based prejudices. For example, a 1966 study on occupational mobility and racial tolerance cited evidence that "the higher one's class of origin or class of destination the more likely that one prefers to exclude Negroes from one's neighborhood." But the authors refused "to contemplate seriously" that such an unflattering finding could be true. Hamilton comments that "years of training" in effect brainwash sociologists into a kind of "perceptual distortion," whereby they see only such data as seem to support their preconceived notions: "It seems likely that such perceptual distortion goes on continuously, social scientists either 'not seeing' contrary evidence . . . or, if seeing it, not remembering it."

## THE STEREOTYPE ON THE SCREEN

If sociology creates the official stereotypes, Hollywood and the networks create the ones we know best. No sooner had the news media discovered the working class and found it to be reactionary, bigoted, and male, than the scriptwriters set to work to exploit the entertainment possibilities of this interesting new social grouping. Roughly speaking, television was drawn to its humorous possibilities; Hollywood, to its supposed potential for violence. The result was two overlapping images: on television, the blue-collar male as buffoon; and in the movies, the blue-collar buffoon as mass murderer.

The blue-collar—and of course, white—buffoon, best represented by Norman Lear's Archie Bunker, was perhaps the inevitable replacement for the perennial black buffoon represented by *Amos 'n' Andy.* For decades, black stereotypes had been natural targets for white derision, their racial "otherness" augmented by rural simplemindedness. But by the sixties, the civil rights movement had revealed "racial humor" as racist, or, at the very least, tasteless and déclassé. Besides, most American blacks were no longer country folk with amusing drawls; they were (or were increasingly represented as) fast-talking, "street-smart" urbanites. In the early-seventies "black-exploitation" films such as *Superfly,* and in countless others since, blacks have both the mental edge and the fashion advantage: They dress slickly and expensively, hustle for a living, and dispense a cynical wisdom unattainable through the supposedly safe, bland experience of whites.

Meanwhile the white Middle Americans had, in fleeing to the suburbs, come to seem like a new kind of peasantry. In the stereotypes of the entertainment media, they were ill-at-ease in the city, ignorant of hip, urban slang, and preoccupied with that most degenerate form of agriculture—lawn maintenance. Urban blacks were setting styles in music, language, and clothing; Middle Americans were prone to such fashion errors as white socks and checkered slacks. The demographic upheavals of the fifties—the black migration northward, and white flight to the suburbs—followed by the black insurgency of the sixties, had one seldom-noted cultural consequence: Jokes about "niggers" became archaic and unfunny, and "Polish jokes" took their place.

*All in the Family,* the sitcom featuring Archie Bunker, was the longest-running Polish joke of all. Bunker (Carroll O'Connor) was not Polish, of course, nor a member of any identifiable ethnic group (by 1970, when the show premiered, a comedy targeting any particular white ethnic group might have faced pickets and boycotts). But as middle-class prejudice would have it, Archie was parochial, patriarchal, ignorant, and given to gross malapropisms. For example, he paid taxes to "the infernal revenue service." And as the conventional interpretation of the backlash would have it, he was belligerently racist, anti-Semitic, hawkish, and deeply threatened by "women's libbers," "faggots," and hippies.

The show was popular and controversial, and especially controversial because it was so popular. Did people watch it to laugh at Archie? Or for the *frisson* of hearing him utter illicit epithets like *nigger* and *kike* on prime-time TV? Or did they simply want to be reassured that, however bitter the arguments between Archie and his liberal, professionally oriented son-in-law, this unaccustomed political turmoil was still "all in the family"? The effect though, was to impress the blue-collar stereotype onto a generation of viewers. Well into the eighties, literate and often quite liberal people would use *All in the Family* as a major sociological reference point, and refer to white working-class males conveniently as "Archie Bunker types."

*Joe* (1970), Hollywood's first major contribution to the stereotype, was Archie Bunker with an armory. When we first meet him, Joe (Peter Boyle) is knocking back boilermakers in a rundown Queens bar, declaiming, for anyone who will listen, a litany of classic backlash sentiments:

> The nigguhs are getting all the money. Why work? You tell me—why the fuck work, when you can screw, have babies, and get paid for it. . . . The social workers—ever noticed that?—they're all nigguh-lovers. . . . I sweat my balls off forty hours a week. . . . [But the blacks:] Set fire to the cities and you get paid for it. Throw a few bombs and you get paid for it. . . . Liberals: 42 percent of all liberals are queer. . . . The rich white kids—hippies—sugar tit all the way. . . . Sex, drugs, pissin' on America. I'd like to kill one of them.

In the end, he does kill perhaps a half-dozen of them, huddled helplessly in a rural commune. But until that ghastly climax, it is hard to know whether Joe is meant to be a joke or a public menace. Like Archie, he is a buffoon. He pronounces *orgy* with a hard *g*, and is clearly as eager to participate in one as to annihilate the hippies who, at least in this movie, party night and day. Even the sound track mocks him with a folksy refrain: "Hey, Joe, don't it make you want to go to war once more?" But unlike Archie, who could be perversely lovable even at his nastiest, there is something dangerously off about Joe. When he learns that a black family has moved in down the block (with real nice furniture, "for coloreds," his wife explains soothingly), he goes down into the basement to stroke his guns. When he happens to meet someone who has actually killed a hippie—a well-off executive who has murdered his daughter's drug-dealer boyfriend—he becomes obsessively attached to his improbable new pal. Joe emerges as a maniac who has been barely kept in line by his pallid marriage and dull job. It is easy to forget, as the plot fades from memory, that in *Joe* it was the executive and not the steelworker who first killed a hippie and who, in the final bloodbath, shoots his own daughter.

*Taxi Driver* (1976) carried the theme of the demented worker one step further. Travis Bickle (Robert De Niro) represents the working class in a stage of surreal degeneration: he has no visible family, no real friends, no union worth mentioning, no on-the-job camaraderie. Here, the "limited associations" and parochial world of the working class have narrowed down to one man in a filthy apartment. Travis is even stupider than Joe or Archie; when asked in the opening interview for the taxi job whether he is "moonlighting," it is clear that he has no idea what that odd compound word means. He does not read newspapers and demonstrates his impatience with TV by kicking his set over during a tedious love scene. He has been deprived, by the scriptwriters, of even a reactionary ideology to focus his rage.

Below him is the chaotic street life of drug-dealing and prostitution, represented by a pimp who exploits underage girls. Above him is the cold, condescending world of the middle class, represented by a presidential candidate who insists on speaking in a phony populist first-person plural about how "we the people" suffered in Vietnam, from unemployment, etc. It's a toss-up which one of these sleazy characters Travis will turn his homicidal fury on first. The climactic scene, as in *Joe,* is mayhem: bodies everywhere, blood dripping from the walls and forming puddles on the floor. But Travis is at peace: This blue-collar worker has finally—and for reasons inscrutable to the audience—done his work.

In Hollywood's decade-long meditation on the working class—roughly 1970 to the early eighties—blue-collar environments, like war zones, were invariably settings for masculine mayhem. Hollywood's blue-collar men were, at any age, perpetual boys—embracing, punching each other's biceps, mock wrestling, rolling on the floor together—all with a masculine exuberance that most white-collar men would have left behind in high school. In *Blue Collar* (1978), the autoworker heroes (Harvey Keitel, Richard Pryor, and Yaphet Kotto) drink, horse around, and even have what Joe would have called an "orgy" together.

But in Hollywood, there is always an element of danger in blue-collar high jinks. In *The Deer Hunter* (1979), the steelworker heroes (Robert De Niro and Christopher Walken, among others) get into an improbably childish quarrel over a pair of hunting boots. A gun is drawn. After the hunt, though, tensions subside when they all shake up their cans of Rolling Rock and squirt each other, in a kind of phallic play appropriate to a junior-high-school locker room. In *Saturday Night Fever* (1977), Tony Manero (John Travolta) and his friends carry the horseplay too far. When one of them dies in a fall from the Verrazano-Narrows Bridge, Tony starts thinking of upward mobility; his working-class environment has become a health hazard.

More often, the working class itself is a monstrous threat, like the savage slaughterhouse workers in *The Texas Chainsaw Massacre* (1974), who are described by critic Robin Wood as "an exploited and degraded proletariat" preying on the "affluent young." In *Looking for Mr. Goodbar* (1977), the heroine (Diane Keaton) is undone by her taste for murderous, blue-collar hunks. In *Assault on Precinct 13* (1976), a refreshingly interracial blue-collar army attacks the police in a human wave, much like the masses of zombies in *Night of the Living Dead*. The difference between war zones and blue-collar settings is that in Hollywood's wars, boys become men; in the blue-collar world, men become boys—often very bad boys— and are likely to remain so for life.

The violence and roughhousing were symptomatic of another role played by Hollywood's blue-collar men: Like the poor, they symbolize the personal and collective past. They are, first of all, out of style, meaning that their tastes are ones that the middle class has long since abandoned. In a trivial but important way, the archaic condition of the working class is often signaled by food cues: In *The Deer Hunter,* a story of steelworkers drawn from small-town innocence into Vietnam, one of the circle of buddies ceremoniously eats a Twinkie dipped in mustard. It is the Twinkie—all sugar and refined flour—as much as the mustard, that caused health-conscious middle-class viewers to giggle.* In *Twice in a Life-*

---

* In 1975, the left community in Minneapolis—many of whose members were graduates of the student movement of the sixties—was torn by what became known as the "Twinkie wars." The issue was whether the local food co-ops, which were largely controlled by the left, should sell healthful, unprocessed foods (brown rice, fresh vegetables, etc.) or familiar commercial foods like Twinkies.

*time* (1985), another tale of steelworkers confronted with the challenges of modern life, the camera underscores the hero's proletarian status by drawing our attention to the white bread and Budweiser on the dinner table.

But the most archaic feature of Hollywood's blue-collar men is their values. They are deeply loyal—not to abstract ideals or ethical principles but to a narrow circle of friends and family. *The Deer Hunter* is a prolonged celebration of blue-collar male bonding; *The Godfather* (1971), which is about "ethnics," a stereotypical category overlapping with the working class, hinges on primitive allegiances forged in the old country. Very often, movie plots revolve around a test to blue-collar loyalties: Terry Molloy in *On the Waterfront* has to decide whether to stick with his pals in a corrupt longshoreman's union or adopt the more middle-class outlook of his girlfriend. Tony Manero has a similar choice between the blue-collar boys or his upwardly mobile dance partner. The construction worker hero of *Bloodbrother* (1978), played by Richard Gere, has to choose between his violently dysfunctional family and the therapeutic values represented by a kindly physician. In *Twice in a Lifetime*, a fifty-year-old steelworker (Gene Hackman) is torn between his tight-knit, family-centered community and his new love. His closest friend and coworker advises him to stay with his wife; his son, who has moved into a middle-class occupation and the thoroughly modern state of California, advises him to follow his heart.

Now, there are two ways to look at the past, or at a social group which has been assigned the symbolic burden of the past: as something to be reformed or overcome, or as something to be revered and restored. In movies like *Bloodbrother*, *Saturday Night Fever*, and *Twice in a Lifetime* the archaic

---

The latter position was upheld by some as the "proletarian line," while the advocates of whole grains were denounced as "petty bourgeois." This peculiar contest was emblematic of the strife occurring throughout the ex–New Left in the mid-seventies, a time when Marxist-Leninists among the left were earnestly trying to overcome their middle-class backgrounds and "proletarianize" themselves through menial labor and what they fancied to be proletarian lifestyles. For example, the Twinkie faction in Minneapolis also insisted that couples within its ranks formalize their unions through marriage.

blue-collar life must be transcended for more cosmopolitan vistas. But in *Rocky* (1976) the hero—described by critic Pauline Kael as the "embodiment of the out-of-fashion pure-at-heart"—triumphs, in spirit at least, against the cynical, cosmopolitan world represented by the black champion, Apollo Creed. In *The Godfather* the old-world values of the Mafia patriarch (Marlon Brando) are upheld against his college-educated son's cold-hearted obsession with the bottom line.

Outside of Hollywood, middle-class reveries on the working class began to divide along similar lines during the 1970s. From one point of view, the working class was not only archaic but obsolete, its boyish violence a sign of arrested development. In *The Greening of America*, for example, Charles Reich slotted blue-collar men into the lowest stage of "consciousness," below white-collar conformists and far below the psychically liberated hip types who represented the highest stage of human development. The working class became, for many middle-class liberals, a psychic dumping ground for such unstylish sentiments as racism, male chauvinism, and crude materialism: a rearguard population that loved white bread and hated black people.

In the alternative, more conservative view, the archaic qualities of the working class were transformed into something precious—the "traditional values" which the middle class saw slipping from its own grasp. The boyish physicality of the working class stood for a kind of manliness that white-collar professionals had long since surrendered to the bureaucracy. The parochialism of working-class life represented an admirable holdout against the intrusions of an increasingly cosmopolitan consumer culture. The economic injustice that made some men "workers" could be interpreted positively as a collective addiction to hard work and self-discipline. In this view, the "forgotten" working class stood for what the middle class itself had lost, or always seemed to be on the verge of losing: the capacity for self-denial and deferred gratification, the very traits required for middle-class success.

Both of these views, however, arose out of a common stereotype, and both were confused in the middle-class mind with personal memory, regret, and nostalgia. To middle-class men, the blue-collar stereotype could never be such a distant "other" as the poor, especially the black poor. Here were blood brothers, personified, in personal memory, by the high-school teammate left behind in one's hometown pumping gas, the Korean War buddies who had come back to factory jobs, the father or grandfather with callused hands and a knack with tools. Yet the blood between the classes, as anyone could see through the lens of the media discovery, was mostly bad.

To look at a male figure associated with the personal and historical past is to find both the father and the son, the man and the boy, someone to look up to and someone to move beyond. The middle-class image of the working class contained both figures, and was colored with nostalgia as well as contempt. The "worker" was both a throwback to childish, outmoded values *and* he was a collective superego, holding out for hard work, tract houses, and processed food against the mad drift of the psychedelicized culture at large. It helped, of course, that he himself was never invited to participate in the great middle-class enterprise of image-making and social "discovery."

## BEYOND THE STEREOTYPE

America's blue-collar workers *were* in revolt in the late sixties and early seventies, but not along the right-wing, traditionalist lines sketched by the media. The late sixties saw the most severe strike wave since shortly after World War II, and by the early seventies the new militancy had swept up autoworkers, rubber workers, steelworkers, teamsters, city workers, hospital workers, farmworkers, tugboat crewmen, gravediggers, and postal employees. For all the talk of racial backlash, black and white workers were marching, picketing, and organizing together in a spirit of class solidarity that had not been seen since the thirties. Nixon's "silent majority" was yelling as loud as it could—not racial epithets but the historic strikers' chant: "Don't cross the line!"

And something new was happening among the blue-collar work force. Young workers, many the same age as the campus rebels, were wearing their hair shoulder length, smoking pot, and beginning to question the totalitarian regimen of factory life. As Stanley Aronowitz reported from the mammoth GM plant at Lordstown, Ohio, "Long hair, marijuana, and rock music is [sic] shared by nearly all young workers in the plant." Young workers were bringing a new dimension to blue-collar insurgency—a rejection of the endless tedium of assembly work. In the massive 1970 GM strike, in which 400,000 autoworkers walked out, the central demand was "thirty and out": retirement at any age after thirty years of service, at a generous pension. More commonly, the blue-collar revolt against work was carried out covertly, outside of union channels. Workers (especially on the grueling auto-assembly lines) were staying home on Mondays, getting high at work, and finding ingenious ways to slow down the assembly line and catch a few moments of rest.

There was even the possibility, in the late sixties, of an explosive convergence of the working-class insurgency and the student movement. Certainly many student radicals dreamed of such an alliance; and if the powerful also thought of it, they had reason to fear. All over the world, radical students plus discontented workers (or peasants) had been the classic ingredients of revolution. In France in 1968 striking students and workers (blue- *and* white-collar) almost toppled the government of Charles de Gaulle. American students borrowed many of their tactics (strikes, occupations) from the blue-collar uprisings of the 1930s; and workers in the sixties were catching the antiauthoritarian spirit of the student radicals. The civil rights movement had already spilled over into the black industrial working class, with the formation of militant groups like the League of Revolutionary Black Workers. Potentially, students and workers of all races might have agreed on the need to end the war, to democratize the workplace, and to open up the universities to all comers.

But the middle-class stereotype of the working class helped ensure that America's radical students and insurgent workers would not get together. Students, like their elders, came to think of blue-collar workers as racists, hardhats, and "Neander-thals." An anecdote from the early seventies illustrates the power of the stereotype. Two young leftists, recent Ivy League graduates I knew through friends in Boston, undertook to pro-letarianize themselves, as the expression went, by taking fac-tory jobs, cutting their hair short, and donning freshly pressed flannel shirts. To their surprise, the workers they had hoped to uplift looked like nothing so much as the hippies these earnest young radicals had left behind on the campus. Furthermore, the workers native to the factory refused to speak to them. As it turned out, the workers decided that the oddly dressed new-comers were narcotics agents and gave them a wide berth.

Everywhere, the middle-class stereotype proved to be too durable to be affected by the facts. When *Time* reported on the blue-collar "blues" in 1970 and documented the revolt against boring, repetitive work, it could not resist prefacing the story with the familiar stereotype. Only two pages before the obser-vation that "young workers are revolting against the job itself, or at least the way it is organized," we find this description of the American worker:

As psychologists and social researchers have confirmed, he believes in God and country—if not necessarily in equality and the right of dissent. He is convinced of the virtues of hard work, the necessity of saving and a steady, ordered way of life.

In their voting habits, too, blue-collar Americans were not, at the time of their discovery, shifting to the right. Nor was much of anybody, except perhaps for the media people who were now so anxious to document a surge of right-wing popu-lism. The 1968 presidential vote told the story: 50 percent of manual workers polled voted for Humphrey, 35 percent for Nixon, and 15 percent for Wallace. Blue-collar workers had been splitting their votes in similar proportions for a dozen years; in the 1956 presidential election, 50 percent voted Dem-ocratic and 50 percent Republican. In contrast, only 34 percent of the supposedly more liberal "professional and business" class voted Democratic in 1968, up only two percentage points from 1956.*

There was no excuse for omitting these facts from the media's 1969 discovery of the working class. Whatever provocation it had supposedly endured from militant blacks, hippies, or student protesters, the blue-collar working class remained steadfastly more liberal than the middle class, at least on the major economic and foreign-policy issues that distinguished the parties. Even Kevin Phillips, the conservative strategist who optimistically announced "The Emerging Republican Majority" in 1969, had to admit that the blue-collar vote was Democratic and that it was so by reason of clear-cut class interests:

> Fears that a Republican administration would undermine Social Security, Medicare, collective bargaining and aid to education played a major part in keeping socially conservative blue-collar workers and senior citizens loyal to the 1968 Democratic candidate.

And in their exhaustive analysis of the 1968 election results, Richard M. Scammon and Ben J. Wattenberg firmly insisted that the class contours of American politics remained what they had always been: The "elite" of "doctors, bankers, and businessmen" was Republican; while "those plain people who work with their hands" were Democratic.

Nor was there any evidence, in 1969, of a general "Middle American" shift to the right. It is true, as Phillips and Scammon and Wattenberg emphasized, that most Americans were conservative on what they termed the "social issues": crime, obscenity, demonstrations, drug use. Over 80 percent of Americans polled in 1968 wanted stricter laws on obscenity, a "stronger stand on student disorders," and opposed the legali-

---

* The percentage of blue-collar workers voting Democratic did go down in 1972, but remained higher than the Democratic vote by "professionals." According to the University of Michigan's Center for Policy Studies, 34 percent of professionals polled voted for George McGovern, compared to 39.4 percent of blue-collar workers and 52.6 percent of unskilled workers.

zation of marijuana. However, these opinions hardly represent a "shift," since even four years earlier there were no student demonstrations and no nude or pot-smoking hippies to disturb public sensibilities. On more traditional issues of economic justice, Americans were becoming not less but more liberal. For example, a comparison of polls taken in 1965 and 1968 showed sharp increases in the number of Americans who "often feel bad" about hunger in America, the treatment of American Indians, and the neglect of old people—with smaller but still significant increases in regretful feelings about slum conditions and the way "Negroes [are] treated." Perhaps most strikingly (and this must surely be counted as a judgment on a "social issue"), the number of Americans who at least professed a willingness to vote for a black presidential candidate was rising sharply: from 38 percent in 1958, to 59 percent in 1965, to an overwhelming 70 percent majority in 1970.

If there was a single, legitimate excuse for declaring a rightward shift among the blue-collar working class, it was George Wallace, who sought the presidency as an independent in 1964, '68, and '72. To the national media he was a foreign and repellent presence, with his heavily brilliantined hair, huge, red-jeweled Masonic ring, and defiant mispronunciations (e.g., *report* for *rapport*). But to his followers, he was a working-class rebel whose campaign literature raised the defiant question, "Can a former truck driver who married a former dime-store clerk and whose father was a plain dirt farmer be elected President of the United States?"

In the summer and fall of 1968, Wallace was showing strong support among white, northern blue-collar workers. A September Gallup poll found 25 percent of the nation's union members prepared to vote for him, and a survey of white males in the smokestack city of Gary, Indiana, found 38 percent of blue-collar men for Wallace, compared to 12.6 percent of white-collar men. Worse, some polls suggested that the more a person identified himself (or, more rarely, herself) as "working-class," the more likely he or she was to support this apparently racist and right-wing upstart.

Trade union and Democratic Party leaders were alarmed.

The workers were expected to follow their unions' instructions and vote for the Democratic candidate, Hubert Humphrey. But here they were, breaking ranks to follow a third-party maverick whose ideology was being nervously compared to fascism. To middle-class liberals, blue-collar support for Wallace was another case of the "politics of unreason." "Even in our well-educated society," an article in the liberal *Christian Century* commented condescendingly, "it is a mistake to assume that voters are rational people."

Working-class support for Wallace was not, however, as solid or extensive as it often appeared in the media. Most of the northern blue-collar support Wallace could claim in the summer of 1968 evaporated in the voting booth. When all the votes were counted and analyzed, it turned out that, in the North, blue-collar workers favored Wallace by only one percentage point over white-collar workers. Only in the South was there a major class differential. Blue-collar workers there gave Wallace 42 percent of their votes, compared to 23 percent from white-collar people. Even Kevin Phillips, who might have had reason to hope otherwise, concluded that "there was no reliable Wallace backing among blue-collar workers and poor whites as a class."

Furthermore, such support as Wallace had among northern workers was not something that genuine conservatives, like Phillips, could easily claim. Polls showed that Wallace voters were far more liberal than Nixon supporters on economic issues, though not on the emerging new "social issues." Among Wallace supporters, there was a decisive political cleavage by class, with his blue-collar supporters being more liberal on welfare-state issues than his white-collar backers. Also, confusingly, many of those who supported Wallace in the summer of '68 had supported the liberal and adamantly pro–civil rights candidacy of Robert F. Kennedy in the spring—before his assassination abruptly cut off the prospects for a *liberal* interracial, working-class constituency.

The working-class support Wallace did attract—transient and "unreliable" as it was—only partly reflected a racist backlash against black gains. George Corley Wallace was undeniably a high-profile racist and segregationist, but he was also, though many liberals appeared not to notice, a liberal on economic issues. He had been attacked by critics in the Alabama state legislature as "downright pink." The economic platform of his American Independent Party stressed expanded social welfare programs and the rights of labor. On the eve of the 1968 election, the head of the American Conservative Union was moved to denounce him as a danger from the left. "True conservativism," he said, "cannot be served by George Wallace. At heart he is a Populist with strong tendencies in the direction of a collectivist welfare state."

Even the national press occasionally caught the leftish undercurrent in Wallace's pitch. As the *Washington Post* observed:

> He is talking about poor people, "ordinary folks," and if you strip him of the Southern accent and some of the surrounding rhetoric you might mistake him for a New Left advocate of the poverty program, urging the maximum feasible participation of the poor and the return of local government to the people, "participatory democracy!"

Pollster Sam Lubell reported that "most of these Wallace supporters maintain, 'Wallace is for the workingman. He couldn't be for anyone else.' Some even talk of the Wallace movement as 'the start of a new labor party.' "

But Wallace was not a populist visionary with a plan for a more generous welfare state and a better deal for labor. He appealed to the resentments rather than the hopes of the "ordinary folks." Only those resentments were not, as many superficially concluded, solely about race. Wallace himself argued that the backlash that he symbolized and fomented sprang from class anger rather than race hatred: "I don't believe there is a backlash in this country against people of color. I think that is a journalistic expression. I think it was coined by the news media." The only real backlash, he believed, was against "the theoreticians and the bureaucrats," whose crimes, of course, included school busing and other integrationist measures.

In fact, Wallace had dropped overt references to blacks when he entered the national political scene in 1964. It is true that he didn't *have* to mention race to get a racist message across; he remained a symbol of intransigent segregationism no matter what he said. But what he did say, in the line of vituperations, was directed almost entirely at the white professional middle class: "the over-educated ivory-tower folks with pointed heads looking down their noses at us," "the liberals, intellectuals and long-hairs [who] have run the country for too long," and the "intellectual morons" with their "sissy attitudes." The self-appointed experts and intellectuals had had their day; the people he listened to were "the workingman in Ohio," "the cab driver in California," "the clerk in Indiana." Wallace saw himself leading their revolt against the "phonies" and "social engineers" in Washington, whom he promised to throw into the Potomac, along with their briefcases.

Wallace's appeal to class anger worked. A detailed survey of blue-collar Wallace supporters in Gary, Indiana, showed that their strongest resentments were not against blacks (though they were indeed strongly resentful of what they perceived as black gains), but against the white-collar middle class. "Northern Wallaceites often regard their working-class group as unjustly held back in comparison to white-collar workers and professionals," the study concluded, and this "class comparison" was politically more decisive than racial resentment. In fact, so effective was Wallace's anti-middle-class populism that it was adopted by the party that traditionally represents the professional middle and upper classes. In the sincerest form of flattery, Vice President Spiro Agnew dedicated himself to attacking the "effete corps of impudent snobs who characterize themselves as intellectuals."

## REASONS FOR ANGER

Much of this chapter has been about the contempt of the middle class for the working class—the insulting stereotypes, the snobbery disguised as sociology, the blindness that allowed the working class to be "discovered" in the first place. The most shocking message of the backlash was that the hostility went both ways. To mainstream sociologists, working-class antagonism to the professional middle class was part of the old American problem of "anti-intellectualism," which popped up from time to time among the ignorant and resentful. More sensitive observers in the late sixties and early seventies suggested that there were solid and immediate reasons for working-class hostility: One was the war in Vietnam. Poor and working-class youths fought; middle-class youths, exempted from service by their student deferrals, were free to protest on college campuses, burn their draft cards or, if they were of a mind to, the American flag.

Another reason for hostility was the longstanding economic disadvantage of working-class Americans—a circumstance that was painfully highlighted, though in opposite ways, by both the civil rights and student movements. Despite the general prosperity of the sixties, blue-collar workers' real earnings were declining, eaten away, in large part, by wartime inflation. Middle-class liberals had imagined that there was only one disadvantaged group, the poor, which, in the imagery of the late sixties, increasingly meant the black poor. The income gap between the middle class and the white blue-collar working class was invisible and usually ignored. In one of the more socially conscious scenes in *Joe*, the hero asks his new friend, the executive Bill, "Whaddya make an hour?" With some amusement, Bill explains that he is paid not by the hour but by the year. He makes $60,000 a year (admittedly a very high executive salary for the time); Joe makes $4 an hour.

The fact that the white working class was itself poor relative to the middle class contributed to the tangle of racist and anti-middle-class sentiments often expressed, for example, by working-class Wallace supporters. As has been explained many times since the late sixties, it was not middle-class suburban liberals who were affected by school busing and other forms of "social engineering." Nor did executives and college professors have much to lose from black demands for equity in hiring. Most blacks had no hope of finding a place in the executive suites or faculty lounges; they were aspiring to blue-collar jobs, such as in the building trades, where color-blind hiring would have meant, among other things, that a white worker could no longer expect to pass his job along to his son.

This is not to say that white working-class people were or are "naturally" more racist because they are more likely to be in contact with black people. A common explanation for the presumed higher levels of racism among white workers is that they are likely to be on the front lines of integration—in "changing" neighborhoods and in blue-collar work situations where blacks might hope to be employed. But a detailed analysis of 1964 survey data showed that, among northern manual laborers, those having the most contact with blacks—in their neighborhoods and jobs—were the *most* favorably disposed toward integration. The highest levels of intolerance were found among those northern workers who had the least contact with blacks.

Blue-collar people did not resent middle-class liberals so much because they were, as Joe would have put it, "nigger-lovers" but because of their air of moral superiority and contempt for the whites who would actually have to make room, in their schools and workplaces, for black progress. As a schoolteacher from a blue-collar family put it in Robert Coles's 1971 study *The Middle Americans*:

> They [middle-class liberals] can cry with sympathy for some insolent, fresh-talking Negro demonstrator . . . but if we even try to explain our problems, they start telling us how wrong we are, and how we need to be more "open" . . . and "accepting."

Relative poverty also gave blue-collar Americans a somewhat jaundiced view of the student movement. To people who could not afford college educations, student protesters seemed like "rich kids" who simply failed to appreciate their good fortune. "A bath, a haircut and a good old-fashioned strap would get most of them back in line," the wife of a $10,000-a-year sewer-equipment salesman told *Newsweek.* "But their mothers are too busy at cocktail parties and bridge clubs to be mothers." Even blue-collar people who agreed with the student demonstrators found it hard to like them. A forty-three-year-old steamfitter in Coles's study seconded his wife's opinion that "some of the students are good, mean well [and] are on the workingman's side against the big corporations." But he still "shout[ed] at the demonstrators" on the TV news, explaining that "a certain kind of professor" and student were arrogant "snobs."

Finally, economic deprivation gave the working class a very different perspective on the problem of affluence. In the late sixties, affluence was still a vexing issue to intellectuals of the middle class: a goal, certainly, for the poor, but a millstone and possibly a threat to more fortunate Americans. But material excess was not an aching social problem to people who earned $4 an hour, and the tackiness of mass culture was hardly an affront to men, like the plumber quoted by *Newsweek,* who could not afford a color television set. In the Gallup poll commissioned by *Newsweek,* 54 percent of college graduates agreed that America was "becoming too materialistic," compared to only 36 percent with a grade-school education. One reason the middle class seemed like snobs was that they appeared so disdainful of the consumer options—the tract house, the matching furniture sets, the second car—that the working class still aspired to. As historian William Leuchtenberg observed:

> Campus *sans-culottes* scoffed at split-level respectability, but workers who had scrimped to achieve lower-middle-class status and the appurtenances of the consumer culture felt a fierce protectiveness about their achievements.

In fact, very few middle-class adults were *sans-culottes,* and fewer still were prepared to combat affluence by rejecting their own material comforts. But they were, as ever, struggling to redefine the "tasteful" away from the common and mass-produced. As a result, the cultural gap between the classes was beginning to take a new form: not simply more, and more expensive, things for the more fortunate but the contrived appearance of less. For the middle class, a search for tasteful authenticity in red wine and unprocessed food (boeuf bourgignon and other foods of peasant provenance for the adults, lentils for the young); for the working class, the affordable comforts of Budweiser, tuna casserole, and TV dinners.

## AN ANCIENT ANTAGONISM

But working-class hostility toward the middle class was not the bitter product of one turbulent decade. To the working class, the professional middle class *is* an elite. Money is only part of its perceived advantage. The other difference, which middle-class people have traditionally not liked to acknowledge, arises from the division of labor between the two classes. People in both classes must work for a living, but, as John Kenneth Galbraith has observed, all work is not the same. For most people, meaning working-class people, work is "fatiguing or monotonous or, at a minimum, a source of no particular pleasure." Only in the professional middle class is work seen, and often experienced, as intrinsically rewarding, creative, and important. But to admit the difference, Galbraith argued, would be to acknowledge a deep and disquieting inequality:

> In both [capitalist and communist] societies it serves the democratic conscience of the more favored groups to identify themselves with those who do hard physical labor. A lurking sense of guilt over a more pleasant, agreeable, and remunerative life can often be assuaged by the observation "I am a worker too."

The difference, though, goes deeper than comfort. It is, more fundamentally, a difference defined by an inequality of power. Relative to the working class, the holders of middle-class occupations are in positions of command or, at the very least, authority. Their job is to conceptualize, in broad terms, what others must do. The job of the worker, blue or pink collar, is to get it done. The fact that this is a relationship of domination—and grudging submission—is usually invisible to the middle class but painfully apparent to the working class. As autoworker John Lippert wrote (in discussing the hostility of his coworkers to college-educated leftists): "In the experience of most people in the plants, colleges train people (e.g., teachers, social workers, engineers) to do one thing: to keep the workers in line."

Historically, the antagonism between the classes is as old as the professional middle class itself, and stems from the fact that one of the purposes of the modern professions was in fact "to keep the workers in line." The period from roughly 1870 to 1920, in which the professions took shape and the professional middle class emerged, was also a period of violent clashes between the working class and its traditional antagonist, the capitalist class. In strike after strike—from the coal fields of Tennessee to the mines of Colorado to the mills of Massachusetts—workers confronted the armed power of capital or its proxy, the National Guard.* In the 1880s, the Knights of Labor, with 700,000 members, declared that "the attitude of the Order to the existing industrial system is necessarily one

---

* The entire bloody history of American labor struggles is neatly forgotten by most celebrants—and critics—of Middle America. Reeve Vanneman and Lynn Weber Cannon give a fascinating example in their highly informative book *The American Perception of Class.* In 1980, columnist David Broder sought to explain Ronald Reagan's appeal to Middle America by citing the town of Coeur d'Alene, Idaho, as a "community where families were strong and unions were weak . . . where employers looked out for their employees!" Coeur d'Alene, Vanneman and Cannon remind Broder, was

> the site of two of the most violent labor conflicts in U.S. history. In 1892 armed miners attacked a struck mine defended by private guards hired to protect imported strikebreakers. The miners succeeded in dropping 100 pounds of dynamite into an operating mill, destroying it, and killing one strikebreaker while wounding others. At another mill, company guards opened fire on the striking miners, killing 5 and wounding 14. The miners fought back, captured the mill, and sent the guards out of the county. This victory was followed by the capture of another mine, where the miners again forced the nonunion workers to flee the county.

of war." In the 1900s, the revolutionary Industrial Workers of the World attracted a million members; and the Socialist Party's Eugene V. Debs won 900,000 votes in the presidential election of 1912. Throughout this period, the knee-jerk capitalist response was repression: armed guards to break strikes, beatings, jailings, and lynchings to crush the militant leadership of the working class.

The emerging professional middle class stepped into the fray in the role of peacemakers. Their message to the capitalists was that nonviolent social control would in the long run be more effective than bullets and billy clubs. Mines and mills did not have to be hotbeds of working-class sedition; they could be run more smoothly by trained, "scientific" managers. Working-class families did not have to be perpetual antagonists to capitalist society; they could be "Americanized" by teachers and social workers and eventually seduced by ad men and marketing experts. Almost every profession or would-be profession, from sociology to home economics, had something to offer in the great task of "taming" the American working class.

The professionals' stance as neutral mediators barely concealed their own class interests. In the Progressive Era ideology of the professional middle class, all social problems could be transformed into technical problems, and technical problems could only be solved by expanding the new class of professional experts. As historian and reformer Fredrick Jackson Turner explained in 1910, it was necessary to train a huge cadre of "administrators, legislators, judges, and experts . . . who shall disinterestedly and intelligently mediate between contending interests." The most dangerous conflict—and the greatest challenge—for the new experts was the conflict between workers and capitalists:

> When the word "capitalist classes" and "the proletariate"
> [*sic*] can be used and understood in America, it is surely time
> to develop such men, with the ideal of service to the State,
> who may help to break the force of these collisions.

And in 1907, Edward A. Ross, one of America's first sociologists, advocated "social engineering" to control class conflict, warning that it might soon be necessary to "turn over the defense of society to professionals."

Professionals, of course, cost money—in salaries for professional managers and engineers, in charitable contributions to welfare agencies, in public expenditures for teachers. But the ultimate decision of American capitalists, as they moved into the twentieth century, was—to put it somewhat crudely—that a cadre of professionals was cheaper than an army of Pinkertons.

The profession of management was born on the front lines of the early-twentieth-century battle between labor and capital, and its story illustrates the tensions between the working class and the emerging middle class. Since the story has been so well told elsewhere, I will be recklessly brief: Until the early twentieth century there was no profession of management—or, for that matter, of engineering. The reason, as the virtual inventor of scientific management, Frederick Taylor, later observed ruefully, was that "the shop was really run by the workmen, and not by the bosses." Manual and mental labor had not yet been sorted into distinct occupations; skilled craftsmen dominated both the technology and the organization of the work process. This left the employer in the vexing situation of being unable to comprehend or control the labor he paid for. Only the workers could judge, for example, how long a given job should take, and hence how much they should be paid.

Taylor's contribution was to show how the intellectual command of the production process could be stripped from the workers and concentrated in a more reliable cadre of middle-class managers and engineers. Through a careful analysis of the production process, the complex and intellectually demanding work of the craftsman could be broken down into simple, repetitive motions to be divided among less-skilled workers. Henceforth, no mere worker would be able to comprehend or control the entire process; each would be reduced to a few repetitive motions, such as turns of a wrench. Meanwhile the manager or engineer, armed with a stopwatch, now oversaw the work process, determining who would do what and, crucially, how fast it should be done.

Henry Ford's assembly line sealed the new division of labor into the hard steel of heavy machinery. America's working class began to be transformed into an army of wrench-turners, required neither to think nor to create—in fact, usually required *not* to think or create. The creative functions (such as designing new products) were removed from the shop floor to the engineer's workstation; the day-to-day decision-making was lifted into the clean and quiet offices of management. This "rationalization" of production did not succeed in taming the working class, which rose up with a new burst of militance in the 1930s. But it did greatly enhance the day-to-day power of employers over their blue-collar hirelings, while—not incidentally—providing employment for growing numbers of educated, white-collar men.

Outside of the industrial workplace, other professions consolidated themselves by offering to "mediate" class conflict or by usurping skills that had belonged to the working class. Social workers and teachers provided invaluable services to the urban poor, but in an ideological context that stressed "Americanization" (patriotism as opposed to class or ethnic identity) and middle-class gentility—or, as they insisted on calling it, "right living." Medicine achieved its professional monopoly in part through a campaign to discredit and outlaw indigenous healers, especially midwives, who had played a key role in every ethnic working-class community. (This was a dubious "reform," since as late as 1910 midwives were achieving lower rates of stillbirths and maternal mortality than the professional physicians who sought to eliminate them.) Public-health officials introduced the sanitary measures that eventually curbed epidemics of infectious diseases, but they also incurred lower-class resentment by their heavy-handed policing of immigrant ghettos.

Today, few people retain any active memory of these historical insults to the working class. But resentment persists in the form of the common perception that middle-class professionals and managers don't really *do* anything—certainly nothing that justifies their superior pay and status. Middle-class functions like supervision and management, and even conceptualization and innovation, are shadowy undertakings at best. To workers who may feel justifiably that they would be more productive without so much professional and managerial interference, middle-class occupations are likely to look like scams for avoiding "real" work.

This was, in fact, the first lesson I was given, as a child of upwardly mobile working-class parents, about the class our family aspired to join. My father, who had been a gandy dancer for the Union Pacific Railroad and a copper miner in Butte, Montana, could not say the word *doctor* without the virtual prefix *quack*. Lawyers were *shysters,* as in *shyster-lawyer;* and professors were without exception *phonies.* These judgments were cynical and confusing, since my father's life strategy had been to escape back-breaking manual labor by joining the ranks of the quacks and the phonies. Later, as an adult, I asked him if these attitudes had been common among his co-workers and drinking companions in Butte in the forties. Yes, of course, he said, because everyone could see that doctors, lawyers, and white-collar managers "didn't do a goddamn thing," yet got paid better than the men who daily risked their lives in the mines.

In interviews with blue-collar chemical workers conducted in the late seventies and early eighties, David Halle found the same universal judgment: It is only workers who actually work. Consider this exchange.

RESEARCHER: Are lawyers working men?

WORKER: . . . No! They don't really work. They just sit and hire people who do the work. . . .

RESEARCHER: Are big business[men] working men?

WORKER: Of course not, they just sit on their butts all day.

RESEARCHER: Am I [professor] a working man?

WORKER [*bitterly*]: No! You're not a working man. . . . You don't breathe in all these fumes, all these chemicals and shit.

Sociologists Richard Sennett and Jonathan Cobb encountered the same resentment in their research for *The Hidden Injuries of Class.* Describing the obstacles to their study, they reported:

Trust was finally established when people felt they could express anger to us about the barriers they felt between people in our class and theirs. "You mean, Dick," a plumber said to Richard Sennett, "you mean you make a good living just by sitting around and thinking? By what right? Now don't take this personally—I mean I'm sure you're a smart fellow and all that—but that's really the life, not having to break your balls for someone else."

It is not only that middle-class professionals appear not to work. What work they do often takes the form of harrassing those below them. Consider this account of a shop-floor encounter from Mike Lefevre, a steelworker interviewed by Studs Terkel:

> This one foreman I've got, he's a kid. He's a college graduate. He thinks he's better than everybody else. He was chewing me out and I was saying, "Yeah, yeah, yeah." He said, "What do you mean, yeah, yeah, yeah. Yes, *sir*." I told him, "Who the hell are you, Hitler? What is this 'Yes, sir' bullshit? I came here to work, I didn't come here to crawl. There's a fuckin' difference."

As a consequence of his assertiveness—a quality prized among professionals but regarded as a "bad attitude" in most blue- and pink-collar work situations—Lefevre reported he "got broke down to a lower grade and lost twenty-five cents an hour, which is a hell of a lot." Similar experiences produced the kind of bitterness expressed by a forty-one-year-old garment worker interviewed by Sandy Carter:

> I know they [technical and managerial employees] do work, but they don't do work like I do. They keep their eye on us; they make sure that everything runs smooth. But we're the ones who do the production. They're just here to make sure we do it like they want.

Or this from a young steelworker:

> As far as I'm concerned I got no use for the intellectual, the so-called expert, who sits around all day dreaming up new ways to control my life.

Outside the workplace, the class conflict continues. How, after all, do working-class people, with their supposedly limited range of associations, encounter the professional middle class? Not, in most cases, as friends or co-workers but in the role of teachers, social workers, or physicians. All of these are "helping professions," full of generous-spirited people, but they are also roles that confer authority and the power to make judgments about others. The teacher will determine whether your child's difficulties stem from a behavior problem, a learning disability, or a simple lack of effort. The social worker, who may have vastly different notions of what constitutes "normal" family life, will scrutinize and diagnose your intimate problems. The physician will pass judgments on your habits and lifestyle; he or she will very likely also treat you (if you are a poor or working-class patient) in an unconsciously patronizing or condescending manner. No wonder, then, that in Sennett and Cobb's study, working-class respondents felt "that an educated, upper-middle-class person was in a position to judge them, and that the judgment rendered would be that working-class people could not be respected as equals."

For working-class people, relations with the middle class are usually a one-way dialogue. From above come commands, diagnoses, instructions, judgments, definitions—even, through the media, suggestions as to how to think, feel, spend money, and relax. Ideas seldom flow "upward" to the middle class, because there are simply no structures to channel the upward flow of thought from class to class. Graduate-school courses do not invite "ordinary" people to speak to classes of professionals-in-training. Managers (outside of experiments in improving the "quality of work life") do not solicit new approaches from their subordinates. Members of the helping professions seldom invite suggestions or criticism from their clients, especially clients perceived as lower class. There is simply no way for the working-class or poor person to capture the attention of middle-class personnel without seeming rude or insubordinate. In the imposed silence of working-class life, hostility thrives. As a forty-six-year-old mother of three, diagnosed as suffering from a "character disorder," said of her social worker:

God I hate that woman. She makes me feel so stupid. Seems like everything that I do is wrong—the way I am with my kids, with my husband, even my sex life. She knows it all. Personally, I think her ideas are a little screwed up, but I can't tell her that.

The delusion of "knowing it all" is more than an individual failing. The structure of the professions, with their steep educational barriers, seems to assure that no outsider has anything to offer. The autodidact, the talented amateur, have been so thoroughly excluded that the possibility of their existence—in large numbers—has been virtually forgotten. Within its fortress of "expertise," the middle class imagines it is the sole repository of useful information—even information about the lives of those who dwell outside the moats. Recall the sociology text that commented that the working-class person "often fails to realize that his story is neither understandable nor interesting to the other person."

The most ubiquitous one-way channel of communication between the classes is television. By the sixties, most Americans, including the poorest, had been drawn into the homogeneous national culture created by network television. There they encountered many kinds of people, including black-power advocates, student protesters, and experts commenting on movements and social trends. But they definitely did not encounter people like themselves. "In the land of the media, whether it is movies, magazines or TV," Floyd Smith, president of the International Association of Machinists, told *Time* in 1970, "Daddy always goes to the office, not to the factory."

Network executives, you will recall, acknowledged having completely "forgotten" the working-class majority. *Its* activism —the upsurge of strikes and militant job actions in the late sixties—was scantily covered relative to the movements of students or minorities, and was never framed as a "crisis," a challenging new phenomenon with its own media heroes and personalities. For example, *Time*'s 1970 article on the blue-collar labor insurgency featured none of the individual insurgents. Only one of the accompanying photos showed actual strikers, and none of them were identified by name. The other photos—hardhats marching on Wall Street, Charlie Chaplin in *Modern Times*, and a poster for the movie *Joe*—illustrated the stereotype but had nothing to do with the story.

In fact, in the sixties it was hard to find a blue-collar worker in the media at all. A report titled *Work in America*, commissioned by the federal government in 1971, observed:

> Today, there is virtually no accurate dramatic representation —as there was in the 1930's—of men and women in working-class occupations. . . . Research shows that less than one character in ten on television is a blue-collar worker, and these few are usually portrayed as crude people with undesirable social traits. Furthermore, portrayals tend to emphasize class stereotypes: lawyers are clever, while construction workers are louts.

So on the eve of their discovery, the working-class majority found on their screens a dramatic new image of the American polity. People were jumping up and down, as it were, with their grievances, their visions, their demands for a better world or a fair share—but never "people like us." In Robert Coles's study, the working-class responses fairly ache with a sense of exclusion and neglect. A fireman's wife told him: "The world hears those demonstrators making their noise. The world doesn't hear me, and doesn't hear a single person I know." And a gas station owner's wife said ruefully:

> If you're a student at a fancy college, then anything you say, the television people are there to take it all down. They put those doped-up hippies and radicals on the screen every other night. Maybe it's our fault. We don't want the attention. . . . Maybe if we talked more, we'd get the attention. But who wants it?

Perhaps most important, television was a new channel through which middle-class professionals could address the working class. At work they gave orders. In schools and social agencies they judged and condescended. Now here they were in one's own home, as televised commentators and experts, scolding, moralizing, carping. As John, a Polish-American machinist, explained:

> I turn on that television station we've got, and it's better than a comedy show. The way they speak on those talk shows! The announcer, with his phony English accent! And the things they say, it makes you want to go and smash the damn set! They're full of long lectures, and they're always "reconsidering" something. . . . There are times when I completely agree with them, but it's their *attitude* that gets you. They're conceited.

It was a mystery to many middle-class observers why so much antagonism identified with the backlash was directed at the media. Spiro Agnew targeted the media for some of his most vicious attacks, as have right-wing populists ever since. It was not that the media had become "too liberal," or that people inevitably shoot the bearer of bad news. What media leaders could not see, as they agonized over the alienation of Middle America, was that the bearer, in this case, was himself bad news. He looked like a "conceited" professor or, worse, like management. Only, in this case, you could not even risk twenty-five cents an hour for the satisfaction of talking back. There is no talking back to TV. You can shout at the screen, like the frustrated viewer quoted above. Or, like Travis Bickle of *Taxi Driver,* you can kick it over.

At the time of its discovery, few mainstream, middle-class commentators could imagine the real sources of working-class hostility. The easy explanation, and the one dictated by the blue-collar stereotype, was that the working class was hostile to middle-class liberalism; and the easy solution was to become less liberal. This was the direction in which many erstwhile liberal intellectuals, repelled by the student movement, were already heading. The stereotype of the reactionary, authoritarian, blue-collar worker helped legitimize their rightward drift. And since the stereotype was a middle-class creation, this was also, in a sense, its function: to provide a spiritual touchstone for an emerging middle-class conservatism—and a cultural home for the "traditional values" of the middle class.

But, if anything, working-class anger should have shown that middle-class liberalism had not gone far enough. It had been shaped by the discovery of poverty, and defined by a concern for the poor—usually imagined as a tiny minority, huddled in their "pockets of poverty." The middle-class, liberal imagination had not anticipated the possibility that huge numbers of people, in many respects thoroughly "ordinary," were also in some sense deprived, neglected, and downtrodden. It was one thing to talk about "equality" and "social change" in relation to a minority, quite another to imagine reform on the scale of the American majority. Middle-class liberalism began to fall back in confusion; it was simply not up to the challenge.

But the fact that the working class was "discovered" in a mood of acute hostility had one clear psychic consequence for the middle class as a whole—liberal, conservative, or uncertain. It could no longer imagine itself as the core of the great American majority. It could no longer pretend to represent the universal welfare, the universal perspective. Here was the true majority, the existence of which had been barely suspected, and it was an angry, embittered majority, hostile, apparently above all, to the middle class itself. In discovering the working class, the middle class discovered a negative, and hideously unflattering, image of itself: an isolated elite, pretentiously liberal, and despised by authentic, hardworking Americans.

## CHAPTER FOUR

# THE "NEW CLASS": A BLUDGEON FOR THE RIGHT

IN THE 1988 PRESIDENTIAL CAMPAIGN, almost two decades after the discovery of the working class, Americans were presented with a striking inversion of class rhetoric: A multimillionaire Republican—scion of the old Yankee upper class and enthusiastic defender of the anti-labor economic policies of the Reagan administration—attacked his Democratic opponent for being, among other things, a member of an "elite." "It's the ultimate triumph of the populist revolution in Republican politics," commented conservative analyst Kevin Phillips. "Here we have the nation's leading preppy—an ornament and offspring of the Establishment—winning as a barefoot populist."

The elite that George Bush charged his opponent with belonging to was the "liberal elite," and he was only echoing what had become since the 1970s the central intellectual insight of the American right: that liberalism represents the interests of an elite as opposed to the needs of "ordinary," "mainstream" people. Or to state this proposition in its full Orwellian glory: Liberal notions of economic justice and equality are only a camouflage for the ambitions of a narrow and selfish social elite.

Until the 1970s, the American right had been small and

aristocratic in temperament. On domestic issues it was pro-business, anti-labor, and opposed to liberal measures to aid the poor and lift the burden of racial discrimination. The New Right, which emerged in the mid-seventies and reached full strength with the election of Ronald Reagan in 1980, was no less committed to the old right's economic agenda and no less loyal to the interests of big business and established wealth. But it was opposed to at least one elite—the "liberal elite" that had first come under fire in the Wallace and Agnew campaigns. And this made it, rhetorically speaking, the ally of the "little guy," the Middle American, even the blue-collar worker, against the cynical manipulations of the "liberal establishment."

In the intellectual theories of the right, the liberal elite is much more than a political antagonist. It is a *class,* known formally as the New Class. Right-wing definitions vary, but it is always defined as a slice of the professional middle class: in particular, a slice calculated to exclude people, such as corporate employees and professionals in private practice, who may indeed be likely, by virtue of their occupations alone, to be pro-business and anti-liberal.

Paradoxically, though, the New Class so defined also includes the intellectuals of the right—journalists, commentators, think-tank residents, authors, speechwriters, and the like. If there was a wicked and domineering New Class, they were as much a part of it as the liberals they excoriated. At one level, simple opportunism dictated this "class treason" on the part of the right. The events of the sixties had seemed to show that the middle class was inclined at least to liberalism, while the working-class majority was inclined to bigotry and reaction. If all this was true—and the media's discovery of the working class seemed to leave little room for doubt—then the obvious strategy for politically ambitious members of the middle class was to renounce their own kind and embrace the dubious populism represented by Spiro Agnew and, more recently, George Bush.

But the right's rhetorical hatred of the New Class was not only a matter of opportunism. It reflected what was, by the seventies, a widespread uneasiness within the professional middle class—a growing awareness that this class was indeed an elite, estranged from the concerns of "ordinary," working-class Americans. On the left, there was a parallel revulsion against the middle class, which some remnants of the student movement now denounced, in the classic terms of Leninist invective, as a selfish and vacillating "petty bourgeoisie." What had begun as class-consciousness—an awareness of the middle class as one class among others—seemed to degenerate, in the seventies and eighties, into self-hate.

On the right, the glimmer of self-awareness embodied in the notion of the New Class was to remain weirdly stunted: The New Class is always "someone else"—an alien group whose one clear function is to serve as a rhetorical bludgeon in the war against liberalism. And at least at the level of rhetoric, this weapon has been effective: The word *liberal*, having spent so much time in the company of *elite* and in association with a malevolent New Class, has been discredited and rendered almost useless. In this chapter, we follow the notion of the New Class from its origins on the left to its unfortunate denouement in the policies of the right.

## THE NEOCONSERVATIVES AND THE NEW CLASS

The idea of a left-leaning and power-hungry New Class originated among a small group of intellectuals centered around the journals *Commentary* and the *Public Interest*. Introducing these "neoconservatives" in 1977, *Newsweek* announced:

> In intellectual circles, the social thinkers who were once the driving force of Democratic liberalism—men like Arthur Schlesinger, Jr., and John Kenneth Galbraith—have been upstaged by a group of "neoconservative" academics, many of them refugees from the liberal left, including Daniel Bell, Nathan Glazer, Irving Kristol, James Q. Wilson, Edward

Banfield, Seymour Martin Lipset and Sen. Daniel P. Moynihan of New York.

Some of them were in fact refugees from Marxism; many of them began their move to the right in the sixties, where we last encountered them analyzing the "lower classes" and denouncing the student movement. The idea of the New Class was something they had first come across on the left and which they refurbished in the 1970s for the purpose of discrediting the left.

Even the term *New Class* betrays its origins, for in the standard Marxist description there were only two noteworthy classes in capitalist societies—the proletariat and the bourgeoisie. From a strict Marxist point of view, any other group qualifying as a "class" would have to be new, for Marx could hardly have overlooked anything as important as a major social class. The heretical idea that there could be a previously unsuspected social class in industrial societies had been incubated in that part of the American left—usually called anti-Stalinist or Trotskyist—which had parted company with the Communist Party over the issue of the Soviet Union. To the Communists, the Soviet Union was a "workers' paradise." To the Trotskyists, it was at best a "deformed workers' state," at worst, the left-wing analogue of fascism.

From the thirties through the fifties, New York City's tiny band of Trotskyist intellectuals wrestled with the problem of what had gone wrong with the Russian revolution, and, almost equally important, how to characterize its disappointing outcome. What *was* the Soviet Union? It obviously wasn't capitalist, but neither was it a "dictatorship of the proletariat," if that unfortunate phrase was supposed to mean that the working class was running things. So who exactly was in charge? Evidently the bureaucrats and something that could be called the intelligentsia were on top, but who, in rigorous Marxist terms, were *they*?

The eventual answer was that the Soviet bureaucracy represented an entirely new, and generally unforeseen, social class. This interpretation received important confirmation in

1957 with the English translation of *The New Class*, by the Yugoslav dissident Milovan Djilas. Djilas had been second in command to Tito during the Yugoslav revolution; now he declared that the revolution had been betrayed by a new class rooted in the "political bureaucracy." All communist revolutions, he argued, had run the same course: Declaring themselves victories of the proletariat, they had succeeded only in replacing the old capitalist class with a new managerial and bureaucratic elite:

> For a long time the Communist revolution and the Communist system have been concealing their true nature. The emergence of the new class has been concealed under socialist phraseology and, more important, under the new collective forms of property ownership. The so-called socialist ownership is a disguise for the real ownership by the political bureaucracy.

It was not at first obvious that there might be a similarly cunning class within capitalist societies like the United States. In the fifties and sixties, a few intellectuals used the term *New Class* to describe the American professional middle class, but without passing judgment on the political ambitions, if any, of this group. Writing in the sixties, David Bazelon, a former Trotskyist turned corporate lawyer and then free-lance commentator, described the American New Class as a politically fractious lot whose membership ranged from Herman Kahn, the nuclear strategist, on the right, to William Kunstler, the radical defense lawyer, on the left—from John Birchers to reform Democrats.

It remained for the neoconservatives to discover a left-leaning New Class within the United States, and in several ways they were ideally situated to do so. As ex-Trotskyists, many of them were familiar with the New Class as an explanation for the power structure of the Soviet Union. Some of them were also aware of Bazelon's theories, which were first published in *Commentary*, a journal that had started out in the fifties on the left. Finally, as leading participants in the intellectual backlash against the student movement, they had witnessed firsthand the "excesses" of middle-class student radicalism. The conservative inference was ripe and waiting to be drawn: that the student radicals of the sixties represented an American New Class no less ruthless and potentially dictatorial than its communist counterpart.

Michael Novak, a former liberal now at a conservative think-tank, took the first step toward this startling conclusion. He stumbled across Bazelon's notion of the New Class in Michael Harrington's 1968 book *Toward a Democratic Left,* where the American New Class was presented in a positive light as a potential "constituency of conscience" for the left. Novak, however, at once saw its utility as a weapon that could be wielded against the left. His reasoning, as set forth in a 1972 article in *Commentary,* was beguilingly syllogistic: The student left belonged to a certain class; this class had its own interests; therefore everything that the left did was aimed secretly at advancing these interests. As he wrote:

> The New Class covers its political campaigns . . . with an aura of morality so thick it would make the righteous Anglo-Saxons of a century ago envious. Because two of its chief causes—civil rights (including poverty) and resistance to the Indochinese war—are morally sound, it has been able to conceal its own lust for power and its own class interests, at least from itself.

The most important of these class interests was "patronage." Referring to the War on Poverty, Novak argued that the left advocated an "activist federal government committed to 'change.' " Why? Because such an effort would generate "hundreds of thousands of jobs and opportunities . . . [for] those whose hearts itch to do good and who long for a 'meaningful' use of their talents, skills, and years."

Soon after the appearance of Novak's article, *Commentary* contributors Lipset and Kahn were identifying their political antagonists in classlike terms as "the new intelligentsia" and "the upper-middle-class progressives." Norman Podhoretz later described the neoconservatives' awakening to the existence of the American New Class as a rebellion, almost, by a heroic band of dissidents:

> Repelled by the sight which the 1960s had vouchsafed of what the adversary culture [meaning the culture of the New Class] might look like in action, and therefore of what it might look like in power, a group of dissident intellectuals . . . appeared on the scene to defend middle-class [i.e., mainstream] values as the indispensable basis of liberty, democracy, widespread material prosperity, and a whole range of private human decencies.

The idea of the New Class finally surfaced in the mass media in a 1975 *Wall Street Journal* column by Irving Kristol. The New Class, as he defined it, consisted of

> scientists, teachers, and educational administrators, journalists and others in the communications industries, psychologists, social workers, those lawyers and doctors who make their careers in the expanding public sector, city planners, the staffs of the larger foundations, the upper levels of government bureaucracy, and so on.

This was of course the group in which Kristol, the sometime professor, editor, and by now neoconservative commentator, could himself claim to be a member in good standing. But he did not introduce it to the readership of the *Journal* in order to establish his own credentials. He introduced—or more accurately, exposed—it in order to warn them. In Kristol's description, the New Class had a political agenda that included the destruction of the capitalist system. In fact, Kristol believed that the power of the New Class had already nearly surpassed that of the corporate elite. "In any naked contest with the 'new class,' " Kristol warned his business readers in a later column, "business is a certain loser."

In the national media, the discovery of the New Class never went beyond Kristol's attacks in the *Journal*. There was, of course, no fanfare on a par with the earlier discoveries of the poor and the working class, no cover stories or television specials featuring professors, lawyers, journalists, and the like as the latest group of "neglected" and "forgotten" Americans. But even as something far smaller than a discovery and more like a rumor circulating among an exclusive readership, the idea of the New Class was to have a commanding impact. In the late seventies the idea took hold as the defining wisdom of neoconservatism—the sine qua non of any sophisticated attack on liberalism or the left. Every liberal goal could now be discredited as a cover-up for New Class ambitions; every supposedly generous impulse could be exposed as a self-serving stratagem. Above all, any effort on behalf of the poor could now be understood as a scheme to fatten the public sector and expand the career opportunities of New Class operatives. As Podhoretz concluded, the New Class "represented itself as concerned only with . . . the good of others (especially the poor and the blacks), but what it really wanted was to aggrandize its own power."

Denouncing the New Class became an almost obligatory rite of passage for men (and occasionally women) moving rapidly from left to right, as if it were the seventies equivalent of the Communist Party—something that intellectuals had to repudiate in order to establish themselves as trustworthy citizens. Indeed, neoconservatives often used the term *New Class* as a substitute for *liberals* or *the left*, suggesting that it was not a class at all but a political party, which everyone was free to join or leave at will. And, like Communist Party defectors in earlier decades, the neoconservatives cherished the conceit that they were the embattled rebels, bravely striking out against a powerful establishment. If the characteristic delusion of the American left is that it has the mass support of "the people," the parallel delusion of the right is that it is a lonely band of risk-takers, willing to stand up for capitalism when the capitalists themselves are too weak or befuddled to fight back.

But why call the ideological enemy a class, when it was actually a very different kind of group, defined more by its suspected political sympathies than by social or economic characteristics? In defining their New Class as media people and intellectuals—plus professional and managerial staff in the public and nonprofit sectors—the neoconservatives identified a potentially important division in the professional middle class. Middle-class people employed by private business probably are, on the whole, more likely to be pro-business, i.e., conservative, in their political views.

But class is not simply a matter of occupation, and it is certainly not simply a matter of what job—for example, public or private sector—one holds at a given time. A man does not change his social class when he moves from an administrative position in the federal government to a similar position with the Chamber of Commerce. Nor is a chemist in private industry in a different social class than her colleagues who teach at the state university. The neoconservatives' New Class was not a class but a set of "suspect" occupations, selected to exclude, for example, most of the readers of the *Wall Street Journal.*

Some conservative definitions were still more selective—to the point of choosing which individuals may be members. In his influential 1984 book *Losing Ground,* Charles Murray defines the elite that he blames for the antipoverty programs of the sixties:

> The group is, with no pejorative connotations, best labeled the intelligentsia. . . . It includes the upper echelons of (in no particular order of importance) academia, journalism, publishing, and the vast network of foundations, institutes, and research centers that has been woven into partnership with government during the last thirty years. . . . Politicians and members of the judiciary (Senator J. William Fulbright and Justice William O. Douglas are examples from the sixties) and bankers and businessmen and lawyers and doctors may be members of the intelligentsia as well, though not all are.

This is not the definition of a class or a coherent social grouping of any kind. It is not even, as Murray claims, a good description of the group of "people who deal professionally in ideas." Rather, it is an arbitrary selection of people who are professionals as well as liberals. Hence the two liberal examples (Fulbright and Douglas) picked out from the larger category of public officials, and hence the humorously redundant explanation that not all bankers are members of the "intelligentsia." Only liberals, apparently, can be members of the intelligentsia he wishes to castigate, raising the question of whether it is possible, in his scheme, to be both a conservative and an intellectual like Murray himself.

Obviously there was some compelling satisfaction to be found in calling the ideological opponent a "class" rather than a group of more humble dimensions, such as "the left." In *The Neoconservatives*, Peter Steinfels suggests that the notion of a class implied an "aura of massiveness and threat." It was also, I think, a more grown-up style of invective than had been employed against the student movement. The attacks on the student movement had focused on the youth of the rebels, and the sharpest weapons had come from psychology: The young were overindulged or driven by unresolved Oedipal conflicts. But by the seventies, many of the youth were approaching their thirties. Moreover, theories of childhood indulgence could not explain the many "fellow travelers," as Podhoretz termed them, within the older generation—professors and public figures such as Dr. Benjamin Spock who had come to identify with the radicalism of the young. The solution was to see the student movement of the sixties as one more manifestation of the New Class drive for power. As Podhoretz "speculated":

The New Class was using its own young people as commandos, sending them out into the streets to clash with the enemy's troops (the police and the National Guard) while the "elders" directed the grand strategy from behind the lines and engaged in less dangerous forms of political warfare against the established power.

In their eagerness to trace every disagreeable feature of the left—or liberalism—to the New Class, the neoconservatives had lapsed into a cartoon version of Marxism, in which all human actions and beliefs can be neatly reduced to economic self-interest. From this point of view, known on the left as "vulgar Marxism," you have only to identify a person's class to know all there is to know about that person's probable opinions on matters ranging from arms control to welfare reform. The neoconservatives should have known better. For one thing, the class analysis that seemed to explain away all their antagonists could not, on the face of it, explain *them*.

To anyone who is not a vulgar Marxist, it goes without saying that members of the New Class, or of the entire professional middle class, can and will write anything they like, within the limits of marketability, including diatribes against their own brethren. Class treason is an option at all socioeconomic levels: from the blue-collar man who becomes a security guard employed to harass striking workers, to the heirs of capitalist fortunes who become donors to left-wing causes. The student radicals who inspired the neoconservatives' move to the right had been class traitors, from one point of view, for attacking the university. In attacking those students as "commandos" of the New Class, the neoconservatives now joined the radicals in betraying—or at least denouncing—their own class. An odd move, but hardly without parallel or precedent.

## A CUNNING SORT OF TREASON

It is possible, without succumbing to vulgarity ourselves, to understand the neoconservatives' animus against their own class as being quite in keeping with the interests of that class, as they understood those interests. For one thing, the neoconservatives steered clear of attacking the central sources of middle-class authority: professionalism and expertise. If they had really wished to undermine the professional middle class, or its New Class subgroup, they could have demanded an end to such cherished defenses as academic tenure. They could have lobbied to loosen the credentialing requirements that limit access to the professions. They might have supported the demands of urban blacks for community, rather than professional, control of the schools, health facilities, and other key service institutions.

Of course, the neoconservatives did none of these things. It was the student movement's assault on professionalism that had roused them to arms in the first place. And it was Daniel Patrick Moynihan, a future neoconservative, who in the mid-sixties had articulated the case for turning the War on Poverty into a jobs program for the experts. In a famous article in the *Public Interest,* he had argued for "the professionalization of reform," meaning especially the War on Poverty. Noting "the exponential growth of knowledge," he had looked forward to the happy day when social change would be left entirely to the experts, making "stupid controversies," "mile-long petitions and mass rallies," as well as other hallmarks of public participation, obsolete.

In fact, it is tempting to interpret the neoconservative diatribes against the New Class as something very different from an attack. It was an announcement, in David Bazelon's view, of "a new strategy" for the professional middle class itself. By the seventies, middle-class opportunities in domestic government and academia were shrinking. The war on Vietnam had swallowed up the War on Poverty; an incipient "tax revolt" threatened future federal activism; economic stagflation and the oil crisis seemed to herald an "age of limits." Making up imaginary social problems and appointing themselves to solve them—which is what the neoconservatives now accused the New Class of having done in the sixties—would no longer have worked anyway. Budgets were shrinking for antipoverty programs and for the cadre of planners, social workers, think-tank inhabitants, and social scientists who were supposed to design and supervise them. If the federal government and the universities were no longer expanding, it was time to find a new patron for the intellectual vanguard of the professional middle class, and the neoconservatives hoped to find one in an obvious place—the corporate elite.

Historically, though, the relationship between the professional middle class and the monied elite has always been tinged with tension and ambiguity. The emerging middle class had depended on the wealthy to subsidize the newly reformed professions and the educational institutions that nurtured them. Men like Johns Hopkins, Leland Stanford, Andrew Carnegie, and John D. Rockefeller underwrote the huge expansion of higher education that took place in the late nineteenth and early twentieth centuries, and without which there would have been no professional middle class. But the professions are by definition—or perhaps we should say by aspiration—autonomous, and not beholden to the mighty. Otherwise they would have no legitimacy in the public's eye: Claims to professional objectivity and neutrality cannot be made from an actual position of servility. Within the early-twentieth-century universities, the struggle for professional autonomy took the form of battles over academic freedom, with the faculty on one side, the capitalist trustees on the other.

Outside the university, the emerging middle class had clashed with the corporate elite over dozens of issues. Drives for "consumer rights"—for clean food and safe products, for example—pitted middle-class reformers against recalcitrant businessmen. Campaigns for "good government" sought to limit the influence of big money (as well as working-class-based political machines) and augment the power of the experts: city managers, advisory "brain trusts," expert consultants. Even the concept of "scientific management" had originated in an attack on waste and inefficiency in business.

Beyond these skirmishes lay a deeper conflict. The professional middle class has traditionally valued science, efficiency, and "rationality." These are, of course, major selling points for professional and managerial services. But rationality implies at least some form of public accountability, for even the public can be expected to learn to reason. Business, on the other hand, has no cause to value such abstractions above profits, and in the early twentieth century resisted even the metric system as an unwonted intrusion by the experts. Not until well into the twentieth century did the modern corporation emerge as a kind of compromise between the classes: The capitalist owners retained ultimate power, but daily decision-making increasingly devolved to managers, engineers, and other professionals recruited from the middle class.

The tension between the middle class and the corporate elite persists to this day and is reenacted in countless battles over professional autonomy: professors may risk firing to express an unpopular opinion; executives occasionally blow the whistle on an unsafe product or unethical procedure. It is expressed, also, in the intellectual pecking order within the middle class: professors tend to look down on executives, "pure" researchers look down on industrial scientists, journalists look down on advertising copywriters. This is snobbery, but it stems from an allegiance to that elusive middle-class value, occupational autonomy—the freedom to direct one's own work according to inner principles rather than externally imposed priorities, such as profit. And it was this that the neoconservatives now proposed to abandon.

In a *Wall Street Journal* column that could have been a cover letter for a job application, Irving Kristol coyly offered his services to the corporate elite. Rather than donating indiscriminately to philanthropic causes that might turn out to be run by antibusiness New Class members, he argued:

A more positive step, of course, would be for corporations to give support to those elements of the "new class"—and they exist, if not in large numbers—which do believe in the preservation of a strong private sector. For the "new class," fortunately, is not an utterly homogeneous entity. It contains men and women . . . who *are* interested in individual liberty and limited government, who *are* worried about the collectivist tendencies in society. . . .

"How can we identify such people, and discriminate intelligently among them?" corporate executives always inquire plaintively. Well, if you decide to go exploring for oil, you find a competent geologist. Similarly, if you wish to make a productive investment in the intellectual and educational worlds, you find competent intellectuals and scholars—"dissident" members, as it were, of the "new class" —to offer guidance.

As Steinfels has noted, he stopped just short of offering his phone number.

If this was treason, it was treason of a very cunning sort.

"We're all careerists," Bazelon says of the middle class. "We're very easy to buy. He [Kristol] opened up a new career line." For masses of young middle-class people, Kristol was anticipating the career choices of the eighties: not sociology or public service but banking and management. For the small intellectual vanguard to which he belonged, he was courting corporate patronage. Business, after all, would be "a certain loser" in any "naked contest" with the New Class; it needed expert help from, of course, the New Class. As B. Bruce-Briggs, the editor of a neoconservative anthology on the New Class, put it, "Intellectual attacks on business require intellectual apologetics; an active bureaucracy requires aggressive lobbyists."

Naturally, one of the things business needed most was a thorough understanding of its antagonist. Neoconservatives soon busied themselves holding seminars and lectures for businessmen on the dangers of the New Class. "What a quintessential New Class activity!" as one such lecturer himself observed. For such efforts, Kristol himself has been rewarded many times over, one of his emoluments being the corporate-funded Institute for Educational Affairs, which promotes research on, among other things, the threat from the New Class.

The corporate leaders who were the targets of neoconservative sycophancy must have found the flurry over the New Class a somewhat murky business. "He sees politics as purely a struggle between intellectuals," one executive complained after having been treated to a neoconservative lecture on the New Class. Certainly businessmen had never been as exercised about the student left as many professors and intellectuals were. But they *were* alarmed by some of the seventies extensions of student activism, especially the environmental and consumer movements. Universities might burn to the ground, and business would go on as usual. But if the public continued to demand safer products and cleaner factories, profits would suffer.

It was comforting, then, to find out that the environmental and consumer movements were coming not from the "public" at all, but from the ever-inventive New Class. William Simon, the millionaire Secretary of the Treasury under President Gerald Ford and cofounder, with Kristol, of the Institute for Educational Affairs, revealed that the "significant" thing about the new movements was that they represented, "above all, the political voice of the contemporary urban elite." Citing Kristol, he warned that this New Class

> combines a morbid economic ignorance with a driving power lust, and it combines hostility to democracy with the illusion that it speaks for the People. . . . If the political ambition of this class is not checked and if it does not acquire the necessary economic education [about the virtues of free enterprise], the dangerous result will be the destruction of freedom.

Robert Bartley, editorial-page editor of the *Wall Street Journal* and a fair barometer of business opinion, wrote in the late seventies that the "concept of the New Class crystallized for me . . . during the wave of student activism." But it was only later, with the emergence of movements for consumer rights, occupational health and safety, and environmentalism, that he became convinced of "something that looks suspiciously like a concerted attack on business, by something that looks suspiciously like the New Class." It was reassuring to know that this New Class was just as money-hungry and unscrupulous as the business class it aimed to displace. Consumer activist Ralph Nader, for example, "claims to live in an $85-a-month apartment," but an investigator known to Bartley "found neighbors willing to testify that he actually lives in an $80,000 (1971 prices) condo owned by his brother Shakeef." Yet, unfairly, it was business that was "perceived to be materialistic," rather than the New Class. "If it is more widely recognized that the New Class has its own materialistic and power agenda," he concluded hopefully, "this disparity will be greatly diminished."

In the long run, though, the most important converts to the neoconservative view of the New Class were not the leaders of major corporations but politically ambitious conservatives.

Twentieth-century American conservatism had had a rather thin intellectual tradition. There was William F. Buckley, Jr., buttressed by the Austrian economist Friedrich von Hayek, but few others. Conservative politicians like Nixon and Agnew were resentful of intellectuals, who—they correctly perceived —tended to be contemptuous of them. All this changed with the arrival of fresh recruits from the left, the neoconservatives, bearing with them the most precious legacy of the left, the notion of class. Now it was possible to understand why there had been no conservative intellectual tradition, and why so many good conservatives hated intellectuals anyway. The intellectuals were part of the New Class, and the New Class hated America.

One vignette, before we move on to the new breed of political thinker who would pick up the idea of the New Class and run with it. In 1969, Daniel Patrick Moynihan, whom we last saw advocating the "professionalization of reform," accepted a job as Nixon's assistant for urban affairs. He greatly impressed the president with a memo attacking "the service-dispensing groups in the society—teachers, welfare workers, urban planners, nutrition experts, etc."—that is, the very professionals he had recently encouraged to take over the business of policy-making. Now he saw them as being in the "resentment business": "They earn very good livings making the black poor feel put upon, when they are, which is often the case, and also, when they are not." Nixon was stirred by Moynihan's explanation of the New Class and its motives, and wrote a note in his diary about what he called "the American leader class":

> It's really sickening to have to receive them at the White House as I often do and to hear them whine and whimper and that's one of the reasons why I enjoy very much more receiving labor leaders and people from middle America who still have character and guts and a bit of patriotism.

There, in ungrammatical outline, was the germ of the New Right's eventual strategy: embrace the working class and the business leaders and cast out the "sickening" New Class.

## THE NEW RIGHT AND THE NEW CLASS

The neoconservatives were, and still are, a small group of intellectuals, absorbed with their journals, institutes, and conferences. The New Right was a movement, or would-be movement, with potential constituents scattered in dozens of single-issue groups and fundamentalist Christian denominations. Within the New Right, the neoconservatives have never been entirely trusted: they are too urban, too self-consciously intellectual, and, no doubt, too likely to be Jewish. But the intellectual leadership of the New Right has not hesitated to crib its ideas from the neoconservatives, and the most important of these was the idea of the New Class. With the ascent of the New Right in the eighties, the idea of the New Class emerged from the airy realm of thought to become part of the rationale for actual policy: policies directed, however, not against the New Class or anything resembling it, but against the poor.

By the New Right's own reckoning, it was born in 1974, when four relatively young organizations based in the Washington area—the Conservative Caucus, RAVCO (the direct-mail fund-raising company run by Richard Viguerie), the Comittee for the Survival of a Free Congress (now the Free Congress Political Action Committee), and the National Conservative Political Action Committee—began systematically coordinating their activities. The money came from wealthy right-wingers such as Joseph Coors and Richard Mellon Scaife, as well as from hundreds of thousands of individuals solicited by RAVCO and other organizations, and it came in great quantities. By the late seventies the New Right was already a highly bureaucratic, top-heavy effort, and a haven, inevitably, for legions of middle-class intellectuals, administrators, and political experts.

It had its own think tanks (of which the Heritage Foundation is the best known), its own periodicals (such as the *Conservative Digest*), and an expanding network of sympathetic or subsidiary groups—pro-business, anti–gun control, pro-law-

and-order, and "pro-family." In 1979 the secular leaders of the New Right instigated the formation of a right-wing, religious membership organization, the Moral Majority, and thereby eventually gained a following among white Protestant fundamentalists. A year later, they helped elect their favorite candidate—except possibly for Jesse Helms—to the presidency of the United States.

Ideologically, the New Right could be considered the scrappy progeny of two very dissimilar men: Barry Goldwater, who came to national prominence as the conservative Republican presidential candidate in 1964, and George Wallace. Goldwater contributed the traditional conservative themes: militarism, anticommunism, and the need to shrink the role of government to make way for truly "free" enterprise. But the men who created the New Right recognized that traditional conservatism, especially on economic issues, has an inherently limited appeal. If the right was to move beyond its blue-blood constituency and tuxedoed image, it would have to follow the trail Wallace had blazed into America's smokestack cities and blue-collar suburbs. It would need new issues, and, if it was to successfully mobilize the resentments of Middle America, it would need an enemy.

The New Right found its first new issues in the backlash themes exploited by Wallace and, more successfully, by Agnew. Opposition to school busing and to textbooks perceived as overly liberal had created, in scattered localities, angry constituencies of Middle Americans, which the New Right did its best to cultivate. In the early seventies, the emergence of a mass feminist movement opened up additional targets for the right: the Equal Rights Amendment, which had sailed through Congress in 1972, and abortion, which was decriminalized by the Supreme Court in 1973. In the late seventies, in its effort to court Protestant fundamentalists, the New Right enlarged its concerns to include opposition to gay rights, opposition to the teaching of evolution and sex education, and advocacy for the restoration of organized prayer in the public schools.

It took a certain spirit of opportunism to graft these "social issues"—anti-abortion, anti-ERA, anti–gun control—onto the

162

traditional economic agenda of the right. As direct-mail wizard Richard Viguerie acknowledged:

> We talk about issues that people care about, like gun control, abortion, taxes and crime. Yes, they're emotional issues, but that's better than talking about capital formation.

As the New Right's leaders recognized, the social issues were the only hope for winning the working class and Middle Americans over to an economic agenda that was unabashedly old right—anti-labor and pro-business.

There remained the problem of defining an enemy. In a less tolerant society, the New Right's chosen enemy might have been blacks, who had been the transparent target of Nixon and Agnew's successful law-and-order campaign. In a less sophisticated society, the most convenient enemy might have been Jews, who have done service as scapegoats in American right-wing demonology from Father Coughlin in the thirties to Lyndon LaRouche in the eighties. But Nazism had given anti-Semitism a bad name in all but the most extreme, often paramilitary, fringe groups of the right. And blatant public racism had gone so far out of style that even segregationist Wallace had found it expedient, as a national figure, to drop overt references to blacks. He had, however, found an alternative in the "pointy-headed professors." It remained only to fashion the political targets of 1968—radical students and adult liberals—into a more durable enemy.

The notion of an evil New Class of intellectuals fit in with longstanding right-wing traditions. The John Birch Society—the secret right-wing organization that flourished in the early sixties—fancied itself up against an even more secret group of intellectuals bent on world domination. These "Illuminati" had been scheming to take over the world since the eighteenth century and in their modern form tended to be communists. As described in a 1967 John Birch Society publication, the Illuminati were a

> conspiracy conceived, organized, and activated by professionals and intellectuals, many of them brilliant and cunning and clever, who decided to put their minds in the service of total evil. . . .

163

Their main habitat these days seems to be the great sub-sidized universities, tax-free foundations, mass media com-munication systems, government bureaus such as the State Department, and a myriad of private organizations such as the Council on Foreign Relations.

To the Birchers, the war against communism was almost a lost cause, since even President Eisenhower was "a conscious agent of the communist conspiracy."

When the New Right emerged in the mid-seventies, the neoconservatives' notion of the New Class was ready and wait-ing to be appropriated. The enemy could be updated; it was not a conspiracy but something more modern and rational-sounding—an entire social class. There remained, however, a touch of the occult, a hint of paranoia, in the New Right's no-tion of the New Class—which is still sometimes referred to, albeit in lower case, as the *illuminati*. As Sidney Blumenthal observed, within the New Right, the New Class represents a "secret system . . . a force more insidious than any political movement, more influential than any political party."

The New Right now had four major classes to consider. At the top were the owners and top managers of big business. Just beneath them in terms of wealth, though surpassing them in power, was the New Class. Then came the working class, lumped in with the car dealers, franchise operators, and other inhabitants of Middle America. At the bottom were of course the poor, who were already being recast by the right as an immutable, hereditary underclass.

The potential political alliances among these classes had been at least dimly apparent since Wallace's 1968 campaign. In 1969, Kevin Phillips, a former staff worker for the Nixon campaign, sketched out a new social "map" of the electorate which seemed to offer the right a clear path to power. As he saw it, the liberal elite, or New Class, had thrown in its lot with the poor, and the resulting "campus-and-brownstone liberal-ism," was alien to the blue-collar Democratic rank and file. As he later summed up the change:

Slowly but surely, liberalism lost much of its Jacksonian and Trumanesque moorings in rural Missouri and steelmaking

164

East Baltimore, and led by the ascendent professors, urban planners, social-welfare workers, minority causists and international economists, managed to become increasingly the political vehicle and banner of *those* interests, not of blue-collar Americans.

The New Class alliance with the poor and minority groups left an obvious strategic alliance for the Republicans—with the working class.

Thus, in the New Right's view, American society was polarizing between two mighty blocs: the New Class and the poor versus the rich and their allies in the working class and Middle America. But to rationalize these alliances, which were still more fanciful than real, the intellectuals of the New Right needed to go beyond the fragments of analysis they had inherited from the neoconservatives. They needed to expose what was deeply sinister about the New Class and ultimately perverse about its sympathy for the poor. And they needed to do so in ways that a resentful Middle America could readily take to heart.

In the neoconservative view, what made the New Class dangerous was its ambition. Ever on the lookout for new opportunities, the New Class had stirred up a fuss about poverty in order to employ and enrich its own members. The poor were only pawns in a power grab, noncombatants in a war ostensibly waged on their behalf. The New Right borrowed most of this analysis but took a colder view of the poor, and shared none of the neoconservatives' lingering attachment to the welfare state. By the end of the sixties, liberal notions of the culture of poverty had hardened into a conservative horror of the black poor, who were conceived as shiftless, violent, and addicted to public handouts. If the New Class and the poor were allied, there must be some previously unsuspected affinity between them, some connection that belied the superficial contrast between the excessively ambitious and the excessively lazy.

In his 1975 book *The Making of the New Majority Party*, New Right strategist William A. Rusher revealed the hidden basis of the emerging class alliances. A wealthy Yale-educated attorney and publisher with an interest in wine-tasting, Rusher is one of the New Right's most enthusiastic proponents of working-class populism. America, he announced, is no longer divided between the haves and the have-nots, but between the "producers" and the "nonproducers." The producers are the blue-collar people who make things, plus the capitalists who generously and thoughtfully pay them to do so. Hence there is an obvious affinity between the very wealthy and the working class: Together they *produce*. And together they support everyone else—the swelling population of nonproducers.

In Rusher's scheme, the poor fit entirely into the category of nonproducers, living idly off the dole. (The existence of the "working poor," who make up over 40 percent of the poverty population over the age of fourteen, is seldom acknowledged by the right. Indeed, nothing could be more destructive to "traditional values" than the realization that, for millions of Americans, hard work does *not* pay.) But the poor are not the only nonproducers:

> The great central fact that looms over the America of the mid-seventies is the growth, in the past 25 years, of a whole new economic class [of nonproducers]. . . . They are neither businessmen nor manufacturers, blue-collar workers or farmers. Instead, the dominant members of the new class form a "verbalist" elite.

The goal of the New Class was to "run the United States," an aim in which they were supported by their "huge and apparently permanent welfare constituency." The affinity between the New Class and the poor now made perfect sense: both groups are parasitic, sly, and at odds with the "basic values" held by the producers—haves and have-nots alike.

Labeling the New Class nonproducers made good populist sense, for, as we have seen, this is how working-class people tend to see middle-class professionals anyway—as people who do not work, at least not in any serious, constructive manner. The right had already had some success in tapping resentment against "lazy" welfare recipients, and perhaps hoped to turn the same kind of resentment against the New Class. "Mr. Rusher is right," a commentator wrote in the *Conservative Di-*

*gest.* "The honoring and rewarding of work must become the basic economic *principle* of the new [political] party." He regretted, however, that there was still too much blue-collar "apathy" about the New Class's threat to big business.

From a capitalist point of view, the New Class does, on the whole, earn its keep quite nicely. Even the most woolly-headed "verbalists" are capable of filling a variety of essential capitalist functions: writing advertising copy for new products, teaching others how to comport themselves in a complex and hierarchical society, or, like Rusher and other intellectuals of the New Right, writing pseudo-populist defenses of big business. Whether out of self-interest or a clearer understanding of the New Class's role, the neoconservatives had never gone so far as to suggest that their own class was parasitical and hence expendable. But this was the inescapable drift of Rusher's analysis. "The producers of America," he wrote, "the businessmen, workers, and farmers have a common economic interest in limiting the growth of this rapacious new non-producing class."

Here an ominous tone creeps in. Why just "limit the growth" of this useless and scheming class? Without specifying exactly what should be done to them, Rusher listed three "targets" for the right: First would be the welfare recipients; second, the leftist students and their professors (not that leftists of any kind were a significant force by 1975). "And then," he warned, "it will be the turn of the other non-producers who have recently learned to live, as a matter of right, off the generosity of working Americans."

## PERMISSIVENESS: THE CRIME OF THE NEW CLASS

As the seventies wore on, the New Right's case against the New Class expanded, adding ever more lurid and nasty charges. The right had originally designed its enemy to capture the resentments of blue-collar and lower-middle-class Americans offended by the black insurgency and the student movement; hence a New Class that was power-hungry, trouble-making, and parasitical. But as the right began to forge a constituency among Christian fundamentalists, its image of the New Class changed accordingly. The New Class remained as power-hungry as ever, but at the same time it became irreligious ("secular humanist"), dissolute, and bent on infecting the entire society with its lax morals and hedonistic outlook. In the words of New Right intellectual George Gilder, it had created "an Establishment culture . . . wallowing in a secular hedonist swamp."

The New Right's leaders—both secular and religious—saw America in the midst of moral breakdown: It had abandoned the biblical commandments and was awash with sin. As Moral Majority leader Reverend Jerry Falwell later reflected:

> If ever there was a time when God needed a job done, it was during the 1960s and 1970s. The future of our nation was at stake. . . . I sincerely believe that Satan had mobilized his own forces to destroy America by negating the Judeo-Christian ethic, secularizing our society, and devaluating human life through the legalization of abortion and infanticide. God needed voices raised to save the nation from inward moral decay.

More secular New Rightists emphasized the betrayal not of God but of "traditional values." Hard work, self-denial, and family loyalty were giving way to the mass pursuit of individual gratification. "Hedonism is the spirit of the age," warned New Right columnist Patrick J. Buchanan in 1978. There was abortion, homosexuality, promiscuity, pornography, drug abuse, godlessness, and feminism—the latter conceived by the New Right as a huge upsurge of female selfishness. Underlying this mass breakdown in morality was a single cause, a deep and central cultural failing. This was "permissiveness," a notion the New Right borrowed from the critics of the student movement and now applied to liberalism itself, and of course to the New Class, which was liberalism personified.

*Permissiveness* may be the most indispensable word in the New Right vocabulary. Whatever the problem—from promiscuity to excessive government spending—permissiveness is the cause. In *Post-Conservative America,* Kevin Phillips (who is critical of the New Right but remains one of its intellectual resources) uses *permissiveness* in dozens of contexts. There is "judicial permissiveness," "permissiveness, homosexuality and abortion," permissiveness in education, permissiveness in mainstream (i.e., not evangelical) churches, plus a generalized "permissivism of various economic, diplomatic, sociological and sexual hues." He even warns about a link between permissiveness and imperial decline, buttressing the point with a quote from pop-historians Will and Ariel Durant: "By the time of Caesar, you had a permissive society and a pagan society in the sense of sexual enjoyment with a minimal moral restraint."

So frequently does the notion of permissiveness appear in right-wing literature that it is hard to believe that it can retain any concrete meaning or explanatory power. As a generalized explanation, permissiveness came to occupy the place that *affluence* once held in liberal critiques of America almost twenty years earlier. Affluence, as we saw in Chapter One, was not just a material condition—wealth—but came to be seen as a vague and suffocating atmosphere, hovering everywhere. So too with permissiveness, which could be considered the evil distillate of affluence. In the ideology of the New Right, it is everywhere, explaining everything from individual personality and behavior to the broad cultural outlines of American society. It can be found at every level of social organization, from the individual to the family to the nation. As one writer observed plaintively in the *Conservative Digest*:

> [George] Washington was not a permissive individual. He did not come from a permissive family. So the U.S. did not begin as a permissive society. Is it too late to go back to our beginnings?

The word *permissive* had not always been a catchall code for moral breakdown. Prior to 1966, the word *permissiveness* found little employment outside of discussions of childraising practices. In 1968, as we have seen, it gained wide exposure as a verbal weapon in the intellectuals' backlash against student radicals. At the same time, the word had begun to take on specifically sexual connotations. For example, in 1969 the mass media were referring to "the permissiveness that currently pervades literature, films and the theatre," by which they did not mean indulgent approaches to childraising, but nudity, sexual openness and sexual diversity. In the same year, in the context of an attack on the "hate, depravity, sickness, violence or obscenity" in art and movies, Theodore H. White concluded that "a new babbitry of permissiveness had replaced the old babbitry of conformity."

With the expansion of the concept of permissiveness it was as if the bad "children" represented by the student radicals had gone through a shockingly sudden puberty. "Permissiveness" in the original sense had made them bad; "permissiveness" in the new, sexualized sense included all the wanton things they did. From there, the pubescent, sexualized notion of permissiveness quickly matured into its all-inclusive New Right usage, and credit for this last transformation probably goes to Spiro Agnew and his speechwriter, Patrick Buchanan. In 1969 Agnew quoted Walter Laqueur writing in *Commentary* on "the cultural and political idiocies perpetrated with impunity in this permissive age." Soon after, Agnew was indicting not just parents, not just sexual freedom, but "the total permissive atmosphere that is sweeping the country."

Hence, by the seventies, layers of different meanings had built an extraordinarily evocative power into the notion of permissiveness. Anything could be *permissive*: a person, a class, a society, a policy, a form of behavior. To say that a policy was *permissive* was first of all to say that it was indulgent and superficially kind, but only *superficially* kind. Had not permissive upbringings "spoiled" an entire generation of young people? Had not permissive social policies unleashed a swarm of ills, from crime to obscenity and sexual abandon? Permissiveness was the most deceitful form of leadership possible: cruelty masked as compassion. It was a poisoned form of love —seductive, ubiquitous, and ultimately lethal.

Beyond that, permissiveness revealed the individual wantonness of its practitioners. To indulge others—in, however, a cruel and misguided way—was to betray a fatal failure of self-control. The impulse to give improper liberties to the young or the poor actually grew out of one's own licentiousness and lack of discipline. From a middle-class vantage point, the poor are the social analogues of the young, and both are psychological stand-ins for the id. Let one loose and the other two would come bursting forth. Permissiveness was both a vice and a mark of vice, linking the lenient judge or the liberal legislator to the drug-dealer and pornographer.

The source of the permissiveness that pervaded American culture was, of course, the New Class itself. Somehow the New Right deduced that educated, middle-class liberals—the professors, foundation staff, media people, and others who make up the right's concept of the New Class—are personally given to libertinism, and that societal permissiveness springs from the personal decadence of New Class members. In *Thunder on the Right*, Alan Crawford describes the suspicion, common on the New Right, that "the lifestyles of Easterners [meaning for the most part New Class Easterners] are somewhat racier than the rightists' own, and that this decadence explains liberal political attitudes."

To many thinkers on the right, New Class decadence was decisively revealed by the youthful counterculture of the sixties. Never mind that so many elders of the professional middle class, including quite liberal ones, had been repelled by the hippies; or that, at that time of the right's discovery of New Class decadence, the counterculture had been dead for some years. On the right, images of pot-smoking protesters, nude revelers, and Woodstockian orgies remained vivid long after the counterculture itself had faded into nostalgia. Writing in 1975, Kevin Phillips turned the entire New Class into a horde of hippies (though his imagery is even more outdated, suggesting early-sixties Beats as well as hippies):

Conceiving themselves unfettered by the past, the new elite thought that *society* could be unfettered—and old restraints cast aside. Aided by the revolution in oral contraceptives,

171

moral standards were thrown off, from King's Road in London's Chelsea to San Francisco's North Beach. What had become promiscuity became openness, naturalness, and freedom . . . drugs were tolerated and even encouraged.

As if having second thoughts about locating the entire liberal elite, from, say, Eugene McCarthy to Chief Justice Earl Warren, in some North Beach "pad," Phillips added the qualification that "none of these attitudes have ever been *universally* shared by the emerging knowledge elite" (emphasis added).

Perhaps the right's strongest secular indictment of New Class decadence is a 1982 essay by New Right theorist Samuel T. Francis, then a legislative assistant to Senator John East. Francis, himself the holder of a typically New Class Ph.D. in history, began by explaining that the New Right's insights do not derive from any tainted New Class sources. They are not "premeditated in academic seminars, calculated with precision in the inner sanctums of tax-exempt foundations, or debated in the stately prose of quarterly and fortnightly journals." Rather, they spring fully formed from a populist sense of injustice, and thus do not require supporting evidence.

Having established his license to say just about anything, Francis proceeds to contrast the liberal elite's "cosmopolitan ethic" with the "domestic ethic" supposedly upheld by the white working class. Conveniently, from an employer's point of view, the workers still uphold "the duty of work . . . the social and human necessity of sacrifice and deferral of gratification." The New Class's "cosmopolitan ethic," on the other hand, "idealizes material indulgence, the glorification of the self, and the transcendence of conventional values, loyalties, and social bonds." What kind of person exemplifies this self-serving ethic, and hence the spirit of the New Class? As Francis suggests, "Its most perfect (though extreme) expression is perhaps Mick Jagger, but a more typical and vapid form is portrayed in advertisements that tell us What Kind of Man Reads *Playboy*."

There is something schizophrenic about the character of the New Class as seen by the New Right: How could any group of people be so recklessly self-indulgent and yet so successful at imposing their will on everyone else? Or, to use Francis's images, how much "precision" could one expect from "inner sanctums" that were no doubt clouded with marijuana smoke? Would not the "stately prose" of the fortnightly journals be overcome with the beat of rock 'n' roll, and the minds of the technocrats dulled with sexual surfeit? Unfazed by this paradox, Francis asserts that New Class decadence and ambition are not only connected but logically inseparable:

> These lifestyles, values and ideals . . . represent the logical outgrowth of its [the New Class's] own structural interests: large, social-engineering government in alliance with corporations, universities and foundations, the mass media, unions, and other bureaucracies.

Somehow, in ways that resist explanation, the entire bureaucratic edifice of New Class power—government, universities, foundations—rests on a secret libertinism, which these institutions in turn propagate into the rest of society as permissiveness.

## PERMISSIVENESS VS. TRADITIONAL VALUES

Like affluence, permissiveness crystallized the middle-class fear of going soft, giving in, and eventually losing the will to succeed. While the liberal critics of affluence had yearned for some new challenge to invigorate the professional middle class, the New Right believed that the middle class—or at least the supposedly liberal, New Class slice of it—was no longer capable of regenerating itself from within. The only hope lay in imposing, by law and force if necessary, the traditional values so essential to middle-class success.

What had happened, between the fifties and the seventies, to make the threat of affluence—or, more precisely, the fear of yielding to it—seem so much more urgent and intense? Certainly "affluence" had not increased. Incomes had risen in the prosperous fifties, but the seventies were a decade of stagnation and decline: an international economic crisis, rising unemployment and inflation in the United States, and diminishing opportunities for the professional middle class.

There had, of course, been a "sexual revolution," manifested even to nonparticipants as a loosening of old standards governing public behavior and entertainment. The government had more or less given up its decades-long fight against literary obscenity in the early sixties, when books like *Lady Chatterley's Lover* and *Tropic of Cancer* were finally allowed to enter the country. In the sixties, best-sellers, like *Portnoy's Complaint* (1969), became shockingly explicit; movies, led by *Bonnie and Clyde* (1967) and *The Graduate* (1967), became more "adult" in their treatment of violence, drugs, and, increasingly, sex. By the seventies, nudity (at least partial nudity) and obscene language had become commonplace, if not obligatory, features of the Hollywood spectacle, leading President Nixon to promise a "war on smut." Literature on sex itself had become more available and accessible. Unlike the "marriage manuals" of the fifties, seventies sex classics, like Alex Comfort's *Joy of Sex* and Nancy Friday's *My Secret Garden,* were nonmedical in tone, enticing, and approving of a wide variety of sexual practices. Television, however, remained tediously bland throughout the sixties, perking up only with the arrival of Norman Lear's adult sitcoms (*Maude* and *Mary Hartman*) in the mid-seventies.

Even when viewed from a great distance, the sexual revolution contributed to the uneasy sense that America was becoming a more permissive society. But temptation is not the same as permission. If there is one clear and ubiquitous source of permissiveness—in the narrow, old-fashioned sense of the word—it lies, as it always has, in the consumer culture. The American economy depends on the willingness of the American people to buy things they do not need (or did not think they needed yesterday) and cannot necessarily afford. For this we do indeed need "permission," which takes the form of the ceaseless campaign to convince us that it is all right to spend and to indulge ourselves, and wrong-headed to defer almost any gratification.

To their credit, the neoconservatives had understood, in

varying degrees, that modern capitalism is at odds with their traditional values—hard work, self-denial, and family loyalty. Daniel Bell (a neoconservative until he abjured the label in the eighties) devoted a book to the "cultural crisis of modern capitalism," by which he meant the conflict between traditional values and the permissive, hedonistic message of the consumer culture. "Modern capitalism," he wrote in a later article, "has been transformed by a widespread hedonism that has made mundane concerns, rather than transcendental ties, the center of people's lives. . . . Without the hedonism stimulated by mass consumption, the very structure of business enterprises would collapse."

And if one thing had changed, between the fifties and seventies, to make America a more permissive society, it was the consumer culture. Advertising became bolder, and the marketing emphasis began to shift from the family, with its soap powders and heavy appliances, to the individual, with his or her more interesting, self-centered needs. Recall that in the fifties advertising had bogged down in the "creative problem." Bored with pushing the suburban ensemble of goods, perhaps because they were bored with their own suburban lives, advertising people were producing lackluster copy and numbing commercials. Then, in 1965, Madison Avenue underwent a collective fit of inspiration known in the industry as "the creative revolution." As historian Stephen Fox describes it:

> The ads grew ever more daring and sacrilegious: the Statue of Liberty modeling a Talon zipper; Gunilla Knutson urging "Take it all off" for Noxzema on TV, with stripper music in the background.

The ads also became more arresting: Avis launched its "We Try Harder" theme; and Alka-Seltzer produced the penitent glutton confessing, "I can't believe I ate the whole thing." Mary Wells, the advertising genius who is often credited with launching the creative revolution, exemplified the new spirit with her transformation of Braniff airlines: The fight attendants were dressed up in short, snappy Pucci outfits, and the planes were painted in pastels.

Then, on top of the ongoing "revolution," came a fresh creative infusion from the counterculture. As a Connecticut commuter was quoted in *Newsweek*:

> For years I've been taking the same train to New York that an advertising executive takes. He gets on at Darien, and used to be strictly a gray-flannel, button-down, crew-cut type. But now he wears flowered jackets, broad ties and sideburns down to here. I guess that's what's happening on Madison Avenue.

At the same time, hip young people—exemplifying the gap between the counterculture and the student left—began to invade Madison Avenue. "My God," groaned an advertising executive to *Newsweek*. "We hired a new copywriter the other day—a very good copywriter, too—and he came to work in his bare feet."

In a transformation that we now take for granted, ads became more imaginative, aggressive, and sometimes disconcerting. A famous sixties ad for class rings showed a hand with six fingers. A New York bakery insisted, at a time when ethnic issues were still too touchy for prime time, "You don't have to be Jewish to love Levy's." A cigarette manufacturer congratulated women, "You've come a long way, baby." Rock music, which white, adult critics had only recently rejected as an offensive "jungle beat," began to sell everything from beer to cars. On TV commercials and in magazine ads, black faces began to appear among the white, suggesting a happier world where beautiful, well-heeled people of both races might mingle freely over drinks.

And slowly but surely, ads became sexier. A 1969 Vitabath ad featuring a discretely profiled nude produced a torrent of protest mail but was highly successful. Mary Wells borrowed the idea of "love power" from the counterculture and introduced the slogan "Everybody could use a little extra love these days"—a permissive notion if there ever was one. Another agency promoted a hair product with the slogan "It lets me be me," hinting, as Stephen Fox reports, at "a new sex life for the young woman, against a backdrop of young clothes and rock music." By the eighties, of course, these ads would seem tame. The frontiers of sexuality would shift from hints of a sex life for the unmarried to portrayals of underage temptresses in underwear or too-tight jeans.

There is no way to know how much the sexualization of advertising and the larger creative revolution inspired the New Right's sense of encroaching permissiveness. The standard right-wing list of symptoms of moral breakdown—from abortion and homosexuality to divorce and drug abuse—never includes advertising or any other routine capitalist activity. But a recent *Washington Post* profile of a Mobile, Alabama, fundamentalist family involved in a campaign against "secular humanist" textbooks emphasizes their obsession with suggestive television advertising. At the dinner table, the Websters indulge in a high-spirited critique of offensive commercials:

> Says Sue [the mother], "There was this pineapple commercial . . ."
> Lora groans.
> "Oh, maaan," says David [the teenage son], slapping his forehead.
> "I think it was Dole. It was the most sensuous commercial, and there was nothin' to it. I mean it was *sensuous!*"
> "She was really eatin' it," says John [the father], sucking his fingers seductively.
> "It wasn't selling pineapple!" says Sue, incredulous. "It was selling sex!"

But television commercials are not just an excuse for this family to engage in some dirty talk. They are, the *Post* reminds us, an assault on the Websters' deepest values, which are expressed in regularly scheduled home-cooked meals and a belief in the absolute inerrancy of the Bible:

> TV is to them a mass-media hawking not only of products but also of values, seductive values, values they don't share, values that are wrong, even evil, but values that first must be ingrained in Americans if they are to buy the bevy of items foisted upon them by the marketeers.

Among the potentially evil new values television brings to people like the Websters are some that are, at least implicitly, *anti*family. In the fifties, the consumer culture had focused on the products appropriate to suburban family living, from breakfast cereals to heavy appliances. There had been no range of "lifestyles," only a single acceptable style of living, defined by washing machines, matching furniture sets, station wagons. These are commodities that families consume, in family settings. They are also the kind of commodities that, as Albert O. Hirschman suggests, are most likely to leave a residue of "disappointment." Promising happiness, they do not provide it; yet they remain as enduring reminders of the unkept promise.

In the last three decades, however, the consumer spectacle has inexorably broadened, bringing into sharper focus the kind of products that do not require a family effort to consume, that do not endure, and that serve no purpose other than fun. These are "leisure products"—vacations, wines and liquor, sports cars—and they define a lifestyle very different from that suggested by the station wagon and Bendix. They are for the single, the wealthy, the sybaritic of all ages and conditions. And the numbers at least of the single were growing rapidly: Between 1970 and 1982, the number of Americans living alone nearly doubled, jumping from 10.9 million to 19.4 million.

It remained for American business—ever adept at interpreting the life cycle as a sequence of marketing opportunities—to recognize singleness as a commercially exploitable condition, as opposed to a simple failure to marry. Teenagers had been defined as a distinct market in the fifties, with major consequences for the self-awareness of youth as a social category. In the sixties and seventies, business discovered young, middle-class singles as a fresh and exciting new market. Like teenagers, singles could spend for fun rather than for family; but like married grown-ups, they had family-size wages to spend.

The combination of grown-up incomes and childlike freedom from responsibility made singles potentially the most free-spending, hedonistic subpopulation imaginable. In a report on the new singles market, *U.S. News and World Report* offered a "typical" single, George Drapeau III, a 30-year-old marketing consultant who lives in a two-bedroom cooperative apartment in Mamaroneck, N.Y. Being on his own, he has time to build his business as well as take frequent weekend ski trips, buy a new car every few years and vacation in Europe. "You don't need an extra car or an extra room in the house, and you don't have an extra mouth to feed," says Drapeau.

Marketing people were quick to recognize that young people like Drapeau were no longer simply bachelors (or worse, spinsters), living from hand to mouth until the right mate came along. "We're bullish on those goods and services that either complement or facilitate the life style of people living alone," a securities analyst told Pacific News Service in 1979. According to the New York ad agency Young and Rubicam, those goods and services included liquor, stereo equipment, books, foreign cars, sporting goods, casual apparel, and gourmet foods. As early as 1969, *Advertising Age* had heralded the burgeoning singles market for "leisure-time product lines" and warned that it could mean trouble for the standard, family-oriented, house-and-garden commodity ensemble: "What will this trend mean to the lawn-mower market—to cite one small negative example?"

Lawn mowers were never rendered extinct by leisure products, in part because by the mid-eighties middle-class singles (then absorbed into the category of "yuppies") were themselves investing in houses and lawns. But in the mid-seventies, when the New Right was coalescing into its network of pro-family, pro-business organizations, the clash of lifestyles was in full heat: singles vs. family, pleasure-giving leisure products vs. dull and durable household appurtenances. There was a third dimension to the conflict: spending vs. saving. The family-centered lifestyle required savings, at least for the down-payment on the house. But for the reasonably affluent, the singles lifestyle required only the rapid turnover of discretionary income.

The rise of the leisure-products market, no less than the creative revolution in advertising, amplified the permissive message of the consumer culture. The marketeers' goal had always been to convince Americans to spend, not save, and here was a cornucopia of urgent new reasons to spend *now*, on oneself. In the face of the new lifestyle and the products that defined it, deferring gratification could mean denying one's most genuine impulses and forfeiting the obvious pleasures of life. A 1975 ad for *Psychology Today*, directed to advertisers, expressed the new hedonism straightforwardly. It shows a young woman, sitting on her living-room floor, improbably decked out in scuba mask and flippers, ski poles and tennis racket. The caption says, in boldface, *"I love me."* "I'm not conceited," she assures us:

> I'm just a good friend to myself.
> And I like to do what makes me feel good.
> Me, myself and I used to sit around, putting things off until tomorrow.
> Tomorrow we'll buy new ski equipment, and look at new compact cars. And pick up that new camera.
> The only trouble is that tomorrow always turned into the next tomorrow.
> And I never had a good time "today" . . .
> [But now] *I live my dreams today, not tomorrow.*

Most of the time, of course, we do not need such detailed refutations of traditional values to convince us that the aerobic young people in MTV commercials or the brooding dandies in Giorgio Armani ads are leading enviably rewarding lives. Advertising still shows us the full-time homemaker agonizing over laundry detergents, the responsible dad choosing among life-insurance policies. But it also provides a running endorsement for a very different way of living—more self-centered, more impulsive, more fun. Even a 1986 ad for life insurance, for example, offers hedonism rather than peace of mind. Above pictures showing a grand piano, a vintage car, a helicopter, and a yacht is the message: "All life insurance lets you provide for your children. Ours lets you buy toys of your own." In fact, the demographic shifts toward later marriage and more frequent divorce that inspired the leisure-products boom have also been encouraged by that boom. For the last two decades or more, advertising has been telling us that the "traditional family" with it "traditional values" is just one option, and by no means the most exciting one.

In the clash between lawn mowers and leisure products, the New Right came in on the side of the house, the family, the savings account. Its animating cultural vision is what historian Allen Hunter has called "suburban pastoralism"—nostalgia for the supposedly stable, prosperous, white suburban way of life we associate with the 1950s. A flick of the switch away from MTV and its soft-porn rock videos lies the Christian Broadcasting Network, where the right-wing evangelical shows are embedded in round-the-clock nostalgia: reruns of fifties sitcoms and cowboy shows, and tame commercials for breakfast cereals, kitchenware, and headache relief.

But this New Right utopia is hardly an alternative to the consumer culture—a pure and Christian lifestyle unsullied by materialism. Consider Frances Fitzgerald's description of the Reverend Jerry Falwell's parishioners in Lynchburg, Virginia:

> A number of the Thomas Road Church members live in the new, developer-built houses on the edge of town: comfortable suburban-style houses set on half-acre lawns, with central air-conditioning and kitchens like the ones that appear in detergent advertisements on television. . . . A woman I visited, Nancy James, had just bought a living room suite, and another, Jackie Gould, had ordered a new set of kitchen cabinets and had them installed without—she said, giggling —consulting her husband.

This is a no less a consumerist lifestyle than that of *Psychology Today*'s athletic young hedonist. The commodities are different, as are the messages on how to live and what to buy. But the permissive theme is still present—and powerful enough, in Jackie Gould's case, to override the need for the specific and personalized permission of the head of the family.

Yet even commodities have a moral life of their own, in which lawn mowers play an entirely different role than leisure products. As historian Elaine Tyler May has observed of the fifties:

Purchasing for the home helped alleviate traditional American uneasiness with consumption: the fear that spending would lead to decadence. Family-centered spending reassured Americans that affluence would strengthen the American way of life. The goods purchased by middle-class consumers, like a modern refrigerator or a house in the suburbs, were intended to foster traditional values.

The refrigerator, or the kitchen cabinets, could be seen as a silent testimony to home, family, and hard work. But the adult toys that comprised the "leisure products" market signified—to anyone still anxious about surrendering to the consumer culture—only decadence. At one level, the New Right's "social issues" boil down to the issue of which commodity ensemble—and accompanying lifestyle—should prevail: maple furniture, home freezers, and prayer, or butcher-top counters, scuba diving, and abortion. Both sets of commodities are products of the same consumer culture, but one hinted at a disastrous breakdown of moral values, a triumph of permissiveness.

The New Right, however, was not about to blame permissiveness on capitalism, no matter how indirectly. In the New Right's scheme of things the businessman is not an enemy; he is a "producer," allied with the working class in his allegiance to the traditional values of hard work and self-denial. He cannot be criticized. His economic interests, after all, are at the core of the New Right's economic program.

Hence the central dishonesty of the New Right: Its intellectual leaders pinpointed permissiveness as the source of America's ills. Yet they could not attack, or even mention, the one source of genuinely permissive ideology in American culture. Blaming permissiveness on the New Class only compounds the dishonesty. The New Class—or more broadly, the professional middle class—includes the marketing strategists, copywriters, and miscellaneous corporate hirelings who actually compose the permissive message of the consumer culture. But the same class also produces the most ardent critiques of that ideology, from the liberal intellectuals who fretted about affluence in the fifties to the New Right itself.

## THE POOR AND THE PERMISSIVE STATE

Unwilling to blame permissiveness on capitalism, the New Right blamed the state. To the New Right, the most shocking and pernicious example of the permissiveness that gripped American society was located in the public sector, in the form of government programs to aid the poor. Welfare was a flagrant example; the antipoverty programs initiated in the sixties were seen as a vast outpouring of misdirected, permissive generosity. The New Right's focus on social welfare programs guaranteed that the victims of right-wing policies would not, of course, be the business community, or even the hated New Class, but the least indulged, least permissively treated segment of American society—the poor.

By 1980 the New Right was in a position to turn its ideas, no matter how crackpot or prejudiced, into government policy. Ronald Reagan, the man whom even Barry Goldwater had found too extreme to endorse in 1976, was elected president. In the Reagan White House, ideas from the far right were not only welcome, they were almost the only ideas. Men associated with the New Right moved into key federal positions, and the New Right's Heritage Foundation became a major source of guidance on domestic policy. Among the ideas adopted wholeheartedly by the new administration were the New Right's startling theories of poverty: it had been caused, strangely enough, by past efforts to cure it, in particular, by the New Class–initiated War on Poverty.

The New Right inherited the neoconservative notion that the War on Poverty was solely the invention of the New Class —an error for which the poor themselves could not be blamed. To New Right ideologue George Gilder, whose 1981 book *Wealth and Poverty* was much admired by President Reagan, the New Class actually consisted of downwardly mobile rich people, who had turned against free enterprise because they lacked their fathers' zest for money-making. Their alliance with the poor was based on defeatism, or perhaps just the desire to have "the fashionable image of a progressive 'new class.' " Similarly, Charles Murray, one of the New Right's most respectable social-policy analysts, attributed the War on Poverty to the "intelligentsia," which had, for unexplained reasons, lost faith in the workings of the free-enterprise system and found it briefly "fashionable" to be liberal.

More commonly, though, New Right analysts, like the neo-conservatives before them, explained antipoverty measures as a scheme for New Class advancement in which the hapless poor had somehow gotten entangled. In a well-publicized attack on New York's governor, White House director of communications Patrick Buchanan charged:

> Mario Cuomo's incessant invocations of the poor, the down-trodden, the ill, almost invariably turn up as preambles to budget requests that would augment the power of his own political class—the Welfare statists.

And with his customary Buckleyesque flamboyance, *American Spectator* editor R. Emmett Tyrrell, Jr., recounted the story of the War on Poverty as follows:

> Once [President Johnson] had fattened up the welfare budget, Washington became a city full of quacks adept at dispensing the loaves and the fishes, and making a bundle. Aid to Families with Dependent Children! Food Stamps! Community Action Programs! Housing Assistance Programs! Medicaid! More! . . . What resulted was not an American welfare state, rationally constructed, but a blowsy milch-cow state teeming with superparasites: social engineers, welfare counselors, bureaucrats, nutritionists, social scientists, legal-aid advisors, and charlatans of even more dubious repute.

Within this giant boondoggle, the poor were entirely passive, if they existed at all. Tyrrell claims they had to be hunted down in order to get them to participate: "Sometimes the government had to send out beaters to locate the newly authorized recipients of these so-called entitlements." To William Rusher, the poor were only a "concept," an excuse for New Class aggrandizement. On this point, he cites a *National Review* editorial:

> "The poor" must be understood in a special sense, as potential clients for the redistributive ministrations of the New Class, the middlemen of social justice. Analytically, "the poor," as a concept, legitimates the power-grab of the New Class middlemen in the same sense as "the proletariat" legitimates the power-grab of the Leninists.

The image of the poor as a passive, colorless lot, subject to the "ministrations" of their social betters, has much in common with the liberal view of the poor in the early sixties. But the New Right went much further in obliterating the poor as agents of their own destiny. To the New Right, the New Class had not only discovered poverty but, in a very real sense, had created it.

Their reasoning begins with the assumption, dating from the discovery of poverty, that the poor are victims of a "culture" or a "syndrome" that disables people in the quest for upward mobility. In the view of the right, this syndrome is the product not of despair but of the overly permissive welfare and anti-poverty programs championed by New Class liberals. Welfare, then, or public aid of any kind, is the *cause* of poverty. In George Gilder's somewhat lurid analysis, welfare cripples its recipients by emasculating poor men, who are no longer needed as breadwinners once their wives or girlfriends go on the dole. As a result, the men (at least black men, who are the only objects of Gilder's concern) respond with "resignation and rage, escapism and violence, short horizons and promiscuous sexuality."

In Charles Murray's more restrained analysis, the expanded social-welfare measures of the sixties created poverty by undermining the "fragile assumption . . . that adults are responsible for the state in which they find themselves." Welfare caused poverty by encouraging a culture of "dependency," in which the poor saw no need to form stable families, work for a living, or otherwise honor America's "traditional values."

This was not the fault of the poor, since it was the New Class "intelligentsia" who had "changed the rules," making out-of-wedlock births and idleness more profitable for the poor than marriage and employment. Murray presented an impressive-looking but unpersuasive assortment of graphs and charts to prove that the increase in out-of-wedlock births and fatherless families during the seventies was a result of the thoughtless generosity of the welfare state.

The New Right's analysis of poverty and welfare became, for a time, the conventional wisdom. The War on Poverty had failed; welfare had failed. In fact, they had backfired, inflicting on their intended beneficiaries "divorce, alcoholism, drug abuse, psychosomatic illness, neurosis, suicide," and, of course, more poverty. Or, as a report from the Reagan administration put it in 1986, liberal social-welfare policies had "frayed the fabric of American family life, bringing increased crime, illegitimate birth, drug use, teen-age pregnancy, divorce, sexually transmitted disease and poverty." The only responsible thing to do was to eliminate these noxious programs before they did any more harm. And this was precisely what the Reagan administration set out to do. Starting in 1981 it instituted devastating cutbacks in Aid to Families with Dependent Children, Food Stamps, housing assistance, special nutritional programs for infants and pregnant mothers, and other programs now seen as misguided attempts to aid the poor.

The ingenuity of the New Right's theory of poverty deserves a moment's appreciation. If attempts to help the poor only hurt them, then it is the anti-welfare right-wingers who are the true friends of the poor, and the liberal do-gooders who are their betrayers. I recall a curious statement by Gilder at a 1982 New Right gathering honoring Phyllis Schlafly. She is, he said, the person who has done more than any other American on behalf of the black minority. For a second an uncomfortable silence fell over the crowd, either at the mention of black people (who were otherwise present only as waiters), or at the thought that Schlafley might have a secret life as a liberal. Then Gilder explained: What she had done for blacks was to campaign against welfare, which, in Gilder's view, put her on a moral par with the civil rights leaders of the sixties. The crowd broke into gratified applause for Schlafly—and for the farsighted racial benevolence of their right-wing worldview.

Is there any truth to the New Right's allegation that indulgent social programs created poverty by inciting a moral breakdown among the poor? Sadly, no: *sadly*, if for no other reason than that American antipoverty efforts have been too puny and niggardly to have any of the effects attributed to them. For example, the increase in female-headed households among the black poor in the seventies, which Murray attributed to rising welfare benefits, took place when AFDC benefits were declining, not rising. In the 1970s, the real value of AFDC benefits declined nationwide by almost 30 percent. In the early eighties, at the time the Reagan administration undertook its sharpest cutbacks in social spending for the poor, there was no state in which the combined value of AFDC payments and Food Stamps was enough to bring a poor family *up to* the poverty level.

Furthermore, numerous studies have failed to find a correlation between the level of benefits paid to the poor and the symptoms of "moral breakdown" that supposedly led to higher poverty rates. For example, if welfare benefits cause out-of-wedlock births, there should be higher rates of such births among poor women in states offering higher benefits. The somewhat more generous states, like California, should be sinkholes of squalor, while Mississippi should be a paradise of Protestant virtue. But a highly respected 1986 study found no correlation between benefit levels and out-of-wedlock birthrates. Nor have any studies found welfare to have a significant effect on poor people's commitment to work. A recent government study from the General Accounting Office, based on a review of over a hundred studies and an extensive survey of its own, concluded that welfare does not encourage family breakups or out-of-wedlock births, and that it has little discernible effect on the incentive to work.

But Americans have only to look beyond their own borders to appreciate how ludicrous the New Right's theories of welfare and poverty are. Most European capitalist nations offer far more generous payments to the unemployed and to single parents than the United States does, yet have lower rates of crime, drug abuse, and teenage pregnancy. France, for example, offers single parents welfare payments that amount to about 79 percent of the average wage for that nation. In Sweden, the figure is 94 percent. Yet those nations are hardly awash in the poverty, degradation, and immorality that the right attributes to our "permissive" welfare state.

Strangely, advocates of the welfare-causes-poverty argument always manage to forget that the poor have seemed equally dissolute to middle- and upper-class observers regardless of whether they were under the influence of "permissive" benefits. Recall the middle-class characterizations of the culture of poverty in the early 1960s, before the War on Poverty was waged. Or consider Daniel Patrick Moynihan's description of the "wild Irish slums of the nineteenth-century Northeast," in which "drunkenness, crime, corruption, discrimination, family disorganization, juvenile delinquency" were the rule, without any encouragement at all from government welfare measures. Whether these kinds of behavior represent "social pathology" or the adaptive mechanisms of poor and dislocated communities is an issue we will leave to the sociologists of deviance. The point is that it is *poverty* that causes the poor to live differently from the middle class, not welfare or other forms of liberal intervention.

But the New Right's great social insight—that attempts to help the poor only increase poverty—provided the final gloss to its more general vision of an America ravaged by the schemes and sins of the New Class. Morally abandoned themselves, the personnel of the New Class had nonetheless found time and energy to construct a vast, permissive welfare state, which in turn served to transmit the corrupt values of the New Class down to those erstwhile innocents, the poor. In the abundant words of R. Emmett Tyrrell:

> The welfare state had turned many theretofore toiling Americanos into parasites, and this new class of busybodies lived as superparasites, deriving nourishment from the dependence of the welfare clients.

An ugly picture, this—suggesting a leachlike presence on the body politic, or a hideous pollution, spreading downward.

The Reagan era provided the New Right with eight years to test their theories of poverty and welfare. Inspired by Gilder and Murray, the administration undertook its systematic cutbacks in social programs for the poor. The cuts were justified not only in terms of their supposedly bracing effect on the poor but as a means of reducing the federal budget, although social spending for the poor accounted for less than 15 percent of the total budget when the cutbacks began in 1981. As we know from the admissions of Reagan's former budget director David Stockman, the administration even inflated the deficit—by cutting taxes and increasing military expenditures—in order to justify deeper cuts in social spending.

The cutbacks were never as deep as New Right theory recommended. Murray had proposed, as a "thought experiment," "scrapping the entire federal welfare and income-support structure for working-aged persons, including AFDC, Medicaid, Food Stamps, Unemployment Insurance, Worker's Compensation, subsidized housing, disability insurance, and the rest." But the administration was hampered by the organized resistance of labor, minority groups, and women's groups. Even more inhibiting was the mounting evidence that most Americans did not share the right-wing approach to poverty. In a review of public opinion polls taken between 1980 and 1984, Seymour Martin Lipset—certainly no liberal himself—concluded that "Americans, while voting conservative on the presidential level, are programmatically liberal." Asked to choose between military and social-spending cuts, the majority chose to cut the Pentagon, not the poor. Even the most stigmatized programs, the right's most pernicious examples of the "milch-cow state"—Aid to Families with Dependent Children and Food Stamps—were supported by 57 percent of people asked to choose between protecting these programs and reducing the federal deficit.

But the Reagan administration's social spending cutbacks were deep enough to hurt. According to the New Right's theories, poverty should have decreased as the poverty-generating social-welfare programs shrank. Of course, it did not. The poverty rate had declined in the sixties, but it rose again in the late seventies (a decade in which welfare benefits were declining in real dollars) and then rose steeply in the early eighties. In 1983 the percentage of poor Americans was the highest it had been since 1965. The poverty rate declined slightly with the economic recovery of 1984 but remained steadily higher than it had been in the late sixties through the mid-seventies. Whether anyone was saved from poverty by the morally uplifting effects of welfare cutbacks we do not know, but the immediate net effect of Reaganomics was to recruit approximately 11 million Americans into the ranks of the poor.

At the same time, New Right–inspired budget cuts guaranteed that the poor would be not only more numerous but also poorer. In 1968 the poorest one-fifth of American families had an estimated 91 percent of the income they needed for their basic requirements; by 1983 congressional researchers estimated they had only 60 percent of the money required for bare subsistence. During the War on Poverty, health care and improved education were the issues that had mobilized poor blacks and Hispanics in inner-city communities. But in the grim new environment of the Reagan years, those became almost "luxury" concerns. Poverty in the eighties meant not only inadequate health care and indifferent schooling but hunger and homelessness. In the name of combatting gross hedonism and permissiveness, the New Right had succeeded in reducing large numbers of the American poor to the condition of their third-world counterparts—beggars, vagrants, and dwellers in makeshift shelters.

The poor were not the only victims of New Right social policy. The erstwhile heroes of New Right ideology—the blue-collar working class—were also badly hurt by Reagan's antiwelfare and antiunion policies. As Frances Fox Piven and Richard Cloward have shown, cutbacks in social programs for the poor undercut the economic position of working-class people generally, in part, by making it riskier for any worker to organize or strike for higher wages. Then, in the recession of 1982–83, millions of blue-collar workers were plunged into unemployment and faced poverty directly. Out-of-work blue-collar men and women found the safety net of public services badly frayed: Unemployment compensation, food stamps, and Medicaid were harder to qualify for and offered less than ever to those who were eligible. The New Right liked to think of itself as championing the traditional values of the working class, and it was convenient that one of these values was self-denial.

The liberal response to the New Right's—and Reagan's—domestic policies was, for the most part, a shameful silence. Many prominent liberal political figures and intellectuals took a public stand against the administration's antilabor and anti-welfare policies, but there was no concerted, ideological rebuttal of the right's economic premises, and no challenge to the fundamental hypocrisy of right-wing populism. In fact, many erstwhile liberals of the middle class moved as quickly as possible to distance themselves from the concerns that had defined liberalism since the sixties. Writing shortly after Reagan's election in 1980, Morton Kondracke, now famed for representing the ostensibly liberal end of the spectrum on public-affairs talk shows, warned of the "danger" that "Democrats will be as reflexive in shielding outworn and expensive Great Society programs in the 1980s as the Republicans were in opposing them in the 1960s."

The warning was either unnecessary or well-heeded. The Democrats offered no defense of the War on Poverty and, through most of the Reagan era, no attack on its right-wing counterpart, Reagan's "war on the poor." Taking a cue from the neoconservatives, one influential group of liberals renamed themselves "neoliberals." As Randall Rothenberg, a leading promoter of the neoliberal label, explained: "The most striking aspect of this new liberalism was its cursory attitude toward the social programs of the Democratic Party's recent past, the programs that, in the eyes of the public, defined liberalism itself." This was, in short, liberalism without the poor or, as it might just as well be put, middle-class liberalism without a conscience.

By the mid-eighties, the neoliberal neologism was barely necessary. There were too few self-proclaimed liberals in public life to make the distinction meaningful, and most of those who remained had edged imperceptibly away from the old goals of equality and social justice anyway. The new, "pragmatic" liberalism of the eighties embraced the right-wing theory that welfare causes poverty, and enthusiastically joined what one reputable liberal termed the "historic bipartisan breakthrough" for a punitive overhaul of the welfare system. But few remaining liberals took any great interest in the downtrodden—poor or working class. Describing the "repackag[ed]," "post-industrial" liberal (with 1988 Democratic candidate Michael Dukakis as the prototype), the *Wall Street Journal* wrote from the depressed area of western Pennsylvania:

> He is self-contained, measured and, above all, managerial. He could be some successful entrepreneur from the pages of *Fortune* magazine. The very words he emphasizes—"invest," "partnerships," "competitive"—are more appropriate to an executive suite than to this valley of the hulks: mile after mile of abandoned steel mills along the Monongahela River, dark and lifeless beneath the greening trees.

By the mid-eighties, liberalism appeared, for all practical purposes, to be dead. Humorist Russell Baker, himself a steadfast liberal, described the breed as near extinction: "The last official count, made in November, showed 20 female liberals and 17 males." And a 1985 *New York Times*/CBS News poll found that of five possible political labels, *liberal* was the least popular, with the exception of the possibly obscure term *populist*.

The right's campaign against the "liberal elite"—or, in more intellectually respectable terms, the New Class—had been an unqualified success. By the eighties, if not the mid-seventies, the expression *middle-class liberal* had the ring of an epithet, as if no other kind of liberal were possible. Even Baker, in his account of the extinction of liberalism, described its remaining representatives in the caricatures made familiar by right-wing populists: "One of the males belonged to the breed classified as limousine liberals. The other belonged to the white-wine-and-brie liberal grouping." The existence of a huge constituency for liberal programs among the poor and the blue-collar working class was all but forgotten, for the word, at least, remained fastened to the "elite." When Jesse Jackson sought to revive an essentially liberal, working-class populism in the Democratic primaries of 1984 and 1988, he had to employ the fresh (though actually quite venerable) term *progressive.*

But the right's campaign against liberal social policies would hardly have been effective if it had not resonated with the self-doubts of those who were still liberal, middle-class intellectuals. If no one refuted the right's theory of the New Class and its motives in the War on Poverty, it was in part because many liberals now believed, guiltily, that they were part of an isolated elite, and disqualified by past mistakes. Even the ultimately elitist notion that antipoverty efforts were tainted with misguided indulgence toward the poor met little resistance and much grudging acceptance. As economist Sar A. Levitan, an otherwise staunch defender of liberal antipoverty efforts, confessed in 1985:

> Ronald Reagan made us realize that in lots of things, we went too far. . . . Permissiveness is the key word. We gave up on old-fashioned standards like punishment for crime, and family values.

Liberal to left-wing journals of opinion rang with mea culpas and accusations that could have been taken straight from the literature of the New Right: that liberals (or leftists) were too tenaciously committed to welfare programs; that they represented a "cosmopolitan" elite out of touch with the majority; that they had slighted the "traditional values" of hard work and family loyalty. In an article on the "dilemma of liberalism," historian Fred Siegel attacked liberal intellectuals for what the right would have called permissiveness—"a binding absolutism that insists on rights without reciprocal obligations"—and went on to trace this failing to the same moral defect the right had located within the New Class:

> Self-indulgence has been raised to the level of a moral imperative, in which individuals have the absolute right to behave as they see fit regardless of the larger consequences.

Above all, the right's attack on the New Class, or liberal elite, rang true because it touched on that perennial fear within the professional middle class of growing soft, of failing to strive, of falling into the snares of affluence. The intellectuals of the right understood the anxieties of their class only too well. They had launched their attack on the poor under cover of a larger moral campaign against permissiveness and self-indulgence. And on these charges, liberals had no defense: not because they had been too permissive or, in all likelihood, self-indulgent, but because this is what they feared.

If the right's target was the New Class, they missed it by a wide margin. They had set out, rhetorically at least, to "limit," chasten, and possibly eliminate the "parasitic" and "rapacious" New Class. But the New Right, for all its populist pretensions, ended up as a vast forcing ground for professional middle-class personnel. Little of its great wealth flowed to the Middle American insurgents that the New Right had supposedly arisen to champion—local advocates of school prayer, segregation, textbook censorship, and miscellaneous pro-family causes. Instead, the New Right created and, in effect, became a dense infrastructure of think-tanks, legal foundations, journals, and lobbying agencies, collectively employing thousands of lawyers, journalists, professors, publicists, administrators, and the like. Charles Murray, for example, was nurtured in a New Right think-tank, the Manhattan Institute, and his attack on welfare was launched with $125,000 donated by right-wing foundations.

The New Right took far better care of its intellectuals than the left or liberals ever had: recruiting them in college, financing campus newspapers for them, grooming them in conferences and special retreats, housing them (between other forms of employment) in its rich, Washington-centered bureaucracy. It is possible for a conservative intellectual to enjoy the life-long munificence of the corporate "milch-cow" so successfully harnessed by the New Right, from his youth as a right-wing campus activist to his declining years in a graciously appointed right-wing think-tank.

The irony is, as usual, lost on its perpetrators. Sidney Blumenthal describes a 1985 gathering of neoconservatives and New Rightists featuring an after-dinner speech by writer Tom Wolfe:

> The ideological spoilsmen—conservative intellectuals with think-tank sinecures, foundation executives, political operatives, and federal jobholders—were congratulated on their "courage" for appearing at this lush affair. . . . Then came the rote attack on the New Class, those who really have power, "a class of ruling intellectuals trained to rule a country," Wolfe declared. . . . The conservatives applauded, dispersed into the Washington night, and showed up at their New Class jobs the next morning.

The right's peculiarly self-deceptive relationship to the New Class was essential, perhaps, to its self-respect. If the professional middle class was an elite—and that notion seemed well-founded by the seventies—the intellectual cadres of the New Right did not want to be part of it. Their fictive battle with the New Class infused them, no doubt, with moral righteousness. Whatever they did, they were on the side of the "plain folks," the Middle Americans, the working class. They could make their careers advancing policies designed to hurt the hard-working and the needy—all in the name of combatting a wicked, and fortunately quite invisible and powerless, "liberal elite."

But in the eighties, growing numbers of middle-class people were not bothering to rationalize greed or careerism with arcane ideological justifications. These were Irving Kristol's spiritual children: young, educated, middle-class people eager to throw in their lot with big business. The yuppies, as they were briefly called, had no qualms about being a social elite. They wanted not only to serve the corporate elite, as Kristol and his colleagues in the New Right did so enthusiastically, but to join it.

## CHAPTER FIVE

# THE YUPPIE STRATEGY

L IKE EVERY OTHER SOCIAL GROUP to rise to fleeting prominence, the yuppies were as much invented as discovered. The term was first employed in the press for the modest purpose of explaining Gary Hart's unexpected success in the 1984 presidential primaries. Someone had voted for him, someone young, urban, and professional, and there was brief hope that this new grouping would provide the Democrats with a much-needed new constituency. But what started as a neutral demographic category evolved with alarming speed into a social slur. Four years after their "discovery," Hendrik Hertzberg wrote in *Esquire*:

> *Yuppie* is now understood almost universally as a term of abuse. . . . "You're a yuppie" is taken to mean not "you're a young urban professional" but rather "you have lousy values."

*Yuppie* is a hybrid category—a mixture of age, address, and class. Other social classes are, in the middle-class imagination, age groups too: the poor as children, blue-collar workers as stern though somewhat pitiable fathers. But yuppies were by definition young adults, and thus subject to the moral judgments that older and more established people routinely pass on the young. From one angle, yuppies were the good children so sorely missed by neoconservatives like Midge Decter in the sixties and early seventies. They did not waste time "finding themselves" or joining radical movements. They plunged directly into the economic mainstream, earning and spending with equal zest. To *Newsweek,* the yuppie eagerness to "go for it" was a healthy sign of the "yuppie virtues of imagination, daring and entrepreneurship."

But they were also the very worst children, the apotheosis of middle-class forebodings about the corrupting effects of affluence. No one hurled the still-potent diagnosis of permissiveness at them, perhaps because by the eighties the word referred to so much more than childraising practices. Yet here they were, displaying that dread trait customarily assigned to the poor—"inability to defer gratification"—and even the desperate "orality" Oscar Lewis had once detected in the culture of poverty. Yuppies did not devote their youth to "that patient overcoming and hard-won new attainment" that Decter had endorsed as the prerequisite to adult middle-class life. They did not study; they "networked." They did not save; they spent. And they did not spend on houses or station wagons, but on Rolex watches, Porsches, quick trips to Aruba, and, most notoriously, high-status foods. In its "Year of the Yuppie" cover story, *Newsweek* found them on "a new plane of consciousness, a state of Transcendental Acquisition."

Yuppies, of course, did not turn out to be a new constituency for liberalism. Their "virtues" of entrepreneurship and acquisition made them for the most part conservatives, though not in the fervid, ideological style of the neoconservatives or the New Right. Yuppies thought of themselves as members of an elite whose interests might naturally collide with those of the lower classes: They lived in gentrified neighborhoods from which the unsightly poor had been freshly cleared; they worked for firms intent on minimizing the "labor costs" of blue- and pink-collar workers; their lifestyle was supported by the labor of poorly paid, often immigrant, service workers—housekeepers, restaurant employees, messengers, and delivery "boys." Although they parted company with the New Right on the social issues, such as abortion and women's rights, self-interest kept them reliably Republican.

Yet, despite their political conservatism, everyone sensed

that the yuppies were somehow connected to that last period of youthful assertiveness, the sixties. Some commentators presented them as grown-up radicals, covertly bearing the heritage of the sixties into the corporate rat race of the eighties. It was possible in fact to have been a radical in the first decade and a self-centered hustler in the second, as Jerry Rubin's transformation from rebel to networking impresario illustrates. The very word *yuppie* had originally been coined in 1983 to describe Rubin's transition from a "yippie"—the acronym for the anarcho-hippie Youth International Party organized by Rubin and Abbie Hoffman—to prototypical young urban professional. *Newsweek* saw yuppies as the "vanguard of the baby-boom generation," which had "marched through the '60s" and was now "speed[ing] toward the airport, advancing on the 1980s in the back seat of a limousine."

Actually, the stereotypical yuppie, who was about thirty in 1984, was more likely to have spent the sixties bicycling around the neighborhood than marching on Washington. With equal disregard for the normal length of generations, yuppies were sometimes presented as the rebellious children of sixties radicals, who, in a stunning reprisal, were now horrifying *their* parents with their self-centeredness and political conservatism. Actor Michael J. Fox, the only yuppie actually pictured in *Esquire*'s "Days of Wine and Sushi" cover story, can ordinarily be found in a sitcom whose single sustaining joke is the clash between Fox and his gentle, sensitive, sixties-generation parents.

What yippies and yuppies did share was their class. Despite the frequent confusion of yuppies and baby-boomers in general, yuppies—defined by lifestyle and income—made up only about 5 percent of their generation. They were exemplars not of their generation but of their class, the same professional middle class that had produced the student rebels. Like the sixties rebels, the yuppies were at the cutting edge of their class, a kind of avant-garde, charting a new direction and agenda. They were also, in their own way, rebels. Both radicals and yuppies rejected the long, traditional path to middle-class success, but the defining zeal of the yuppies was to join another class—the rich.

The actual number of demographically official yuppies—people born between 1945 and 1959, earning over $40,000 a year in a professional or managerial occupation, and living in urban areas—was only about 1.5 million, hardly enough to warrant excitement. If yuppies were further defined as greedy, shallow people prone to burble about the joys of real estate investment, like those depicted in *Newsweek*'s cover story, then, as a commentator in the *New Republic* observed, there were probably no more than 113 of them nationwide. But there was certainly a yuppie style of work and consumption, as well as what could be called a yuppie strategy for success, and these embraced, to a greater or lesser extent, many thousands of middle-class people beyond the demographic category. Here I will use *yuppie* in a loose, rather than demographically precise, sense, for someone who adopted the strategy and more or less fit the style. Hardly anyone, of course, deserves to bear the full burden of the stereotype.

But even the stereotype plays an important role in our chronicle of emerging class awareness. With the image of the yuppie, the normally invisible, normally "normal" middle class finally emerged in the mass media as a distinct group with its own ambitions, habitats, and tastes in food and running gear. The class usually privileged to do the discovering and naming of classes had itself been discovered by the media and, with scant respect for its dignity, named with a diminutive that rhymes with *puppy.*

Of course, those who followed the yuppie strategy did not represent all of their class. They were a select segment, just as the right's version of the New Class had been a selected subset of the larger professional middle class. In fact, the two groups —yuppie and New Class—are, technically speaking, complementary. The New Class, as defined by the neoconservatives, was that part of the professional middle class that finds an occupational home in the media, in the public sector, and in the nonprofit world exemplified by the university, the foundation, the social-welfare agency. And the New Class, by the right's definition, was solidly and unrepentently liberal.

The yuppies, on the other hand, represented the more than 60 percent of the middle class that earns its living in the direct service of corporate power, as executives, corporate lawyers, and other sorts of business-employed professionals, consultants, or brokers. They were the fulfillment of the neoconservatives' dream that "intellectuals," or at least members of the professional middle class, might abandon any remaining concerns for the lower classes and become the trusted courtiers of the corporate elite.

But the very frivolity of yuppies—and hence of the very *subject* of yuppies—was a distraction from the deeper changes their appearance signaled. In the eighties, the class contours of American society were undergoing a seismic shift. The extremes of wealth and poverty moved further apart, and, as if stretched beyond the limit of safety, the ground in the middle began to tremble and crack. Whole occupational groups and subpopulations—farmers, steelworkers, single mothers—began to tumble toward the bottom. Other groups—lower-level white-collar employees, schoolteachers, even higher-status professionals and their families—found themselves scrambling to remain in place.

In the confusion, only one group, outside of the very rich, seemed to have a clear strategy for success. And perhaps it was because that strategy involved such a betrayal of traditional middle-class values—such a wholesale surrender to the priorities of profit and the pleasures of consumerism—that the media turned so quickly against those who followed it. Implicit in the media's half-mocking, half-indulgent "discovery" of yuppies was the incipiently liberal understanding that their strategy might not, after all, be the way to go.

## THE POLARIZATION OF AMERICA

It was possible, until the eighties, for a comfortable American to think of class as a form of cultural diversity, parallel to ethnicity or even "lifestyle." The emphasis had been on the *culture* of poverty, or of the supposedly parochial subculture of the working class. In the mass media, class often appeared to be a way of life, even a set of options adding color and texture to an otherwise increasingly homogeneous America. In 1985, for example, a sidebar in *U.S. News and World Report* titled "Beatniks, Preppies, and Punkers: The Love Affair with Labels" juxtaposed, as "categories" of Americans, both faddists and economic groups:

> VALLEY GIRLS, 1981 . . . fun-loving teens with materialistic values and their own style of dress (leg warmers, cut-out sweatshirts) . . .
> UNDERCLASS, 1982 . . . a part of the American population seemingly mired in poverty.
> YUPPIES, 1984 . . . "young urban professionals" . . . [known for their] consumerist lifestyle.

But there is another, much dryer and less judgmental way of thinking about class: as an index defined solely by money—who has it and who doesn't. In the 1980s, this grimmer view of class became harder than ever to avoid. Those who "had" had more than ever, and those who "had not" were more numerous, and more undeniably miserable, than at any time since poverty was "discovered."

Sometime in the late sixties American society had begun to lurch off the track leading to the American dream of affluence and equality. No one could have known it at the time, but those were the last years in which economic inequality among Americans declined. Since then, in a sharp reversal of the equalizing trend that had been under way since shortly after World War II, the extremes of wealth have grown farther apart and the middle has lost ground. Some economists even began to predict that the middle class—defined simply as those with middling amounts of money—would disappear altogether, leaving America torn, like many third-world societies, between an affluent minority and an army of the desperately poor.

There is still a "middle class" in the statistical sense. At least, a graph of income distribution still comes out as a bell-shaped curve, with most people hovering near the mean income rather than at either extreme. (If the middle range of income actually disappeared, the curve would have two humps, rather than one smooth peak in the middle.) But in the last decade the curve has slumped toward the lower end and flattened a little on top, so that it begins to look less like a weathered hill and more like a beached whale. To the untrained eye, the shift is not alarming, but income-distribution curves do not change capriciously. *Any* change commands attention.

The change is evident no matter how you slice up the population—whether you compare the top fifth to the bottom fifth, or the top 40 percent to the poorest 40 percent—and whether you look at individual earnings, household earnings, or employ occult-sounding measures of inequality like the economists' "Gini coefficient." In 1985, for example, the top fifth of American families—those earning more than $48,000 a year—took in 43 percent of all family income, a postwar high. The bottom fifth—families earning less than $13,200 a year—got only 4.7 percent, their lowest share in twenty-five years. Families in a somewhat arbitrarily defined middle range ($15,000 to $35,000 a year) saw their share fall to 39 percent of total family income from 46 percent in 1970. According to the Census Bureau, the income gap between the richest and the poorest families was wider in the mid-eighties than at any time since the bureau began keeping statistics in 1946.

The widening gap between the extremes was in no small part the result of the conscious efforts of the Reagan administration. At the same time that the administration sliced viciously away at social programs designed to help the down-and-out, it rewarded Reagan's constituency of wealth with a series of generous tax reductions. The combination of spending cuts for the poor and tax cuts for the rich produced a massive, government-induced upward redistribution of wealth. Between 1980 and 1984 alone, the richest one-fifth of American families gained $25 billion in income and the poorest one-fifth lost $6 billion.

Meanwhile, income at the extremes was also diverging. The poor faced wages held down by that miserly standard, the minimum wage, which remained, throughout most of the eighties, at $3.35 an hour, or $6,900 a year—more than $4,000 less than what the federal government defined as the poverty level for a family of four. In early 1988, *U.S. News and World Report*, which had once questioned the very existence of "poverty" in the United States, acknowledged that there were now 9 million working American adults whose wages were not sufficient to lift them and their families above the poverty level:

> They are people like Glen Whitbeck, a short-order cook whose $8000 annual salary doesn't stretch to cover his two little girls' medical bills. Or like Charlie Scott, a construction worker whose money woes forced him and his wife into a shelter and then, most recently, provoked a separation. Or Pamela Kelley, a onetime airline-passenger screener who shifted to canned food at home because pot roast was too expensive for her and her two-year-old daughter.

As if rubbing its eyes in disbelief, *U.S. News* noted that the poor of the eighties did not fit the stereotype defined by the culture of poverty and the ideologues of the New Right. The concept of the poor as "shiftless, black urban males unable to hold jobs, or as inner-city mothers on welfare whose sole work experience is the repeated bearing and raising of illegitimate children," the magazine admitted, was "woefully overblown."

At the other extreme, where wages are known more elegantly as "compensation," there is of course no parallel to the minimum wage—no "maximum wage" to contain the greed of the already rich. In the eighties, while the median income of American families actually declined, the compensation of top executives rose dizzily. In 1986, top executives earned an average of $679,000 a year, up 9 percent from the year before. Executive incomes over $1 million (from salary and bonuses) became routine; only incomes over $10 million raised eyebrows. Reporting on then-chairman of NCR Inc. William S. Anderson's annual compensation of $13,229,000, the *New York Times* noted dryly:

The kind of salary reported for Mr. Anderson brings out strong feelings in those who believe that the men at the top of the corporate pinnacle are wildly overpaid, members of an elite that pretty much sets its own pay.

In this decade of political reaction, no conscience, no shame, or, more likely, no fear of the have-nots seemed to restrain the ultra-rich. Consider this society-page description of a party thrown by Malcolm Forbes of *Forbes* magazine ("The Capitalist Tool") in May 1987:

> Mr. Forbes' latest Highland fling (the Forbes clan hails from Scotland) included a regiment of 140 tartan-clad bagpipers and drummers marching through simulated mist. There were baronial Scottish stage sets whipped up by a designer of opera sets. There were 11-foot-tall flower arrangements dense with onopordon thistle, Grucci fireworks, laser beams, and, as party favors, copies of "The Sayings of Chairman Malcolm" for the lads and inscribed Revere bowls from Tiffany for the lasses . . . .
>   Once there, the guests, seated at 106 tables, supped on a meal whose raw materials included 24 hams, 700 baby pheasants, 100 pounds of *foie gras*, 400 pounds of *haricots verts*, 1,500 pounds of Scotch salmon, 24 legs of lamb, 60 country pâtés, 3,000 artichokes, 720 pints of raspberries and strawberries, 150 quarts of cream and 15 gallons of butterscotch sauce. . . . The Forbeses also let them eat "celebration cake" and "capitalist cookies."

No one could any longer imagine that America was the land of one vast, undifferentiated middle class. In cities like Los Angeles and New York, the contrasts in wealth and poverty scandalized European visitors: high-rise buildings where two-bedroom apartments cost more to rent than most Americans earn in a month, while at street level, makeshift cardboard structures sheltered the homeless. The streets carried fleets of stretch limos, their windows discreetly shaded to frustrate the curious, while on the sidewalk, beggars of all ages searched trash cans for edible crusts; breakdancers performed for quarters; hawkers sold ballpoint pens, watches, used clothing, old magazines, drugs.

While these lurid, distinctly un-American images came to characterize the extremes of wealth and poverty, no less dramatic changes were taking place in the middle range of income. For one thing, a middle-level income no longer guaranteed such perquisites of middle-class status as home ownership. According to the National Association of Homebuilders, in 1984 a family needed an income of approximately $37,000 to afford a median-priced home, but in the same year the median family income was only $26,167—almost $11,000 short. That gap marked a sharp deterioration in the prospects of middle-income, mostly working-class people. According to economists Frank S. Levy and Richard Michel, a typical wage-earner in the 1950s faced housing costs equivalent to about 14 percent of his gross monthly pay. In 1984, however, a thirty-year-old man who purchased a median-priced home had to set aside a staggering 44 percent of his income for carrying charges. For the first time in postwar America, a middle-level income no longer guaranteed what we have come to think of as a middle-class lifestyle.

But the big news was that the "middle class," or more precisely, the middle range of income, was becoming ever more sparsely inhabited. If the middle range was defined as lying between family incomes of $20,000 and $50,000, the fraction of families with middle-range incomes declined from 53 percent in 1973 to less than 48 percent in 1984. Some people were climbing out and up, but others were sinking down toward the bottom.*

---

* At this point, there does not seem to be a consensus as to whether more people moved downward from the middle range of income, or upward. Different studies offer different answers. Economist Stephen J. Rose reported in 1983 that three-fourths of those leaving the middle-income range in the late seventies and early eighties suffered decline. Likewise, economist Katherine L. Bradbury, studying middle-income shrinkage from 1979 to 1984, found most of those leaving the middle class heading downward. However, a recent Bureau of Labor Statistics study covering middle-class shrinkage between 1969 and 1986 found that, in that seventeen-year period, "most of the decline in the proportion of families in the middle has gone to the upper class, not the lower."

Many arbitrary factors determined whether a given family moved up or down: Had they purchased a house before the real estate boom of the seventies? Had they refrained from having too many children? Were they able to get help from their parents? By and large, though, the new cleavage in the middle range of income followed familiar class lines. The blue-collar working class was skidding downward, while the professional middle class was holding its own or gaining ground: In 1987 the median income for men with five or more years of higher education was $34,731, and that for women with the same education was $26,399—or $61,130 for a couple. A high-school-educated working-class couple earned a total of $36,888, more than a third less.

The phrase *the disappearing middle class,* which I, among others, used to describe the enormous changes of the eighties, in some ways missed the point. It was the blue-collar working class that was "disappearing," at least from the middle range of comfort. In the New Right's imagination the working class was a precious avatar of "traditional values," a human bulwark against permissiveness. But to the business interests that commanded the New Right's deepest loyalties, the American blue-collar working class—with its once-strong unions and real tradition of workplace defiance—had become a burden.

Beginning in the seventies, the corporate elite did everything possible to shake this burden loose. They "out-sourced" their manufacturing jobs to the lower-paid and more intimidated work force of the third world. They shifted their capital from manufacturing to the quick-profit realm of financial speculation—corporate mergers, leveraged buyouts—leaving American plants and technology to decay. And they led a brutal assault on the wages and living standards of those who still had jobs to cling to. For it is well to remember that what we call the working class, and picture as people striving to make a living, exists in the business literature only as *labor costs.*

The corporate abandonment of manufacturing—or what economists Barry Bluestone and Bennett Harrison have called " the deindustrialization of America"—violently disrupted the life of the blue-collar working class. Between 1979 and 1984,

11.5 million American workers lost their jobs because of plant shutdowns or relocations. Only 60 percent were able to find new jobs, and nearly half of the new jobs were at lower pay than the lost jobs. One study found that laid-off steelworkers in Chicago saw their incomes fall, on the average, by one-half, from $22,000 a year to $12,500 a year, just slightly above the official poverty level.

Throughout America's industrial "rust belt," whole towns and neighborhoods fell into decline as factories shut their doors. There were plenty of alternative jobs in the service sector—as bank tellers, hotel clerks, fast-food workers—but these tended to be low-paid, nonunion, and otherwise foreign to men whose skills lay in working with things, not people. A laid-off copper miner in Butte, Montana, a huge man wearing cowboy boots, overalls, and a scruffy beard, told me indignantly that he had been offered retraining—as a nurses' aide. Usually it was women or young, often black or Hispanic, men who took the proliferating service jobs; and one of the paradigmatic images of the eighties was that of the laid-off steelworker whose homemaker-wife has gone out to support the family on her wages at Burger King.

According to Harrison and Bluestone, though, the biggest reason for the declining fortunes of the working class was not job loss but wage loss. In every industry, employers launched a fierce initiative against labor costs: demanding wage concessions as the price of continued employment; instituting two-tier wage structures whereby the recently hired are paid on a vastly lower scale than those with seniority; replacing full-time workers with part-time employees who do not have to be offered benefits such as health insurance; and, of course, old-fashioned union-busting. In the eighties, law firms did a brisk business in union-busting services to employers, including public-relations drives to discredit the union and psychological methods of dividing and demoralizing the work force. More brutal, brass-knuckle approaches also flourished. Between 1986 and 1988, three New York–area union organizers of my acquaintance were beaten by company thugs, and two Queens factory workers who had participated in an organizing drive were pistol-whipped, in front of their coworkers, by the factory owners.

The Reagan administration set the tone of labor relations in the 1980s by busting PATCO, the air traffic controllers' union, in 1981. The administration then proceeded to all but eviscerate the Occupational Safety and Health Administration and the National Labor Relations Board, which guarantee minimal legal protections to labor. While the ideologues of the New Right extolled the virtues of the working class, the government of the New Right abetted the worst capitalist assault on America's working people since the 1920s.

Middle-class people, professionals and managers, also suffered in the economic dislocations of the eighties. They too lost jobs when plants closed or when government-financed social-welfare agencies shut down their services. They too experienced the stresses of a polarizing society, in which the poor were becoming ever more desperate and the rich were becoming more numerous and brash. While the poor were increasingly to be avoided for safety's sake, the rich presented a different kind of threat to people in the middle: bidding up the cost of real estate to astronomical values and uncomplainingly accepting college tuitions in the range of $20,000 a year. If staying in the economic and social middle ground had become impossible for much of the working class, it had also become a challenge for those whose education and occupation entitled them to believe they *were* the middle class.

But the professional middle class is more resilient than those below it. A laid-off manager is more likely to find a decent-paying job than a laid-off assembly-line worker. Public-sector professionals, like doctors, social workers, and administrators, can switch over to the private sector when the funds for public services are cut. And compared to blue- or pink-collar workers, white-collar professionals are in a better position to negotiate higher pay to meet the rising costs of housing and education. Above all, the young of the professional middle class are flexible. Starting in the seventies, they began to abandon the long, penurious path leading to professional status, and to go for the money.

They didn't have to read Irving Kristol to know which way the wind was blowing. By the early seventies it was clear that the sixties boom in higher education had produced "too many" educated young Americans. In 1968 only 6 percent of new Ph.D.'s had been unable to find jobs; by 1974 that figure had jumped to 26 percent. One study found that among college graduates less than five years out of school only 62 percent had professional or managerial jobs in 1980, compared with 76 percent in 1970. As the *Boston Globe* reported in 1985:

> Gary Rodgers, 44, is a PhD who has taught at Harvard and Yale and written books on Diderot. Unable to get tenure, he settled for a job teaching rudimentary English to Citibank employees. Marie Wellington, 32, is a Harvard PhD in romance languages who had hoped to teach in a tenured position. Today, she is a Berlitz Language Co. manager in Chicago. . . . At Cambridge's Ambassador Cabs alone, there are six PhD's [as cab drivers].

While Ph.D.'s in literature went hungry or learned stenography, jobs for professionals were proliferating in that vast area of endeavor known as "business services." The expansion of government regulation in the sixties and seventies meant more jobs for corporate lawyers. The out-sourcing of manufacturing to the third world meant more, rather than fewer, jobs for American managers, as the United States became one of the great administrative headquarters of the "global assembly line." The shift in business emphasis from manufacturing and distribution to financial speculation created openings for whole armies of brokers, financial analysts, and bankers. Corporate recruiters brought the good news to campuses, where they found, according to one college president, "a new mood on campus": "In the 1960s, there were a lot of social concerns. Now . . . the students want to come to get a skill and have the resources to support a middle-class existence."

The first element of what might be called the "yuppie strategy" was to choose a college major that corporate recruiters would look favorably upon. In one short decade, American campuses went from being hotbeds of dissent to hothouses for the production of corporate cadres. Between the early seventies and the early eighties, the number of students receiving bachelor's degrees in English fell by almost 50 percent, while the number graduating with degrees in business nearly doubled. The social sciences also took an almost 50 percent cut, and mathematics and the natural sciences—which presumably are essential for the future technological competitiveness of the United States—could together claim fewer than 4 percent of the college seniors graduating in 1983.

Students were also choosing to avoid the prolonged deprivations associated with graduate study. In the sciences, for example, the share of doctorates awarded to American students by U.S. institutions fell from 76.3 percent in 1978 to 63 percent in 1986. In that year, for the first time, U.S. universities awarded more Ph.D.s in engineering to foreigners than to Americans. The Americans had, so to speak, a better offer. They were skipping graduate school in favor of corporate jobs offering high starting salaries. As an engineering graduate student explained to the *New York Times*:

> One of the big things is being poor for a long period of time. If you can get a bachelor's and go out and make $30,000 or $40,000 a year, why get $10,000 a year as a graduate student?

There had been a time when ambitious students saw corporate employment as an option for the intellectually handicapped. Now it was the professions that seemed like a dull, low-paid backwater compared to the brisk world of business.

The choice of a pragmatic, business-oriented major was not always made happily. Many of the college students I talked to in the mid-eighties were suffering from what might be called "premature pragmatism." They were putting aside, at far too early an age, their idealism and intellectual curiosity in favor of economic security, which was increasingly defined as wealth. A young woman interviewed by *Newsweek* had switched from social work to sales because "I realized that I would have to make a commitment to being poor to be a social worker." Similarly, a Smith student, who happened to be one of few activists on that campus at the time, told me she had given up her ambition to be a psychiatric social worker because she "couldn't live on that." Instead, she said wryly, she would be going into banking.

To an adult who might have defined social work as an eminently respectable middle-class career, decisions such as these seemed either ill-informed or childishly greedy. But in the shifting economic landscape of the eighties, what had once been a secure middle-class occupation might no longer provide the necessities, such as home ownership, of middle-class life. All over the country, students who had started out wanting to be environmental chemists, special-education teachers, public administrators, or novelists redirected their aspirations to business or law. They did so, in most cases, out of a sullen sense of necessity, trading off personal autonomy, idealism, and creativity for what they hoped would be safety and possibly comfort.

With nineteen-year-olds redirecting their energies from sociology to spreadsheets, a negative, self-centered mood settled over the campuses. UCLA's annual survey of undergraduate attitudes found a steady rise in avarice and a decline in "altruism and social concern." In 1987, for example, a record 73 percent of students reported "being very well off financially" as their top goal, compared to 39 percent in 1970. Only 16 percent were interested in doing something to preserve the environment, compared to 45 percent in 1972. In other areas, students were now at least as conservative as the general public: Only 21 percent favored legalizing marijuana in 1987, compared to 53 percent in 1977. In 1984, only 49 percent believed abortion should be available to married women, down from 68 percent in the seventies. Peter Carlson, a former sixties radical, returned to his old dorm room at Boston University in 1986 to find

> posters of Miss Piggy, Sesame Street's Bert and Ernie, Kermit the Frog . . . a mural-sized photo of a bottle of Cordon Rouge champagne popping its cork, a poster of elegant sushi

arrangements . . . and a cartoon captioned, "Shop till you drop." Almost lost amid this collage of cuteness, I spied a postcard of Ron and Nancy atop a desk. I wondered: Is that a genuine *hommage* or some sort of ironic protest?

It was a genuine *hommage.*

A lucky, highly publicized minority of the new generation of pragmatists leaped directly from the academy to instant wealth. Beginning in the late seventies, graduates of Harvard Law School and a few other elite, business-oriented institutions could expect to be courted with starting salaries above $40,000 a year. In Wall Street's bustling money factories, the goal of amassing a million by age thirty was neither uncommon nor entirely unrealistic. Baby high-rollers were proliferating, and New York's $50-a-lunch restaurants were jammed, by the late eighties, with fresh-faced young people barely above drinking age. These financial prodigies were, in at least one sense, the true descendants of the sixties radicals: They had scorned the arduous apprenticeship traditionally required for middle-class membership—scorned, in fact, the middle class itself.

Most young graduates, however, could expect to attain eventual incomes only in the modest $30,000 to $40,000 range. For the majority who did not enter adult life with a legacy of Manhattan real estate, or who lacked the sangfroid for investment banking, the second rule of the yuppie strategy applied: Marry a financial equal. A 1976 ad for *Psychology Today* laid out the possibility of upward mobility through a new, more androgynous, approach to marriage. The ad, which ran full-page in the *New York Times,* shows a smiling young couple wearing identical pin-stripe jackets. The text begins in large bold letters, " . . . *our bank can't tell us apart,*" and continues:

Which one of us makes $20,000?

We both do. And we like to spend it on the same kinds of things, too . . .

Now that we're married, we have twice as much money and twice as much savings.

We'll be traveling farther. And a lot more often.

We'll also get to play more tennis. Spend more weekends
skiing. Or camping.

And, now, we can have our once-a-month wine and cheese
party, once-a-week.

I guess we know what we want from life.

And with twice as much money we not only can put more
into it, we can get more out of it.

## FEMINISM AND CLASS CONSOLIDATION

In the late fifties, when our story began, marrying
an economic equal was neither necessary nor possible. Most
middle-class—or for that matter, blue-collar working-class—
men could expect to earn enough to support a wife and children. Moreover, most women who intended to marry and have
children did not invest their prime childbearing years in postgraduate education and professional advancement. In 1960,
just over 30 percent of American women worked outside the
home, and most of those did so because their husband's income was plainly inadequate or because their children had
grown up, leaving the house quiet and eternally tidy.

A decade or so later, enough had changed so that the marriage of equals was both possible and, in most cases, necessary.
Most American men no longer earned enough to support a
family unassisted, and most American women—including
wives and mothers—had gone out and gotten jobs. Many married women went to work simply to help compensate for their
husbands' declining earning power. At the same time, later
marriages and the 50 percent divorce rate guaranteed that the
great majority of women would have to support themselves
and possibly their children on their own earnings at some
point in their lives. By the seventies, only the wives of the rich
could imagine that employment was simply an option.

But in the professional middle class, women were working
not only because they had to, not only because they feared not
finding a suitable husband—or any husband at all—but because they wanted to. They were in fact not just "working"—a

part-time job while the children are at school, a stab at catering or some other expansion of a domestic skill—they were pursuing demanding, fast-track professional careers with at least as much energy and intensity as their male colleagues. And this was the result not merely of crude economic pressure but of feminism.

The feminist movement has of course affected the lives of women in all social classes, and it has changed women's lives in ways that have little to do with economics or the dynamics of any particular class. By abolishing the cruder forms of sex discrimination, the movement opened doors for women of all classes, races, and conditions. Women won the right to abortion, the right to equal pay for equal work, the right to equal educational opportunity. And feminists are still working to expand these rights and win new ones—such as subsidized child care, pay equity, and paid maternity leave. Perhaps above all, the feminist movement has won enormous gains for all women in the intangible areas of dignity and self-esteem. But for our story, what is important about feminism is that it helped save the professional middle class from economic decline and at the same time healed it of that subtler form of decline described two decades earlier by Betty Friedan as "progressive demoralization."

Among women's economic gains, perhaps the greatest single achievement of the feminist movement has been the opening up of formerly male professions, such as law, medicine, and management. For most of this century the professions have been the occupational fortress of the middle class, but until recently they were reserved for men. The very traits that early-twentieth-century reformers sought to attach to the professions —objectivity, scientific rationality, and a dispassionate concern for society—were conceived of as quintessentially masculine traits. In 1871, for example, the president of the American Medical Association had this to say on the subject of women in medicine:

> Certain women seek to rival men in manly sports . . . and the
> strong-minded ape them in all things, even in dress. In doing

so, they may command a sort of admiration such as all monstrous productions inspire, especially when they tend towards a higher type than their own.

Throughout the twentieth century, women who aspired to a profession were directed toward those intellectually "softer" occupations—nursing, social work, teaching—that are deemed "semi-professions" by the sociologists and rewarded commensurately by employers. Those who persisted in trying to gain entrance to the top professions often faced harrassment from professors and fellow students, followed by marginalization within their profession. Ellen Richards, for example, one of America's first female chemists, was segregated from the male students when she attended MIT in the 1860s, and eventually consigned to what was felt to be a more suitable "science" for a woman—home economics.

Feminism, when it reemerged in the 1970s, launched a two-pronged attack on the traditionally male professions. On the one hand, women demanded to be let in on an equal footing. On the other hand, they questioned the core assumptions of the professions—their exclusivity, their claims to scientific objectivity and public service. In medicine, for example, feminists simultaneously demanded that women be admitted to the profession and attacked it for its sexism, racism, and greed—qualities that seemed to betray any claims to objectivity and public service. Feminists wanted women to be doctors, but they also wanted to abolish medicine as an elite profession and encourage the skills and participation of more humble health workers, lay practitioners (such as the self-trained midwives who began practicing illegally in the seventies), and the "consumers" of health care. With all the professions, feminists wanted, paradoxically at times, to open them up—and close them down.

This ambivalence reflected a larger quandary. Did feminists want to overthrow what they recognized to be a "male-dominated, capitalist society"? Or did they simply want women to take their place within it? Did they want revolution, or assimilation? The radical answer had drawn confidence from the student left and the black insurgency, but as those movements waned in the early seventies, assimilation began to look like the only practical strategy. I remember how betrayed many radical and left-leaning feminists felt at a 1975 conference held by the New York City chapter of the National Organization for Women, which featured, among the usual workshops on feminist political themes, sessions on how to "make it" in the corporate world. Surely the aim of the struggle was not to propel a few women to the top of a fundamentally unjust hierarchy, in which most women counted for little more than cheap labor. Yet as many quite radical feminists later came to realize, there is no way that an economically marginalized group can be expected to "wait for the revolution," letting moral purity compensate for certain poverty. Mainstream feminism came to stand unambiguously for assimilation, with the proviso or at least vague hope that women would somehow "humanize" the positions into which they were assimilated.

So, empowered by feminism—even if they did not always regard themselves as feminists—women poured into what had been almost exclusively male domains. In medicine, only 9 percent of first-year students were female in 1969; in 1987, 37 percent were female. In law, women had taken only 8 percent of the degrees awarded in 1973; ten years later women took 36 percent. In business, only 4.9 percent of the MBAs graduating in 1973 were women; ten years later 28.9 percent were women.

Not that women have achieved anything like full equality within these professions. A representation of 30 to 40 percent is far short of 50 percent. And within these areas of endeavor, women still find subtle barriers blocking the way to the top. Women doctors are likely to choose, or be channeled into, the relatively low-status field of pediatrics rather than, say, surgery. Women academics are well represented among the junior faculty, sparse among the tenured senior faculty. Businesswomen complain about the "glass ceiling" that stands between them and the boardroom, and feel blocked at all levels by the almost impenetrably masculine culture of the corporate world. But the fact remains that in little more than a decade women increased their representation among the most prestigious and lucrative professions by 300 to 400 percent. As a change in the fortunes of women, that has to be counted somewhere up near the achievement of suffrage.

It was an achievement, however, that was sharply limited by class. The chief beneficiaries of the opening of the professions were women who already had the advantages of good schools, an encouraging home life, and the money and leisure for higher education. A 1976 study showed, for example, that the women clambering into medical school were likely to come from the same class background as the men who were already there. Nor were there gains of comparable magnitude within the traditionally male blue-collar skilled occupations, in part because so many of these occupations were themselves in decline. While the percentage of women in professional training was rising from less than 10 percent up to 40 percent, the proportion of women construction workers and skilled craftspersons did not reach 10 percent.

So while some women moved into positions of visibility and even power, the average working woman, who is not a professional and not likely to be college-educated, is still pretty much where she always was: waiting on tables, emptying wastebaskets, or pounding a keyboard for $5 or $6 an hour. If the recent opening up of the professions has been feminism's greatest victory, it is a victory whose sweetness the majority of American women will never taste.

But it is the change within the professional middle class that concerns us here. The chasm that existed within that class—separating its achievers from its menial laborers, its husbands from its wives—was potentially bridged. A young woman no longer had to secure her membership in the middle class through the tenuous pact of marriage. She didn't have to marry a doctor; she could be one. It remained for the young men of this class to overcome their resentment of the new female competition and understand that they in turn could be married to doctors or lawyers instead of mere wives.

By the seventies this change was well under way. The old notion that a working wife was a sure sign of male inadequacy was hard to find in any class. As I argued in an earlier book, *The Hearts of Men,* the traditional masculine ideal—husband, father, and sole breadwinner—had been going out of style for decades. The reasons for this had less to do with feminism, which did not become a mass movement until the early seventies, than with a consumer culture that was increasingly reaching out to men as consumers in their own right. In the words of the early *Playboy* magazine, which should be seen as a promoter of the new masculine ideology as well as of soft pornography, wives were "parasites," trapping men into lives of perpetual toil to support *their* consumerism. Men earned the money, why shouldn't they spend it on themselves?

Feminism, when it came along, offered a socially conscious rationale for this somewhat churlish attitude. It allowed men, especially young, middle-class men, to insist that they were not fleeing from their traditional responsibilities but joining in the general effort to overcome obsolete and restrictive sex roles. As psychologist and men's liberation advocate Herb Goldberg argued in the 1970s, if women were tired of being sex objects for men, men were equally weary of being "success objects" for women. Besides, quite apart from the men's liberationists, the old pressures on men to "prove their masculinity" by marrying young and singlehandedly supporting a family were relaxing. By the eighties, no one thought it odd if a man of thirty or so remained single, apportioning his earnings among the products advertised in such places as *Gentleman's Quarterly, Metropolitan Home,* and *Connoisseur.*

The women's magazines complained that men—meaning eligible men with attractive incomes—were suffering from "fear of commitment." Many men, however, were displaying a justifiable fear of making the wrong commitment. The young men—stereotypical yuppies, although the word had not yet come into widespread use—who were interviewed for a 1984 article I wrote on the "new man" did not rule out marriage, but they were concerned with finding a mate who could "pull her own weight," who "would not be a burden"—as if they were selecting a companion for an upstream rafting trip. And while this is hardly scientific evidence, I have often polled college lecture audiences, first asking the women how many of them would like to be full-time homemakers. One or two brave hands go up for this unstylish option. But when the young men are asked how many of them would be willing to support a full-time homemaker wife, the response is a few snickers, and no hands.

Women had once married men who looked as though they would be reliable breadwinners, and men had once married women who simply looked good. But now both sexes were determined to find proven wage-earners. As Harvard economics professor David Bloom told *Time* in 1986: "A pairing-off based on economics is occurring. Higher-income men and higher-income women are tending to find each other." Mimi Lieber, a New York–based marketing consultant, told me in a 1986 interview:

> We're seeing a changing pattern of marriage. It used to be that looks determined how well a woman married. But today the little dime-store girl is not being picked up by the college student. The doctor isn't marrying a nurse, he's marrying another doctor.

The frequency with which college men once married pretty dime-store clerks should probably not be exaggerated. College itself, as a social experience, helped ensure that young middle- or upper-class men would end up with young women of similar backgrounds. But marriage had provided at least a limited avenue of upward mobility for young women of humble origins, and that avenue was now all but closed. In the fifties, for example, an office romance meant the occasional dalliance between a boss and his secretary. Thirty years later, according to the *Wall Street Journal,* office romance was "flourishing" because "women routinely work beside men as professional and managerial peers."

Besides, a certain social opprobrium now attaches to the man who socializes with women far below him in the occupational hierarchy. Just as a professional woman who fell in love with a blue-collar male would be a subject of wonder and scorn, the executive who dallies with a pink-collar worker would be revealed today as insecure and lacking in judgment.

In the 1988 movie *Working Girl,* an ambitious secretary pretends to be an upper-level executive in order to carry out a major deal. In the process she becomes romantically involved with an attractive male executive from another firm. When he finds out about her deception, she challenges him: Would you have fallen in love with me if I were just a secretary? He is abashed, because the answer, of course, is no.

It is as if, in climbing into the middle class on the strength of their own achievements, the new executive and professional women had pulled up the ladder behind them. Of course, they had not done so themselves. *Men* were choosing to marry for money, as well as for love or for looks. But upwardly mobile young professional women had much to gain from the tightened "pattern of marriage" within the class. Seen as economic partners as well as helpmates, women are more likely to be equals within their marriages. They are also less likely than in the past to be displaced by any of the far more numerous women—secretaries, flight attendants, cocktail waitresses— who lack professional credentials and impressive resumés.

Viewed from outside and "below," then, the professional middle class has simply become a more impregnable fortress. Once only men had had to scale its walls, devoting their youth and young adulthood to preparation and apprenticeship. Women could drift in on the strength of their charm or of so slight a credential as a bachelor's degree in French literature or art history. Today, however, almost no one gets in—male or female—without submitting to the same discipline and passing the same tests that were originally designed to exclude intruders from below.

Almost as soon as the class consolidated itself through its new androgyny, an unaccountable weariness seemed to overcome middle-class feminism. In 1963 Betty Friedan had blamed the "feminine mystique" for the "progressive demoralization" of the professional middle class—men, women, and children. The full-time housewife, she argued, had become a menace. Bored, tranquilized, suffering from "housewife's syndrome," she was not even up to the one job assigned to her— raising children to be ambitious, disciplined members of the middle class. Excluded from the "battle with the world," she had no way of transmitting the skills required for that battle. The "wasted energy" of housewives, Friedan predicted, would continue "to be destructive to their husbands, their children, and to themselves until it is used in their own battle with the world."

Two decades later, no one could complain that women were insufficiently engaged in the "battle," dazed noncombatants in the world of men. A new problem had arisen in the middle class: whether anyone would have children at all. To the individual professional woman, the problem was experienced as the inexorable ticking of the "biological clock": How would she find a husband before her fertile years ended, and find time from her career for childbearing? To conservative intellectuals, it was the problem of the "birth dearth." There was no shortage of population globally, nor even a shortfall among Americans in general. But the birthrate among the educated, affluent, white population had fallen drastically. If there had been a question in the early sixties of whether the middle class could reproduce itself as a class, there was now a question of whether its members would reproduce at all.

At the same time, *raising* the children began to loom as a bigger challenge than ever. In the early seventies, ambitious middle-class mothers counted themselves lucky to find a day-care center or a reliable baby-sitter to mind the children while they rushed off to work. But a decade later, with mounting competition for admission to the "good" private colleges—and even to the first-rate urban nursery schools—women were thinking twice about paid child care.

The concern was expressed in various ways: "I don't want to miss the early years"; or "I don't want to leave my child with just *anyone*." But the real issue was the old middle-class dilemma of whether "anyone"—such as a Jamaican housekeeper or a Hispanic day-care worker—was equipped to instill such middle-class virtues as concentration and intellectual discipline. For many young middle-class couples the choice was stark: Have the mother work and risk retarding the child's intellectual development, or have the mother stay home, build up the child's IQ, and risk being unable to pay for a pricy nursery school or, later, private college. Unfortunately, feminism had not advanced to the point where these were a *father's* agonizing choices.

Attuned to the new doubts among middle-class women, Betty Friedan announced in 1981 a "second stage" for American feminism. In the first stage, she wrote, "Our aim was full participation, power and voice in the mainstream, inside the party, the political process, the professions, the business world"—in short, assimilation. But where once women had been stymied by the feminine mystique, she wrote, they were now afflicted by a "feminist mystique" which required them to be brittle, masculinized strivers. Just as she had once quoted dozens of frustrated housewives, Friedan now cited battle-weary career women, anguished over their desire to have children before their childbearing years ran out. Thus the second stage would suspend hostilities between men and women. It would "involve coming to new terms with the family" and must be launched "so we can live a new 'yes' to life and love, and can *choose* to have children."

Many feminists found Friedan's proposed truce premature. She did not claim that the struggle for equality was over, but she now saw many familiar forms of sexism as "first stage problems"—as if they required little more than a mop-up operation. For many middle-class women there was some truth to this. Problems of sheer economic injustice, of stinging discrimination, were not looming as large as the problem of when and how to start a family. But a far larger number of women remained, as always, in stereotypically female jobs, paid far less than men in jobs requiring similar levels of skill and responsibility. For these women, Friedan's announcement that feminism had moved on to a less militant second stage was, at the very least, insensitive.

Friedan was only one sign of the new quietism of middle-class feminism. In academia, women's studies—long the most reliable reproductive organ of middle-class feminism—began in some quarters to take on a detached and esoteric air. Reviewing an important new anthology of highbrow feminist scholarship in 1987, Catherine Stimpson—herself a leading pioneer of women's studies—found the contributions strangely "eccentric in focus, uneasy in spirit." On the campuses, the mood among young career-oriented women was reportedly "post-feminist" and dominated by the conviction that, whatever indignities women had suffered in the remote past (say, 1970), the way was now open for any young woman of spirit to rise straight to the top of whatever lucrative and rewarding field she might choose.

Middle-class feminism is not, of course, all there is to American feminism. A 1986 Gallup poll found that a startling 56 percent of American women considered themselves to be "feminists," and the degree of feminist identification was, if anything, slightly higher as one descended the socioeconomic scale. Black women, for example, who are economically disadvantaged relative to white women, professed to be feminists at the rate of 65 percent. But middle-class white women provide the public face of feminism; they direct and staff its major institutions. And by the late eighties, middle-class feminism seemed, even to many of its own stalwarts, to be tired: tired of defeat at the hands of the New Right over issues like the Equal Rights Amendment, but also exhausted from its own successes.

Even in the face of the new problems confronting working women, however, few are likely to trade in the "feminist mystique" for the old feminine one. For above all, the assimilation of women has almost doubled the economic resources of the middle class, helping save it from the decline experienced by the working class and lifting it, in fact, well out of the middle range of income. The $60,000-plus a year that a professional couple can expect to earn by pooling their incomes puts them financially well ahead of over 80 percent of American families. By assimilating women, what we have called the middle class became, in strictly economic terms, the upper middle class.

## THE CONSUMER BINGE

The hallmark of the yuppie—male or female, married or single—was consumption. The yuppie of stereotype drove a $40,000 foreign car, vacationed vigorously in all seasons, and aspired to a condominium with an intimidating address. Even those who could not afford the big-ticket items—condos and Porsches—infused their daily lives with extravagant details: salad dressings made of raspberry vinegar and walnut oil, imported mineral water, $100 sneakers, $50 meals at the restaurant of the moment. Yuppie spending patterns represented a new, undreamed-of level of capitulation to the consumer culture: a compulsive acquisitiveness bordering on addiction, a mental state resembling the supposed "present-orientation" and "radical improvidence" of the despised underclass.

Yuppie consumerism was not simply a distortion built into the stereotype. America was on a consumer binge, or as some economists put it, in a new stage of "hyperconsumption." Someone was spending, and it was not the laid-off industrial worker or unemployed woman on a dwindling welfare allowance. In fact, even during the recession of 1982–83, even after the stock-market crash of 1987, sales of luxury goods boomed. The truly rich—roughly the 5 percent of Americans who hold over 50 percent of the nation's wealth—accounted for a disproportionate share of the boom, particularly in the markets for yachts, gems, jets, real estate, and such collectibles as classic cars. But at the low end of luxury—which includes vacation trips, restaurant meals, and sports cars—America's newly rich, double-income business professionals were holding up their share of the binge.

In defense of yuppie spending habits—and it is a tribute to the enduring anxiety of the middle class that they still needed *any* defense at the height of Reagan-era profligacy—*New Republic* editor Michael Kinsley described the yuppies as engaged in a kind of compensatory spending. The $40,000 or so that a young business person might earn did not, after all, measure up so well when compared to the purchasing power enjoyed by his or her parents a few decades ago. It would hardly be enough to cover the house, station wagon, stay-at-home spouse, and three children that the white-collar man of the fifties expected as a matter of right. So, in Kinsley's argument, the raspberry vinegar, *crème fraîche*, and so forth had to be seen as "affordable luxuries":

They serve as consolation for the lack of unaffordable luxuries like a large house. You may not have a dining room, but you have a dining room table, and everything on it can have a complicated explanation involving many foreign words.

But the compensatory-spending argument misses the profound change in middle-class attitudes toward consumption. In a previous generation, a young couple who lacked the money for a house and other family-oriented purchases would simply have skipped the raspberry vinegar (or its fifties equivalent) and saved their pennies. Spending was the reward for saving; and "leisure products," which include all the yuppie favorites, took second place to the moral solidity represented by a house and heavy appliances. The profligacy of the yuppies, which set a standard for all the middle class as a whole, was the surrender to hedonism that middle-class intellectuals had been warning against for over thirty years.

The consumer binge of the eighties is all the more startling when contrasted to the trend that immediately preceded it— the fashionable austerity of the seventies, symbolized by Jimmy Carter's low-budget 1976 inauguration and the popularity of E. F. Schumacher's *Small Is Beautiful*. "Voluntary simplicity," as this brief interlude of abstemiousness has since been termed, gave concrete expression to the middle-class fears of affluence that had been voiced since the fifties. The counterculture and student movement of the sixties were its immediate inspiration; the oil shortage of the early seventies and the new environmentalism imbued it with a high sense of moral purpose. A 1977 Harris poll found Americans increasingly concerned with "learning to get our pleasure out of nonmaterial experiences," rather than "satisfying our needs for more goods and services." According to a study by the Stanford Research Institute, this attitude was particularly strong among young, educated, middle-class people, who were no longer likely to be political activists but at least tended "to prefer products that are functional, healthy, nonpolluting, durable, repairable, recyclable or made from renewable raw materials, energy-cheap, authentic, aesthetically pleasing, and made through simple technology." These preferences easily accommodated the new marketing emphasis on "leisure products," such as sports equipment, cameras, and stereos. The requirements of being functional and healthy did not, however, extend to such eighties favorites as *crème fraîche* and Beluga caviar.

Voluntary simplicity echoed the "simplicity movement" of the emerging middle class in the Progressive Era. Both movements sought a way to express middle-class political aspirations in the form of personal behavior, or, in seventies terminology, "lifestyle." In the early twentieth century, middle-class simplicity had meant fewer and plainer items of furniture, looser clothes, and lighter meals. In the 1970s, the trend was to minimalist (or high-tech) decor, blue cotton work shirts, "health foods," and a horror of strong drink and cigarette smoke. Both movements embodied a principled rejection of the endlessly wasteful, endlessly seductive, capitalist consumer culture. And both movements ended by trivializing that rejection as a new set of consumer options: in the 1970s, natural fiber over polyester, whole-grain bread over white, plain oak furniture over high-gloss department-store maple.

No one in the 1970s expected voluntary simplicity to fade with the mere turn of a decade. It was a "quiet revolution," according to the Harris poll summary, a "major transformation of Western values," according to the Stanford Research Institute. Moreover, voluntary simplicity seemed to have become the very hallmark of middle-class existence—not only an ethic but a set of behavioral cues that distinguished the middle class from those both above and below it. The poor and the working class smoked and ate cheeseburgers; the middle class carved out nonsmoking environments for itself and eschewed red meat, American cheese, and grease in all forms.

So entrenched were the new middle-class tastes that it began to appear as if the classes could no longer coexist in the same physical space. I recall the dilemma faced by a group of young doctors in Chicago who wanted to invite other hospital workers—aides, orderlies, technicians, nurses—to a party. The doctors, friends of mine and dedicated reformers of the medical system, hoped to celebrate in the most generous and egalitarian fashion possible. But, they agonized, would their working-class co-workers submit to the obvious (middle-class) rules: no smoking, no hard liquor, and no junk food? The doctors finally realized that they would have to make a sacrifice, at least for one evening, of their values and possibly their health.

But it was more common for middle-class practitioners of the new simplicity to simply retreat from the challenge of mixed environments. Health was usually the immediate rationale, but health had become a nebulous metaphor for other distinctions, and disguised a growing disdain for the white working class. In the early sixties, middle-class commentators had, perversely enough, seen the poor as the victims of a consumerist mentality, the slaves of sensation and impulse. As the seventies wore on, the blue-collar working class began to take the place of the poor in the moral hierarchy of the middle class. The poor themselves once again dropped from view, leaving the working class—with its tasteless home furnishings, high-fat diet, and unwholesome addictions—to serve as an object lesson in the perils of succumbing to the consumer culture.

So how was the middle class able, within a few short years, to throw itself into the consumerist binge without losing its sense of identity—its fragile autonomy from the leveling force of the consumer culture? The short answer is that it was *not* able to. The binge was experienced as a capitulation every bit as profound as the switch from relatively autonomous careers in the professions to get-rich-quick trajectories in the business world. But the short-term answer was that the middle class was able to construct a new identity around conspicuous consumption, redefining it not as surrender but as a pious form of work.

## THE EMBRACE OF AFFLUENCE

One of the unappealing features of 1950s-style mass-marketed affluence, from a middle-class point of view, was that it allowed for only "minute distinctions" between the middle class and those immediately below, the working class. One might have more and better, but "better" was not distinctively different: thicker carpets, a car with more options, museum prints rather than dime-store reproductions on the walls. In the eighties this problem was decisively resolved. The mass market disappeared and was replaced by two markets, which we know as "upscale" and "downscale." The change reflected the growing middle-class zeal to distinguish itself from the less fortunate, and at the same time it made such distinctions almost mandatory for anyone hoping to inhabit the social and occupational world of the successful and "upscale."

Everywhere in the retail industry there were signs of the new market polarization. Department stores, for example, faced the choice of specializing in one end of the class spectrum or the other—or else going out of business. Undifferentiated chains, like Korvette's and Gimbel's, which had aimed at both blue- and white-collar middle-income consumers, were forced to close, while Sears and J. C. Penney anxiously tried to "reposition" themselves to survive in the ever more deeply segmented market. The stores and chains that prospered were the ones that learned to specialize in one extreme of wealth or the other: Bloomingdale's and Neiman-Marcus for the upscale; K-Mart and Woolco for those constrained by poverty or thrift.

Inside the stores there was hardly any product that could not be found in up- and downscale versions, as if even lifeless commodities were being asked to take sides in an undeclared class war. Beer divided between the familiar American brands and dozens of expensive imports—Beck's, Corona, Heineken, Kirin. Food, of course, divided and subdivided frenetically, but the broad contours of change were reflected in Pillsbury's restaurant strategy: Burger King for the proletariat; Bennigan's well-appointed, trendily stocked restaurants for the yuppies. The auto industry had always had its Cadillacs and Chevys, but now there was a fresh segmentation among the imports, with Mercedes and Audis for the affluent, Toyotas for the masses. Even the most phlegmatic commodities, home appliances, began to sort themselves out as manufacturers added high-tech features to create an upscale line. According to a market analyst for the Bear Stearns brokerage firm:

There is a consumer out there who doesn't want chain-store labels on things they buy. Kenmore [the Sears brand of appliances] is a good name but not a yuppie name. When they have friends over, these people do not want those friends to see names like Sears or Kenmore. They want people to see names like Sony or Kitchen Aid.

The split in the mass market followed the deepening fault lines within American society and was a response to those underlying shifts. Downwardly mobile people have little choice but to go for the discount goods, while the upwardly mobile are eager to transform their money into the visible marks of status. No doubt, too, the pressure to consolidate one's financial position through marriage heightened the importance of small and subtle class cues. A "nice guy" or a "good-looking gal" would no longer do, and since bank accounts and resumés are not visible attributes, a myriad of other cues were required to sort the good prospects from the losers. Upscale spending patterns created the cultural space in which the financially well matched could find each other—far from the burger-eaters and Bud-drinkers and those unfortunate enough to wear unnatural fibers. In fact, upscale department stores found a new use as cruising grounds for affluent singles. At the height of the consumer binge, a popular dating activity was a joint mission to a high-priced store like Bloomingdale's.

Whatever the reasons, the yuppie spending pattern, (whether indulged in by demographically official yuppies or not) represented a frantic positioning—an almost desperate commitment to the latest upscale fad. In the fashionable intellectual discourse of the time, possessions were important only as "signifiers," elements of an ever-shifting language that spoke of wealth and promise. The trick was to understand the language as it changed from month to month, leaving behind the ignorant and the less than affluent. As soon as an affordable fad—the example is often given of pita-bread sandwiches—sedimented down to the general public, it would be rendered useless as a mark of status and abandoned by the cognoscenti.

Hence that favorite magazine and newspaper filler in the mid-eighties, the list of what's in and what's out, calculated to both mock and alarm the status-conscious reader. For example, in 1985 the *Miami Herald* published a largely predictable list of what's "hot" and "not hot": Conservatives, dinner parties, and gilt were hot; liberals, cookouts, and minimalism were not. The joke was at the end of the long lists, where, under *hot,* one found *what's not hot,* and under *not hot,* of course, *what's hot.*

But there was a certain consistency to the dominant upscale tastes. Conservatism had triumphed over liberalism, gilt over minimalism, expensive over modestly priced. The obvious impetus was the sudden visibility of the truly rich, who reentered public consciousness with the triumphal display of the 1981 Reagan inauguration. The rich, of course, are always with us. But throughout most of the postwar period they had not been too eager to announce their presence, as a class, to the potentially resentful public. All this changed with the ascent to power of the New Right, whose populist language conflicted openly with its aristocratic allegiances. According to historian Deborah Silverman, the Reagan era introduced a "new cultural style" consistent with right-wing politics:

> A style aggressively dedicated to the cult of visible wealth and distinction, and to the illusion that they were well earned; a style that adopted the artifacts of Chinese emperors, French aristocrats, and English noblemen as signs of exclusivity and renunciation; a style of unabashed opulence, whose mixture of hedonism, spitefulness, and social repudiation was captured in the slogan "Living well is the best revenge."

Not to mention the even nastier and more popular slogan "He who dies with the most toys wins."

What was pathetic and ultimately embarrassing about the stereotypical yuppie was that he or she was such a poor copy of the truly rich. People who have yachts and private jets do not have to agonize over "what's hot" and "what's not." People who employ their own chefs do not have to engage in yuppie-style "competitive eating" to establish their place in the world. In moving from minimalism to gilt, from voluntary simplicity to a parodic profligacy, the upwardly mobile middle class began to lose its own fragile sense of dignity. The rich can surrender to hedonism because they have no reason to remain tense and alert. But the middle class cannot afford to let down its guard; it maintains its position only through continual exertion—through allegiance to the "traditional values" of hard work and self-denial. In the eighties, the middle class came dangerously close to adopting the presumed wantonness of the poor—that is, the actual wantonness of the very rich.

## THE WAR AGAINST SOFTNESS

The big difference is that young business and professional people *work*. The truly rich, like the courtiers who surrounded Nancy Reagan, do not work but drift easily from fashion show to award dinner, from winter townhouse to summer home, from one vaguely "cultural" entertainment to another. But those who wish to succeed in such richly remunerative fields as corporate law and finance banking must work, at least in their early years, seventy or so hours a week. Most of those who merely wish to participate in the consumer binge must also work beyond the required eight hours a day. And those who only want to *look* as if they hold important positions in lucrative fields must at least *look* as if they are overworked. Work was essential to the yuppie style, not only as the means to wealth and hence indulgence but as the moral antidote to indulgence.

If one side of the yuppie style was conspicuous, status-oriented consumption, the other side was conspicuous and no less status-conscious work—or if not work, the appearance of work, even in leisure. Social commentator Benita Eisler has described what she calls the "New Upper Classes" in America as the "deserving rich" because they work—steadily and compulsively—and have in the process been "morally regenerated." Certainly the more affluent participants in the yuppie style fit this category. Work gave them back the dignity they lost, if only subconsciously and spiritually, in the conformity of yuppie consumption. In fact, any extravagance could be justified as a form of psychological renewal required by the excessively hardworking. *Newsweek* described a twenty-eight-year-old Denver lawyer who had once studied to be a regional planner (and whose life would surely have been simpler if he had pursued his original goal):

> He would like to marry someday, but he is in the Yuppie bind of having to work hard to afford the kind of luxuries that make hard work possible: a Saab, vacations in the Orient, carte blanche at all the top health clubs in town. He has a feeling that if he had to spend his leisure hours cleaning out the basement instead, his 12-hour days at the office would seem a lot less bearable.

In daily life, the hallmark of the yuppie style was a frenetic busyness. Traditional aristocracies are conspicuously idle; the upwardly mobile middle class was conspicuously busy. Those who wished to appear successful ordered their lives by their appointment books, budgeting even social interactions down to the minute. One of the young, urban, professional men interviewed in 1984 by my research assistant, Harriet Bernstein, boasted of having reduced the time it took for him to arrange his evening date to five minutes a day, and for most practitioners of the yuppie style, even courtship had to double with some equally worthy pastime—shopping, jogging, or eating dinner. The long three-martini business lunch of a previous generation gave way to briefer encounters—the business breakfast or the phone call by appointment.

Naturally, anyone who in the course of a day shops, jogs, holds down a demanding job, and engages in eating as a form of display will feel pressed for time. Anyone who does all these things while trying to sustain a courtship—or worse, raise a child—will be frantic. But busyness was not only an objective condition, it became an essential insignia of status—and a not entirely ineffective one. To have time and attention for others is to concede their importance. The upwardly mobile professional, rushing from one appointment or deadline to another, concedes nothing to those who are less harried and hence, obviously, less important.

If work was central to the yuppie search for expiation, so too was the simulation of work—exercise. In the eighties, *exercise* itself became a hopelessly generic term, covering proliferating possibilities of exertion: "toning," aerobics, Nautilus workouts, weight training, running, jogging, power walking. The "fitness craze," as trend-watchers termed it, began in the late seventies and soon generated new products and booming new industries: health spas and gyms, exercise classes and videotapes, home exercise equipment, fancy leotards and shoes specialized for running, aerobic dancing, and even walking. Although the craze drew recruits from all classes, it was centered in the upwardly mobile middle class, which quickly turned fitness—or the effort to achieve it—into another insignia of social rank.

Almost by definition, the true work or paid employment of this class does not involve physical exertion. In fact, exemption from manual labor is the most ancient privilege of the "mental worker," from village scribe to Madison Avenue copywriter. He or she does not bend, lift, scrub, shovel, haul, or engage in other potentially damaging exertions for a living. Freed from external command, the body becomes a seemingly autonomous realm, the one zone in which the mental worker feels entirely free to exert his or her own will. Within the scope of the body, particularly the musculature and digestive system, one is safe from the encroachments of meaningless work and joyless acquisition. Inner standards can be met, high goals achieved, all within this one small realm where discipline and purity still have their clear rewards.

In earlier decades, the middle class had also sought redemption through the body. Dieting became a middle-class preoccupation in the fifties, when it was linked to the rejection of suffocating, mass-marketed affluence. In the seventies, dieting was eclipsed by the new health consciousness, which operated as a kind of internal environmentalism: toxins like cigarette smoke and liquor were to be avoided. "Good" foods—natural, unprocessed, usually vegetarian and appallingly bland—could be indulged in quantity. In many ways, both medical and cultural, "high fiber" became the designated antagonist of saturated fat: Fat was greasy and supine; fiber dry and stiff. It could be counted on to scrub the body's interior clean of lipogenous and toxic residues from the outer world. If you could not defend yourself against addictive consumerism or wanton industrialism, you could at least keep your body slim, detached, and clean.

In contrast to dieting and health-foodism, fitness was exuberantly pro-capitalist. It accepted pollution, metaphorical and real (except in the case of cigarette smoke, which remained a major middle-class concern, even a cause). It accepted consumerism. In fact, the pursuit of fitness could hardly be disentangled from the business of consumption. There had of course been diet foods and health foods, but it was not really necessary to spend more in order to get less (fat, calories, additives). Diets and healthy eating could be pursued cheaply enough as alternatives to conventional consumption. But fitness was a commodity itself, from the health-club membership (several hundred dollars a year for a well-equipped but unpretentious club) to the shoes (easily $100 for an impressive pair) and the various optional paraphernalia (hand weights, stationary bicycle for home use, etc.). To be fit in the fullest sense—which involved cardiovascular capacity, muscle tone, flexibility, and strength—one had to spend money, one had to indulge.

But this was a form of consumption in which indulgence was perfectly matched, second by second, with obvious, visible effort. It was consumption made strenuous and morally renewing, "working out" as a balletic imitation of true work, in which the hedonism of consumption could be confronted head-on and vanquished with the slow burn of pyruvic acid in the muscles. In the words of Jane Fonda, "No pain, no gain," and, what was equally important, the certainty that no gain would be made except through the redemption of pain.

In a practical way, too, the fitness craze balanced the extravagant oral indulgence of upscale, middle-class life. The dieters of the past had not eaten, or had eaten only tasteless, punitive substances such as cottage cheese and dry toast. Health foodists had transformed eating into a ritual of purification, in which brown rice and bean sprouts symbolized autonomy from an overbearing urban-industrial society. The yuppie style, in contrast, was one of aggressive, infantile orality. Nouvelle cuisine, with its tiny portions of blanched vegetables and fish, provided continuity with earlier concerns about body weight and purity. But after nouvelle cuisine faded, food lost its moorings in nutrition and its ancient links to health. Food became edible status. And since symbols of status are all-too-quickly publicized through television, food became fad, nimbly outrunning the tastes of the masses: from austere nouvelle cuisine to thick, creamy sauces, from Continental-style foods to the "new American cuisine," from fancy to Tex-Mex, from the exotic to meatloaf.

Dieters were not welcome at this feast. The only way to keep ahead—to eat significantly, impressively, competitively —was to keep in shape. If fitness was consumption, it was also penance, a continual balancing of calories ingested with calories expended, a socially acceptable equivalent of bulimia. But fitness not only looked backward at the last meal, it looked ahead to the next. Fitness literature emphasized that regular, strenuous exercise made for a more manageable appetite and efficient metabolism. In a very real sense, eating was what one got in shape *for.* The fit could eat more without the usual depressing, frumpy, and of course downscale results. And, in a society that associates obesity with gluttony, the fit are also *permitted* to eat more without exciting disgust.

But the fitness craze was not solely penance. The mental/ manual division of labor is hurtful to those who must sit as well as to those who must lift and strain for a living. For young office workers, exercise was not only simulated work but simulated play. Ordinarily, only children are permitted to move their bodies freely and vigorously in public. The regimented exercise class, the clothes that distinguish a runner from a fugitive, the cruel resistance of a Nautilus machine—all these things allow adults to regain the lost muscular license of childhood. For a generation that had, all too early, renounced the dreams of youth for the sober detail of the balance sheet, fitness was fun—a covert extension of childhood.

Fitness, or the effort to achieve it, was also instrumental to grown-up purposes. It quickly became, like tastes in food, another class cue. Being fit in the fullest sense was a proof of having money and, beyond that, almost certain proof that one had not earned that money through manual labor or muscular exertion. As a twenty-four-year-old banker told *Newsweek*, "Fitness is another way of signaling to people that you are serious." The fit or soon-to-be-fit matched money with work (or its public representation, the workout), indulgence with discipline, intake with output. They could be found in health clubs and spas, at marathons or on jogging trails. In the eighties, these venues replaced the singles bar as the reliable place to meet suitable members of the other sex. In an exercise class or in the lineup to use a Nautilus machine, good looks were restored to their place in the rituals of mating—but only as the hard new appearance of fitness, and then only as clue to deeper things, such as income and occupational rank.

Finally there was the observable goal of fitness. Dieters sought thinness; weight lifters, who were often of dubious background and occupation, sought the menace of bulk. But those who pursued fitness aimed at a new kind of outcome, known as "definition": The outline of the body had to become more clearly enunciated in hard, though not exaggerated, curves of muscle. For women as well as men, the standard of beauty moved away from mere slimness. Legs that were too thin could be as unsightly as legs that were too fat; beauty lay in the clear line of muscle, precisely nurtured by the right balance of toning, weight training, and aerobics. To achieve definition was to present a hard outline to the world, a projection of self that was not sensitive and receptive—as therapies in the seventies had aimed at—but tough and contained. Definition offered proof that one could hold one's own against the encroaching hedonism—that one could eat, gorge, binge without the horror of dissolving into softness.

## YUPPIE GUILT

The term *yuppie* disappeared from the media almost as swiftly as it had appeared. In 1986 the editor of a major monthly magazine told me she found the term "tiresome" and never wanted to hear it again. Apparently many other editors felt the same way, and editors are in a position to decide which words the rest of us will hear, or at least see. In England, the editor of the *Daily Telegraph* ordered a "complete ban" on the word itself. The rise and fall of the word could be followed in the *Readers' Guide to Periodical Literature,* which listed nineteen entries under *yuppies* in 1984. For 1985 there were twenty-six entries. By 1987 the number of entries had sunk back to nineteen. Today the term is as out of style as nouvelle cuisine and sushi, the yuppie food fads which faded in the mid-eighties, to be replaced by heartier fare. Other groups have seen their stereotypes stick for decades; not so the middle class, which was able to take the first clear caricature to come its way and render that caricature useless as cliché.

For the professional middle class, which had both coined the term and then retracted it, the lifespan of the yuppie label represented a moment of unaccustomed self-exposure. A 1985 Roper poll found that 60 percent of adult Americans knew what yuppies were (compared, for example, to the only 34 percent who could name the Secretary of State). No other term describing the educated middle class, in whole or part, had ever earned such widespread usage. The *New Class,* for all that it exercised the New Right, remained a recondite notion, and even its more colloquial versions, like *liberal elite,* never managed to conjure up a clear and definite imagery.

But the yuppie—perhaps especially the female yuppie whose odd uniform of skirted suit and sneakers symbolized the compromise between capitalism and feminism—was as familiar a caricature as the Bud-drinking worker in a T-shirt. Americans knew, roughly, how yuppies looked. And they did not like what they saw. In the Roper poll, the great majority found yuppies "overly concerned with themselves." In a 1987 *Newsweek* poll, yuppies placed third among "things the respondents said were losing favor." Stockbrokers placed second, beaten only narrowly by "drugs."

Not that the media coverage had been all bad. (At least not until the stock-market crash of November 1987, for which yuppies were unfairly blamed.) *Newsweek*'s cover story had found yuppies an energetic, sober lot, and only occasionally lapsed into sarcasm, as in this description of yuppie courtship: "It's important to know that someone shares your taste in tableware, and it's better if you both jog than if one of you bikes instead."

By and large, the tone of the early coverage was that yuppies, with their predictable obsessions with food, money, and fitness, were *cute*. And that may be what hurt the most: The idea that the professional middle class, or at least some significant segment of it, could be so easily labeled and patronized. *Other* people occupied definable social classes, and these classes could be readily caricatured as welfare mothers or "hard-hats." But the middle class still fancies itself a set of self-determining individuals, not a group driven by common interests and instincts. Probably very few people read about yuppies and thought, "Oh my god, that's me!" But many in the middle class could see some part of themselves, some emerging constellation of tastes (for coarse-grain mustard, linen suits, or frequent workouts), and realize that they themselves had been labeled, caricatured, and fingered as part of some larger conformity emanating from beyond their individual will and judgment.

It hurt even more that this pattern of conformity could be almost entirely defined by material goods, purchases, brand names. A half-indulgent, half-mocking article in *Metropolitan Home* offered a simple quiz to determine whether the reader was a yuppie:

> Do you currently own or covet:
> A BMW, Saab, Volvo, or Mercedes.
> A Krups coffeemaker, Braun juicer, or Teraillon kitchen scale . . .
> Anything designed by Perry Ellis, Ralph Lauren, Issey Miyake, Merona Sport, Calvin Klein, or L.L. Bean . . .
> Canned pâté for a real emergency.

The unpleasant implication was that *things* had more power than one knew: the power to speak for one, to announce one's social name or type. In some curious way, the ownership had reversed, and the coveted, upscale brand name had migrated from the thing to the person.

There were defensive reactions to what was quickly denounced as "yuppie-bashing." A self-described "young urban professional writer" in the *New Republic,* which normally sets somewhat higher standards for invective, was reduced to calling the *Newsweek* cover story on yuppies "ultra-stupid," and asking rhetorically whether we are "possibly talking here about the worst cover story of the decade?" A writer in *Glamour* complained that, as a result of the "negative assessment of yuppies . . . a growing number of my peers feel compelled to apologize for their life-styles." Yuppies were not as materialistic as they had been depicted, she insisted, citing the example of a young New York attorney who had taken a pay cut so that he could now work two days a week at "a center for spiritual growth." But such excursions from the life of getting and spending should hardly be necessary. "Isn't it time," she asked, "to stop putting ourselves down for being what we are: people who have usually *earned* the right to enjoy a few material comforts?"

Some of the coverage of yuppies had the quality of a debate, and indeed there was more than one vantage point within the class that produced the yuppie style. Older people (that is, people born before 1945) resented yuppies for their youth, for their refusal to follow the usual arduous path to middle-class membership. "They have no concept that you ought to spend your younger years scraping along and saving," a middle-aged economist remarked to me. "They want to start life with everything their parents had in middle age, only more of it." There was even deeper resentment from those elements of the professional middle class who had not followed the "yuppie strategy." To those who remained in such traditional middle-class occupations as teaching, research, and journalism, yuppies were an abomination, like a younger brother turned criminal. The harshest anti-yuppie sentiments I heard were not from blue-collar workers but from a group of midwestern college teachers, still earning sub-yuppie salaries of around $30,000 a year.

But in the end there was no real debate. The yuppie style was an embarrassment, even to its most ardent practitioners. It was too conformist, too anxiety-ridden, and, in an America increasingly polarized by class, not even cute. In the years of yuppie excess, the poor had become visible again. It is a sad testimony to the middle-class solipsism of the eighties that the poor had literally to go outdoors to make their presence known. The homeless, who captured media attention in the middle of the decade, are not a special breed, as they are sometimes presented, but only the unluckiest of the poor. Their own homes had been torn down, or renovated and gentrified to make room for the rising corporate-administrative stratum represented by the yuppies. Or they had been driven out by skyrocketing real estate prices, bidded up by the rich and nearly rich. The homeless stood—literally, on so many city streets— as a shocking refutation of the ongoing consumer binge: the other side of the story.

There was also something exhausting about the yuppie way of life, with its neurotic layering of "compensatory spending" and compensatory suffering. The strategy had been to renounce the usual perquisites of middle-class life—an interesting, prestigious profession at a middling income—for quick money. But the strategy necessitated the style: The loss of an intrinsically rewarding profession had to be compensated for by strenuous consumption, and the strenuous consumption had to be compensated for by equally strenuous exertion— five-mile runs, ninety-minute workouts. The middle class does not make large amounts of money easily or endure their effects with a clear conscience and glad heart. It would have been easier and more satisfying, as many college students may now be beginning to see, to be a "poor" social worker or regional planner and achieve at least the traditional dignity of the middle-class professions.

No small part of that dignity derives from the intellectual commitment—no matter how attenuated or pretentious—of the middle class. It is, after all, the *professional* middle class that concerns us here, people whose bid for comfort and respect is based on their claims to some special knowledge.

Even the most philistine young finance banker must have a college degree or more, and hence some rudimentary exposure to a tradition of critical inquiry and aesthetic appreciation.

But the yuppie style was totally indifferent to that tradition. It had its own system of snobbery: not books and theater but food and restaurants. The student rebels of the sixties had been accused by their academic critics of being anti-intellectual; the yuppies were simply *un*intellectual (and interestingly, the neoconservatives have not risen up in condemnation). With a workday devoted to the "bottom line" and a leisure life divided between consumption and penance, the yuppie style was—to borrow a yuppie word—ultra-stupid.

In an article titled "Confessions of a Reluctant Yuppie," Peter Baida, a young hospital administrator, related the following story:

> A couple of years ago . . . my wife and I gave what might be called a Yuppie dinner party. All six of our guests were young professionals with degrees in law or business from top-ranked schools. At one point I mentioned that my wife recently had finished reading Proust and that now I had begun. "Who is Proust?" one of our guests asked. I thought someone else would answer, but all eyes turned toward me. Suddenly I realized that not one of our guests knew who Proust was.

No doubt they knew what Brie was, or pesto or Chardonnay, but this "reluctant yuppie" had expected the dinner table conversation to rise above the level of the dinnerware and what was on it. "I don't hate yuppies," he concluded, affirming that he himself was "right to go to business school." But "they—we—make me sad."

The stock-market crash of 1987 did not spell the end of yuppiedom or, as some excited commentators believed, the end of "the world as we know it." The consumer binge continues, though with less fanfare and more restrained advertising. On campuses, young people are still shelving their more idealistic aspirations for careers of corporate servitude or self-seeking entrepreneurship, though in slightly fewer numbers than before. On downtown streets, young people in expensive clothes still stroll on mild evenings, talking of leveraged buyouts and good things to eat.

But the crash did signal a turning point in middle-class consciousness—a moment of revulsion, however fleeting, against the materialism and greed now localized in "yuppies." A few months after the crash, *Newsweek,* which had practically defined yuppies in its 1984 cover story, announced that they were now in "disgrace." More decisively, the *Wall Street Journal* declared that "conspicuous consumption is passé"; it had in fact sunk to the lowest level of middle-class opprobrium, normally occupied by white bread and polyester, to become "tacky":

> Yuppies have become a bore and, under the circumstances, something of an embarrassment. Thus, Madison Avenue is trying to wipe them out . . . yuppies are now to be replaced in Madison Avenue's eyes by stay-at-home "couch potatoes" or some other group with similar buying characteristics but better values than yuppies exhibited.

Advertising would continue, of course, to promote upscale consumption and to seek out people whose "buying characteristics" were thoroughly yuppified. But the message would change. As one ad man told the *Wall Street Journal,* "It was as if people were saying it's OK to be greedy. That now is definitely déclassé."

There were even signs, in the late eighties, of a search for "better," and possibly more liberal, values. *New York* magazine, a reliable purveyor to yuppie tastes, ran a 1986 cover story on the novel possibility of "Doing Good." Or as the headline put it more aggressively: "HAD IT WITH PRIDE, COVETOUSNESS, LUST, ANGER, GLUTTONY, ENVY, AND SLOTH? IT'S TIME TO START DOING GOOD." *Newsweek* found "signs of increased altruism" in the land, and announced, two years in advance, that the eighties—the decade most frequently likened to the fifties —were over.

So, in some sense, our story has come full circle. We began

in the late fifties, when affluence had suddenly become tedious and the joys of materialism had begun to pale. Then too, middle-class commentators sought new "values"—which meant, at the time, new challenges to revive a stagnant liberalism. They found them in the gross inequalities of class and race that had somehow survived the general "affluence." They discovered the poor—that is, the most visibly miserable Americans—and found in them a new mission for liberalism. To Arthur Schlesinger, Jr., who led the search for issues and challenges in the fifties and early sixties, a "cycle" is about to begin again: "There is a lot of pent-up idealism. That will increase, and in the 1990s we'll enter a phase that will be much like the 1930s and the 1960s." The possibility remained, of course, that the repudiation of greed would be as transient and superficial as the yuppies that immediately preceded it.

## CHAPTER SIX

# THE NEXT GREAT SHIFT

THERE IS NO RULE that history must move in cycles, that a shift to the right must be matched by one to the left, or that, in some numerological accounting, the nineties will resemble the sixties. Despite repeated announcements of the "end of greed" and increasingly testy calls for "new values," the professional middle class remains, on the whole, committed to the pursuit of wealth: sycophantic toward those who have it, impatient with those who do not, and uncertain about what, if anything, was left behind in the heat of the chase.

Part of the problem is "structural," which is the economists' way of saying that it's no one's fault. Things simply cost more —so much more that we are frequently invited to sympathize with the middle-class breadwinner who can no longer get by on upwards of $100,000 a year. As one reports:

> My wife and I are baby-boomers in our mid-thirties. We are both professionals with master's degrees; our combined annual income this year will be about $115,000. . . . By any measure of income distribution we are way up there in the top 5 percent of American families. Something is terribly wrong.

The writer goes on to detail the current and future expenses of families like his own: monthly mortgage payments of $4,500,

commuting and child-care costs for the two-career couple, payments to private retirement funds, plus the prospect of college
costs, for the two-year-old, that "could exceed $100,000 an-
nually."

It is hardly greed that impels a man to want the best education for his children or a comfortable home for them to grow
up in. These costs are real and, since each family faces them
alone—without the possibility of exerting collective pressure
—nonnegotiable. Something indeed is "terribly wrong" when
the once-modest expectations of the middle class can be met
only with what is a far from middling income.

But it is also true that the expectations of the professional
middle class have been becoming somewhat more immodest
over time. If the above baby-boomer were a city-dweller, he
might have added the thoroughly "necessary" expenses of a
summer house and private schools for the children, and concluded that $200,000, or even more, was barely sufficient to
sustain a "middle-class" lifestyle. Again, much of this expense
can be counted as blamelessly "structural." Just as suburbanization ratcheted up the cost of middle-class living in the postwar years—necessitating the second car, the houseful of
furniture and appliances—so too has the "reurbanization" of a
sizable segment of the professional middle class in recent
years. There is no way, in this class, to live next to the con-
densed squalor of the cities without access to safer spaces: the
$8,000-a-year nursery school, the $10,000 summer rental, the
well-patrolled $500,000 co-op apartment.

Finally, add those details of yuppie "extravagance" that
must be deployed to signify one's social rank. At some point—
which, in the professional middle class, may long since have
passed—these too become almost "structural" requirements:
not options but socially mandated "necessities" demanded by
the pace of life, and demanding, in turn, an ever-faster pace of
work. And still the end is not in sight. In the spring of 1987 the
*New York Times* detailed the budget crunch of a young family
earning $600,000 a year.

Under these circumstances, the imagination contracts to fit
the task at hand: getting ahead, staying abreast, earning
enough. The "best minds," in the judgment of their college

professors, continue to spurn the more demanding disciplines for the speedier rewards of finance banking and corporate law. A narrow path has opened up, leading from the middle class directly to great wealth, and all those with quick minds and pointy elbows are crowding onto it. Increasingly, the professions, such as medicine, engineering, and scientific research, that require sustained concentration and the vaunted ability to "defer gratification" are left to lower-status people: immigrants from the third world, women.

Even within the New Class occupations that ought, if right-wing theory is any guide, to harbor masses of the more liberal-minded, a frantic repositioning is taking place. The once secure and even stodgy professoriate divides between the "star" professors, at one extreme, who earn near six figures and teach few courses, and, at the other extreme, the growing intellectual proletariat of part-time faculty, who commute from campus to campus to piece together a living. Journalism still has its financially marginal free-lance writers and hardworking local newspaper reporters. But now it also has a growing cadre of celebrity pundits, men like George Will, who move easily from print to television, from television to the corporate-lecture circuit, commanding five-figure fees for a single appearance in the flesh.

The continued existence of the professional middle class, as a class, may eventually be in question. One chunk is moving up, perhaps to join en masse the corporate elite from whose hand it now securely feeds. The lawyer specializing in mergers and acquisitions, the professor with his own bioengineering firm, the celebrity commentator—these mingle now with heads of companies, even heads of state. Meanwhile, another layer—less plucky or perhaps more stubbornly independent—sediments toward the white-collar end of the working class. The engineer, the lawyer handling routine cases, the teacher of unmarketable subjects like history or English—these may find themselves increasingly in the social orbit of computer programmers, travel agents, medical technicians.

But until new lines are drawn, the hustle is on. Everywhere, the scent of money intoxicates and clouds the mind. I attended a meeting of a group, mostly professors by occupation, dedicated to encouraging young people in the arts. When the question arose of whether to accept corporate sponsorship for a certain undertaking, there were many worried statements about "compromise," for, indeed, the corporation was seeking legitimation for a product that might well offend artistic sensibilities. Finally someone rose to clarify the issue: The question is not whether we sell ourselves, he said, but whether we sell ourselves for a high enough price. Titters arose, in honor not only of the sexual innuendo but of the larger resonance of his question. In the professional middle class, which once fought to secure the autonomy of its occupational redoubts, there is today no larger question than: What are we worth, and who will buy?

When more is not enough, but only serves as a springboard to further excess, then we have entered a state analogous to physical addiction. It does not matter that the "more" is often structurally decreed, that the costs of a decent way of living elude the frugal as well as the self-indulgent. The driving need is still the same. So it is fitting that the national obsession of the late eighties—replacing terrorism and missing children— should be drugs. The most dangerous current drug is an affliction, primarily, of the black urban poor, suggesting that a highly targeted approach to treatment and prevention might be in order. But in the media, the problem is always "drugs," as if the problem were everywhere and everyone were at risk.

The indiscriminate hysteria over drugs reflects that old anxiety at the heart of the middle class: the fear of falling, of losing control, of growing soft. "Drugs," as an undifferentiated category, symbolize the larger and thoroughly legal consumer culture, with its addictive appeal and harsh consequences for those who cannot keep up or default on their debts. It has become a cliché to say that this is an "addictive society," but the addiction most of us have most to fear is not promoted by a street-corner dealer. The entire market, the expanding spectacle of consumer possibilities, has us in its grip, and because that is too large and nameless, we turn our outrage toward something that is both less powerful and more concrete.

The fear of softening focuses, most naturally, on the young. The hardworking middle-class breadwinner has no reason to fear that his or her ambition will be blunted by a winter vacation or a mortgage on a second home, but the children may already be thoroughly numbed. Every week brings us news of their declining intellectual performance relative to the children of Japan, Korea, and western Europe. In the affluent suburbs, Caucasian children, descended from the ambitious immigrants of another era, are inexorably surpassed by the children of fresh immigrants from southern and Pacific Asia. The white children compete through consumption (clothes, cars, the splendor of the "sweet sixteen" party); only the more recent arrivals have the stamina to compete for grades. Sensing the problem, anxious parents float proposals to require uniforms in the public schools, as if discipline could be acquired by physical contact. But the only hope—the only white hope, that is—may be that the immigrants will, in a generation or two, desist from striving and join the rest of the sleepwalkers in the mall.

As anxiety over consumption grows, so too, no doubt, will the volume of voices demanding a return to "traditional values" and their pedagogical equivalent, "basics." The clamor for tradition is not, as many seem to think, part of an overdue pendular swing away from the hollow modernism of disposable loyalties, short attention spans, and easy comforts. "Traditional values" are merely a counterpoint to modernism, perhaps an inevitable feature of it. The broader the path to what appears to be laxity and surrender, the louder the calls for discipline and struggle. For the "New Class" is not, as the intellectuals of the right have liked to think, the locus or agent of hedonism. It is the locus of the most acute *conflict* over hedonism, the nexus of the most pronounced tension between modernism and tradition, consumerism and self-discipline. The intellectuals of the right, as usual, forgot themselves.

So there is no guarantee that anxiety over affluence and consumption will lead, once again, to a rebirth of liberalism. Certainly at the more fortunate, monied end of the professional middle class, where family incomes surpass those of over 80 or even 90 percent of Americans, there is little impetus for a leftward shift. As the urban middle class withdraws from public spaces and services—schools, parks, mass transportation—it also withdraws political support for public spending designed to benefit the community as a whole. Couples who send their children to private school, commute to work by taxi, and find their clean air at Aspen or Cancún will understandably prefer a tax cut to an expansion of government spending. The suburban middle class has of course long since withdrawn, geographically and often mentally, from the challenges of a diverse and unequal society. They may vote for a liberal Democrat at the local level, but favor conservatives at the centers of national power.

At all levels, political allegiance is increasingly determined by class. As Thomas Byrne Edsall of the *Washington Post* reports, the Democratic Party now finds its stronghold in the lower two-thirds of the income distribution, while Republican loyalty ascends straightforwardly as a function of wealth. The liberal elitists and "limousine liberals" of right-wing populist rhetoric are now, unfortunately, almost as rare as Republicans on the welfare rolls.

Meanwhile, class polarization continues, and develops a perverse, self-reinforcing dynamic of its own. As the professional middle class withdraws from public services, those services lose their most adamant advocates and critics. The schools deteriorate into holding bins. The parks are abandoned to the purveyors of drugs. Public hospitals, long since deserted by the middle class, regress to their ancient function of concealing the homeless, the disturbed, and the contagiously ill from public view. As the public sector declines—starved of funds and preyed on by corrupt municipal governments—so too do the opportunities available to the poor and the working class. The elaborate educational barriers to the professions are hardly necessary when huge numbers of potential aspirants can barely read above the third-grade level.

But if the middle class can no longer see the abandoned poor, the poor can still see *them.* In the past the lower classes lived in ignorance of the habits and indulgences of the rich. Servants were the only messengers between the classes, bringing the tenement news from the townhouse. Today television, that great enforcer of emulation, brings the most decrepit ghetto dwelling intimate glimpses into the "lifestyles of the rich and famous," not to mention the merely affluent. Studying the televised array of products and comforts available, seemingly, to everyone else, the poor become more dangerous. There are no models, in the mainstream media, suggesting that anything less than middle-class affluence might be an honorable and dignified condition, nor is there any reason why corporate advertisers should promote such a subversive possibility. If young black men in the ghettos—as well as many white ones in the suburbs—seem to prefer the underground economy of drugs and crime and temporary hustles to the drudgery of steady work at the minimum wage, they have at least been well educated as *consumers.*

Of course, as the poor become dangerous—addicted, short-tempered, diseased—the middle class withdraws still further from contact. Better to *close* the park, as some affluent lower-Manhattanites have argued, than risk mingling with those who have no other space in which to sleep or pass the time. Better to block off public streets, as some Miami neighborhoods have concluded, than allow free passage to the down-and-out. Even our city streets are less likely than in the past to offer the promiscuous mingling of "others." Suburban malls have drained downtown shopping areas and left them to the poor; the new urban skywalks lift the white-collar population into a weatherproof world of their own, leaving the streets to the overlapping categories of the poor, blue-collar workers, and people of color. And the more the poor are cut off or abandoned, the less they are capable of inspiring sympathy or even simple human interest.

So the nervous, uphill financial climb of the professional middle class accelerates the downward spiral of the society as a whole: toward cruelly widening inequalities, toward heightened estrangement along lines of class and race, and toward the moral anesthesia that estrangement requires. The professional middle class was born with the delusion that it stood outside of the class struggle—waged then between the workers and the "robber barons"—as neutral arbiters and experts. But at least that delusion carried with it a sense of responsibility—to mediate, to plan; to compensate, in other words, for the reckless shortsightedness of the monied class. Today, no such sense of mission animates the middle class. It has, in large numbers, joined the problem.

We need a revival of conscience and responsibility in the middle class. But from what ground is it likely to spring? What crisis might inspire it? What exhortations would have the power to call it forth? Alas, the questions have a tiresome, hectoring tone. Even the words *conscience* and *responsibility* begin to grate, suggesting only a slight improvement on the "traditional values" of conservative cant, especially self-denial. Guilt is not a fruitful basis for political renewal, any more than moral superiority, which is often only the mirror image of guilt.

The student left of the sixties, which is the most recent example we have of a largely middle-class movement of conscience, foundered between moral superiority and guilt. Its early years of expansion and optimism were tainted, too often, with an overweening sense of superiority toward those "Middle Americans" who refused to confront, as we used to say, their racism and related failings. Then, at the end of the sixties, came the discovery of the working class, and the left's subsequent discovery of its own, all-too-elite, position in the scheme of things. The student left woke up abruptly to the fact that it was not working-class, not "third-world," and hence had no place in the canonical theories of revolution. The movement was only, as Columbia student leader Mark Rudd once put it in a moment of perfect self-loathing, "a weird pile of liberal shit." Dismayed at not being legitimate agents of change, the activists drifted off—a few to vanguard organizations claiming a direct affinity with "the people," and most to their neglected studies and careers.

More recently, the right's attacks on the liberal elite have deepened the paralysis of middle-class conscience. One does not have to buy the entire theory of a New Class conspiracy to find in it the grain of a disturbing truth: Middle-class–led reform movements, from the Progressive Era to the War on Poverty, have been marred by an elitist distance from the would-be beneficiaries of reform. They were not intended to promote a vision of mass participation, leading to change from the bottom up, but, at worst, have exemplified Daniel Patrick Moynihan's notion of the "professionalization of reform"—itself an echo of Progressive Era calls for reform led by the "experts."

It is easy to conclude—in guilt and perhaps relief—that the professional middle class has no place in social change: that it is too driven by its own ambitions, too compromised by its own elite status, and too removed from those whose sufferings cry out most loudly for redress. As a thoughtful and liberally oriented young woman wrote to me recently, in considerable anguish: "I know what is important to me morally, but I don't know if there is a role for a white woman from the upper middle class. . . . Other people question my motives and sometimes I do too."

If there is to be a revival of conscience, it will have to be grounded in a deeper shift—in consciousness or, collectively, *class*-consciousness. This book has traced a prior shift in consciousness: from the naïve solipsism of the middle class in the fifties to the thoroughly pessimistic self-assessment that accompanied the conservative mood of the eighties. In this assessment, the professional middle class is an elite that is both estranged from the majority of "ordinary" people and menaced internally by hedonism and self-indulgence. Its goals are suspect, its generosity poisoned.

Clearly, the next great shift demands a second look, from within this class, at who we are and what we want: Power, as the right charges? Wealth, as the yuppie strategy suggests? Or are there other needs, repressed in the prevailing conservatism, which might begin to connect us with the lost "others" of the "lower" classes?

## DISCOVERING THE TRUE ELITE

A good place to start is with the unfinished business of class discovery. In this book, we have traced the discovery of the poor, the discovery of the working class, and, finally, the discovery of the New Class—that partial *self*-discovery of the professional middle class as a whole. In all this, one class had eluded detection, as a class—and that is the rich, or more narrowly, the corporate elite. Their discovery is crucial, for the rich are the genuine elite, relative to whom even the middle class is only another "lower class." If the conservative shift was based on a middle-class awareness of itself as an elite, then it was also based on an unwillingness to acknowledge where power really lies.

The rich, as individuals, are never far from view. They are a cherished part of the entertainment spectacle, their loves, their failed marriages, and their family strains reassuring us that "money does not bring happiness"—only the wherewithal, perhaps, to endure its absence. In the eighties, as the young of the middle class swarmed into the service of the corporate elite, the media amplified its fawning coverage of the upper class. *Vanity Fair,* which started out with mild intellectual aspirations, and *M,* a magazine of male fashion, bring us gossip from the polo fields, photos of the latest debutantes, and reports on the romances of local royalty, such as Princess Radziwill, and on the tastes of billionaire entrepreneurs, led by the sleek and spendthrift Trumps. In the media, the rich are legitimated, enthroned almost, by their association with the remnants of European aristocracy and, in the west, the homegrown aristocracy of Hollywood. If there is any connection between the gross excrescence of wealth and the indisputable spread of pauperism, it is discreetly left in mystery.

In the theories of the right, which still suffuse the mainstream way of seeing things, the rich are not the shallow people we see in magazines, eagerly opening their drawing rooms and formal parties to the stares of plainer folks. Usually, they are not present at all, having been displaced by the craftier and more powerful New Class. Or they are folded into the working class as socially responsible "producers": Middle Americans like anyone else, only somehow larger. Occasionally they are sanctified, as in George Gilder's writings, as remote and kindly patriarchs whose "gift" of capital seeps down to nourish the rest of us.

But capitalists no longer serve as stewards of social wealth —bravely risking, wisely investing, all for the greater good—if indeed they ever did. Consider the sad denouement of Reaganomics. Billions were redistributed upward through tax cuts and other fondly permissive policies: regulatory relaxation, for example, and the official abandonment of wage-earning workers. The idea was that the monied class, sated with all this excess wealth, would then be moved to invest in productive ventures providing decent jobs. But no such "trickle-down" occurred. The business journals still chart the decline of American industry. In technology, we continue to stumble behind the Asian nations that were only yesterday dismissed as mindless mimics. And since the new jobs generated by the economy are mostly low paid and often part-time, the median income for a family of four remains stuck, as it has been for years, just below the truly modest sum of $30,000 a year.

What happened to the immense largesse made available, by conservative policies, to the rich? Some small part financed the visible extravagance of the eighties, aptly represented by Malcolm Forbes's "capitalist cookies," Trump's helicopters, and Nancy Reagan's borrowed gowns. Another smallish part was invested, if the word applies, in hoardable items such as art. But most went to fuel the speculative binge on Wall Street: the corporate takeovers, mergers and acquisitions, leveraged buyouts that have made America, as some economists put it, a "casino society."

None of these speculative activities generates new wealth, new jobs (except for legions of corporate lawyers), new products, or new technology. They are games of chance, carried on at an unprecedented scale, whose only tangible result is a re-shuffling of existing wealth and power among a tiny group of players. The leading players, who are also the leading capitalists of our day, are the investment bankers, some of whom earn tens of millions a year and trade in companies with assets exceeding the wealth of many nations. As economist Robert B. Reich observes:

> Rarely have so few earned so much for doing so little. Never have so few exercised such power over how the slices of the American pie are rearranged.

In the speculative frenzy that has taken the place of industrial capitalism, it is the corporate-financial elite that most clearly exhibits the supposed defects of the poor: present-time orientation and the incapacity to defer gratification. Foreign financers and investors, who seem increasingly to serve as the superego of U.S. capitalism, routinely criticize the American business community for its unwillingness to think beyond the next quarter's profits—its refusal, for example, to invest in the research and plant modernization that might lead to profits in the longer term. Our corporate elite has been entrusted with an unseemly share of the nation's wealth—wealth that ultimately represents the labor of workers, the ingenuity of scientists and technicians, the vanishing abundance of natural resources—and they are gambling it away. If there is one clear lesson of Reaganomics, it is that the *rich* cannot be trusted with money.

Class polarization invites class conflict. There have been too many Wall Street scandals, too many megatakeovers in which giant corporations—and inevitably their employees—are tossed about like poker chips. There has been too much flaunting of extravagance, too much evidence of the bullying power of corporate wealth over politicans and the political process. The media are unlikely to launch a critical "discovery" of the class that sponsors them. But scattered articles, the occasional populist politician of the left, a few recent books—these announce America's accelerating decline toward a plutocracy ruled by the whim and greedy impulse of the few.

The discovery of the rich—and among them, the truly powerful—should have an immediately salutary effect on the professional middle class. The $115,000-a-year couple should begin to notice whose wealth ultimately drives up the price of real estate and education. Students may question the "market forces" that demand armies of lawyers and a diminishing number of scientists and social workers. Liberal intellectuals, still tortured by their imputed membership in a power-hungry New Class, may regain the use of their backbones.

For the American middle class is not, of course, a ruling class. Even its most privileged members find themselves blocked by higher powers. The magazine editor must bow, occasionally, to the financial power of the publisher or the advertisers. Industrial scientists and engineers see cherished innovations dropped because they will not realize quick enough profits. The tenured faculty finds its autonomy checked by the aggregated wealth of the board of trustees. Whatever power can be won through skill, ambition, and strength of will can ultimately be outweighed by the force of capital.

## REDISCOVERING THE "OTHERS"

If the rich, as a class, can be discovered, then it may also be possible for the middle class to rediscover the "lower classes"—not as alien "others" or even as objects of liberal sympathy, but as allies in a struggle to curb the inordinate and growing power of wealth. This is, in fact, almost the defining dream of the American left: that discontented members of the middle class might join the working-class majority in a political effort to redistribute both power and wealth downward, to those who need them most. As the dream unfolds into the future, class ceases to be a meaningful dimension of human variety. The steep gradients of wealth and poverty, power and helplessness, are abolished, and genuine democracy can take root, at last, in level ground.

For the point of discussing class is ultimately to abolish it. Tax the rich and enrich the poor until both groups are absorbed into some broad and truly universal middle class. The details are subject to debate: You can emphasize better jobs and wages or you can offer a guaranteed income that circumvents the labor market. Or you can emphasize services (such as education, health care, housing, child care) that improve the lives of everyone and widen the opportunities of those in need. Probably all of these things should be done, in some considered combination, until America truly begins to resemble what it once believed itself to be: a classless, even-tempered society where the most pressing problems have to do with the "quality of life" rather than the quantity of human misery.

But it is far easier to sketch the alliances required for such an undertaking than to create them in the flesh, easier to see the "others" as distant "constituencies"—the building blocks of strategic fantasy—rather than as potential colleagues and leaders. Even the middle-class left, where the spirit is most willing, has an uneven record of reaching out across the lines of class. Left and right, we are still locked in by a middle-class culture that is almost wholly insular, self-referential, and in its own way, parochial. We seldom see the "others" except as projections of our own anxieties or instruments of our ambitions, and even when seeing them—as victims, "cases," or exemplars of some archaic virtue—seldom hear.

Overcoming stereotypes is perhaps the easiest step, for stereotypes have only to be identified to be disarmed as knowledge. In the last few years, for example, news of the feminization of poverty—and of the widespread existence of the "working poor"—has sapped the power of some of the most noxious and implicitly racist images of the poor. The hard part is to move beyond stereotypes to an understanding that the "others" are as diverse and individual as one's own kind, and also—in ways that may deserve respect as well as worry— distinctly different.

Again, a shift in consciousness is required—an effort of intellect and imagination. Many factors conspire to isolate the classes and keep the middle class from noticing the "others," much less addressing them as fellow citizens. The physical segregation of the classes guarantees that we will move and usually live in separate spaces. Our fragmented welfare state —which includes "welfare" for the poor and an array of tax breaks for the middle class—keeps us from finding common ground in economic issues. In the media, the decline of labor coverage ensures that no one will know of the working class's moments of heroism—or defeat. And even when they are in our presence, we tend to screen out the "unimportant" people: busboys, messengers, nurses's aides, ticket agents, secretaries.

Nor do we usually see the daily efforts and achievements of the "others." Consider, as a brief case study in class insularity, the longstanding middle-class preoccupation with commodities as marks of social status. In the currently fashionable intellectual approach, commodities are "signifiers" in a "language" of status, telling us, for example, who is worth knowing and who may be safely neglected. But this notion, as it stands, is itself limited and class-bound. If all that things signify is degrees of rank, then the language of commodities becomes a conversation among the already privileged, who are alone prepared to decode the shadings of "taste" represented by each consumer option and brand name. If things speak only of status, then they speak only to the status-conscious, and the only news they bring is of arrogance and degrees of wealth.

It is possible, however, to "read" things another way: not only as statements about the status of their owners, but as the congealed labor of invisible others. Whatever it is, someone manufactured it, packed it, trucked it to market, and stood behind a counter until it was sold. When we are prepared to listen, the computerized appliance speaks of Asian women straining their eyes on a distant assembly line; the gourmet take-out food speaks of immigrant workers chopping food in a sweltering kitchen; the towering condominium building speaks of lives risked at high altitude; and everything speaks of the tense solitude of the over-the-road truck driver. Learning to read things this way is a step to breaking out of the middle class's own lonely isolation.

There is a need, also, to learn to *hear* the "others." Strangely, for a society so tightly linked by mass communications, a kind of language barrier divides the classes. From the vantage point of the professional middle class, those "below" do not speak clearly, or intelligibly, or interestingly. Hence the all-too-common, unconsciously patronizing judgment that a particular representative of the poor or the working class is "articulate," implying that the rest are not. Hence, too, the old sociological prejudice that the "lower classes" are limited and parochial in their utterances, or not worth listening to.

We tend to think of the problem, if we think of it at all, as a simple *lack* on the part of the "lower" classes—most likely, a simple lack of vocabulary. Stereotypes of verbally deprived workers come to mind: Archie Bunker with his malapropisms, Ed Norton braying dumbly on *The Honeymooners*. But usually it is the middle class that is speaking the strange language— something sociologist Alvin Gouldner called "critical discourse." This is the language of the academy and also of bureaucracy; and, in his analysis, it defines the professional middle class as a "speech community." It is distinguished, above all, by its impersonal and seemingly universal tone. Within critical discourse, Gouldner writes,

> persons and their social positions must not be visible in their speech. Speech becomes impersonal. Speakers hide behind their speech. Speech seems to be disembodied, de-contextualized and self-grounded.

Relative to the vernacular, critical discourse operates at a high level of abstraction, always seeking to absorb the particular into the general, the personal into the impersonal. This is its strength. But the rudely undemocratic consequence is that individual statements from "below" come to seem almost weightless, fragmentary, unprocessed. Since ordinary speech does not aspire to universality and does not hide the speaker in a gauze of impersonal rhetoric, it is easily dismissed as limited and "anecdotal." Meanwhile, even a truly "limited" idea, when expressed in the impersonal mode common to the middle class, becomes grander than the utterance of an individual person—larger in implication, more consequential.

The way across the language barrier lies, first, through awareness of the middle-class assumptions that automatically denigrate "ordinary" styles of speech. In the longer term, we need a critique of critical discourse itself. Is there a way to "reembody" the middle class's impersonal mode of discourse, so that it no longer serves to conceal the individual and variable speaker? For we may need to find our*selves* in the language of abstraction, if we are ever to find the "others" in the language of daily life. And finding the "others"—not as aliens, not as projections of inner fear—is essential to the revival of middle-class conscience.

What does the professional middle class have to gain, or perhaps to lose, in a more egalitarian future? The problem with middle-class liberalism—perhaps the worst problem—was that it never asked the question. It assumed that American affluence was sufficient to embrace all those in poverty without any loss to those who were not. And it assumed that any gains to the middle class itself would be purely spiritual, leaving the way open for right-wing theories of the liberal elite's "real" motives and agenda.

Compared to the world as seen by middle-class intellectuals at mid-century, ours is a world of scarcity. No one imagines that affluence is a widespread condition, much less a social problem. No one any longer believes that poverty can be abolished painlessly, without an effort at downward redistribution: not in the United States, and certainly not in the world as a whole. Even economic growth—that venerable liberal alternative to redistribution—has reached the limits of the earth's environment and must, sooner rather than later, come to a stop. And surely, if "middle-class" is to be defined by incomes available now to 5 percent or less of the American population, then few can hope to attain that once quite ordinary condition.

But there is one thing that should not be scarce, that should in fact increase, and that is good and pleasurable and decent work: the work of caring, healing, building, teaching, planning, learning. The pride of the professions that define the middle class is that they still contain and represent such work. The tragedy is that they represent such work made scarce. In part, the blame falls on the corporate elite, which demands ever more bankers and lawyers, on the one hand, and low-paid helots on the other—and few, if any, poets, astronomers, or givers of care. But the middle class is also culpable, for its strategy has long been to hoard the best work, to heighten the barriers, to exclude the masses of willing hands.

Professions, as opposed to *jobs*, are understood to offer some measure of intrinsic satisfaction, some linkage of science and service, intellect and conscience, autonomy and responsibility. No one has such expectations of a mere *job*; and it is this, as much as anything, which defines the middle-class advantage over the working-class majority. The working class must work —often at uncomfortable or repetitive tasks—for money, and find its pleasures elsewhere. Only in the middle class (and among the working rich) is pleasure in work regarded, more or less, as a right. As John Kenneth Galbraith observed many years ago:

> For some, and probably a majority, [work] remains a stint to be performed. . . . For others work, as it continues to be called, is an entirely different matter. It is taken for granted that it will be enjoyable.

Work, of the special kind that it reserves to itself, is the secret hedonism of the middle class, its alternative to the less satisfying, and hence more addictive, hedonism of the consumer culture. And, although we seldom think of it this way, the pleasure of work is the middle class's tacit rebuttal to capitalism, a pleasure that cannot be commodified or marketed, that need not obsolesce or wane with time.

It is the pleasure of work—and the sense of being entitled to that pleasure—that is most easily lost in the scramble to get ahead, or simply to stay in place within a recklessly polarizing society. Galbraith's comment provides a measure of the loss that has already been incurred. In 1958 he could fairly observe that a professional would be "insult[ed]" and "disturbed" if it were thought that "his principal motivation in life is the pay he receives." Today, as the more rewarding professions (medicine, for example, and science and teaching) are abandoned for more lucrative careers, few would find such a motivation dishonorable. Even within the more rewarding professions, the traditional perquisites—autonomy, creativity, and service —are easily traded off in favor of greater income.

The more we abandon the ethos of professionalism—and its secret pleasure principle—the more we are dependent on the commodified pleasures of the market. The would-be regional planner turned corporate lawyer, the would-be social worker turned banker, must compensate for abandoned dreams with spending. The costs of heightened consumption demand still longer hours of empty labor—which must, in turn, be compensated with more consumption. Hence the addictive frenzy of the "yuppie strategy." Hence, too, one more source of momentum for the forces of polarization and deepening class inequality.

But even for the middle class, the way out does not lie through a simple revival of professionalism. The elitism of the professions—with their steep and often arbitrary barriers of education and licensing—hurts not only the excluded members of the lower classes, but those who are, by birth, most likely to be included. This is the catch in the strategy of professionalism and the source of so much middle-class anxiety: the barriers erected to exclude intruders from other classes also stand in the way of the youth of the middle class. The barriers ensure that only the hardworking, the self-denying, will make it—and not even all of them. Hence the fear of hedonism, of growing soft and, ultimately, falling. Hard work and self-denial become our punitive "values"—setting us against all those who have not yet made it (the young, the poor) and even against our own desires.

But if we start with what needs to be *done*, we can see that the middle class's anxious sense of scarcity is in no small part self-imposed. There is potentially no limit to the demand for skilled, creative, and caring people, no limit to the problems to be solved, the needs to be met by human craft and agency. The mentality of scarcity may be appropriate to the realm of consumer goods—for the obvious reasons of fairness and ecology —but it has no place in the realm of conscious, responsible, effort and achievement.

In an egalitarian future, there would be enough work to go around, and work pleasurable enough so that all will want it. This is not a matter of "lowering standards," but of opening doors: removing artificial barriers and expanding educational opportunity to all comers. In the process, education itself must change, abandoning its restrictive biases (by race and sex as well as class), downplaying competition. The long process of growing up and preparing for an adult occupational role need no longer be an exercise in "deferring gratification." "Permissiveness" would cease to be a threat and an excuse for class injustice. For growing numbers of people of all backgrounds, the path of self-indulgence would lead straight on from the pleasure of learning to the joy of chosen work.

At the point where education becomes the free exercise of mind, it would inevitably cease to be the mechanism of class reproduction. It would be too exuberant, too playful, to remain in quiet service to social inequality. Everyone would want it; the barriers erected to keep out the "others" would tumble, and the hungry of all ages would swarm in.

This, very simply, should be the program of the professional middle class and the agenda it brings to any broader movement for equality and social justice: to expand the class, welcoming everyone, until there remains no other class.

# NOTES

## INTRODUCTION

PAGE NO.

8 *as perilously skewed as that of India:* Steve Brouwer, *Sharing the Pie* (Carlisle, Pa.: Big Picture Books, 1988), p. 4.

12 *This class can be defined:* For more thorough definitions, as well as history and theories of this class in the United States, see Barbara Ehrenreich and John Ehrenreich, "The Professional-Managerial Class," in Pat Walker, ed., *Between Labor and Capital: The Professional Managerial Class* (Boston: South End Press, 1979); Alvin Gouldner, *The Future of Intellectuals and the Rise of the New Class* (New York: Seabury/Continuum, 1979); and David Bazelon, *Power in America* (New York: New American Library, 1967).

12 *about 20 percent of the population:* John Ehrenreich's calculation in Ehrenreich and Ehrenreich, "Professional-Managerial Class."

12 *the corporate elite:* For an interesting attempt to define an upper boundary, see Michael Albert and Robin Hahnel, "A Ticket to Ride: More Locations on the Class Map," in Walker, *Between Labor and Capital*, pp. 243–78.

13 *some points of commonality:* The reader seeking more theoretical rigor or sociological detail is referred to Ehrenreich and Ehrenreich, Gouldner, and Bazelon.

## ONE: AFFLUENCE, DREAD, AND THE DISCOVERY OF POVERTY

18 *"A number of influential voices":* Vance Packard, *The Status Seekers* (New York: Pocket Books, 1961), p. 2. *"The lower-class people":* pp. 72–73.

19 *"What can we write about?":* Quoted in Peter Schrag, *The End of the American Future* (New York: Simon and Schuster, 1973), p. 88.

19 *"The fundamental political problems"*: Seymour Martin Lipset, *Political Man* (Garden City, N.Y.: Doubleday, 1963), p. 442.

19 *"To be sure"*: David Riesman and Nathan Glazer, "The Intellectuals and the Discontented Classes," in Daniel Bell, ed., *The New American Right*. (New York: Criterion, 1955), pp. 72–73.

19 *"There are still pools"*: Arthur Schlesinger, Jr., *The Politics of Hope* (Boston: Houghton Mifflin, 1963), p. 92. (Originally published in *Esquire,* January 1960.)

20 *"A total ideology is"*: Daniel Bell, *The End of Ideology: On the Exhaustion of Political Ideas in the Fifties* (New York: Free Press, 1962), p. 400.

20 *Schlesinger described Americans:* Schlesinger, *Politics of Hope*, pp. 84–85.

20 *"The paramount goal"*: Quoted in Ethel Kawin, *Parenthood in a Free Nation*, vol. I, *Basic Concepts for Parents* (New York: Macmillan, 1967), p. 105.

20 *"to produce more consumer goods"*: Quoted in Schlesinger, *Politics of Hope,* p. 83.

21 *"the last stubborn barriers"*: Quoted in Allan David Heskin, "Crisis and Response: An Historical Perspective on Advocacy Planning," UCLA (no date) p. 1.

21 *"the refinement of our mass media"*: Schlesinger, *Politics of Hope,* p. 90.

21 *"A liberal was one who"*: Alan Wolfe, *America's Impasse: The Rise and Fall of the Politics of Growth* (New York: Pantheon Books, 1981), p. 28.

22 *The other-directed man:* Arthur Schlesinger, Jr., *Kennedy or Nixon: Does It Make Any Difference?* (New York: Macmillan, 1960), p. 4.

22 *"Contemporary American liberalism"*: Arthur Schlesinger, Jr., *The Politics of Hope,* p. 70.

23 *J. Edgar Hoover blamed:* Quoted in Douglas T. Miller and Marion Nowak, *The Fifties* (Garden City, N.Y.: Doubleday, 1977), p. 280.

25 *"classes are not functionally real"*: Roger Brown, *Social Psychology* (New York: Free Press, 1965), p. 135.

26 *"In addition to the age and sex categories"*: William F. Ogburn and Meyer F. Nimkoff, *Sociology* (Boston: Houghton Mifflin, 1964), pp. 436–37. *"In rapidly changing modern urban America"*: p. 437.

26 *"The major shift to a 'classless society'"*: Arnold W. Green, *Sociology: An Analysis of Life in Modern Society* (New York: McGraw-Hill, 1968), p. 201.  the *"American myth of ideological equalitarianism"*: pp. 459–61.

27 *the lower-class person "sedulously avoids work"*: Green, *Sociology,* p. 207.

27 *"The superego (conscience) tends to be stronger"*: Francis E. Merrill and H. Wentworth Eldridge, *Society and Culture: An Introduction to Sociology* (New York: Prentice Hall, 1957), pp. 319–20.

27 *"matters of good taste"*: Green, *Sociology,* pp. 206–8.

28 *since he was "comparatively insensitive"*: Merrill and Eldridge, *Society and Culture,* p. 318.

28 *"Our complex division of labor"*: Green, *Sociology,* p. 203.

28 *"Social organization consists"*: George A. Lundberg, Clarence C. Schrag, and Otto N. Larsen, *Sociology* (New York: Harper, 1954), pp. 275–76. *"how things happen"*: p. 4.

29 *"The steady pressure to consume"*: Herbert Gold, *The Age of Happy Problems* (New York: Dial Press, 1962), p. 10.

29–30 *many intellectuals worried:* Quoted in Eric Goldman, *The Tragedy of Lyndon Johnson* (New York: Knopf, 1969), pp. 140–41.

30 *Affluence was an appealing target:* Todd Gitlin, *The Sixties: Years of Hope, Days of Rage* (New York: Bantam Books, 1987), p. 12.

30 *Affluence could be attacked:* However, the man who first pinpointed affluence as the American condition, John Kenneth Galbraith, was abundantly critical of the wastefulness of corporate-dominated economy and the inequities it generated. See *The Affluent Society* (Boston: Houghton Mifflin, 1958).

30 *"The loudest complaints about tailfins"*: Stephan Thernstrom, quoted in William E. Leuchtenburg, *The Troubled Feast: American Society Since 1945* (Boston: Little, Brown, 1973), p. 113.

31 *"The general demand that they consume":* Jack Kerouac, *The Dharma Bums* (New York: Viking Press, 1958), p. 77.

32 *The typical dieter:* Hillel Schwartz, *Never Satisfied: A Cultural History of Diets, Fantasies, and Fat* (New York: Free Press, 1986), p. 254. *"Men who were merely plump":* p. 247. *"Americans of the Depression":* p. 235.

33 *Meandering along:* Eric Goldman, quoted in Leuchtenberg, *Troubled Feast,* p. 110.

33 *"Russia more than makes up":* Schlesinger, *Politics of Hope,* pp. 83–84.

33 *Adlai Stevenson had warned:* Quoted in Leuchtenberg, *Troubled Feast,* p. 111.

34 *"The consumer culture":* Gold, *Age of Happy Problems,* p. 7.

35 *"it was hard to know economic struggle":* Gold, *Age of Happy Problems,* pp. 3–4.

36 *"We are now confronted":* Quoted in William H. Whyte, Jr., *The Organization Man* (New York: Simon and Schuster, 1956), p. 17.

36 *the amount spent on advertising:* David M. Potter, *People of Plenty: Economic Abundance and the American Character* (Chicago: Phoenix Books, 1954), p. 178. *"Certainly it marks":* p. 188.

36 *"are likely to generate":* Albert O. Hirschman, *Shifting Involvements: Private Interest and Public Action* (Princeton, N.J.: Princeton University Press, 1982), p. 38. *Durable goods are especially disappointing):* p. 29.

37 *Advertising had become:* Stephen Fox, *The Mirror Makers: A History of American Advertising and Its Creators* (New York: Morrow, 1984), p. 179. *"The creative man has lost":* p. 180.

37 *In reality, the earning gap:* Using Census Bureau statistics, Phil Steinberg calculates that the ratio of professional, managerial, and administrative male incomes to those of all other males was 1.59:1 in 1950 and exactly the same in 1960.

38 *"rather more than the usual number of books":* Russell Lynes, *A Surfeit of Honey* (New York: Harper, 1957), p. 32.

38 *"When a group is either satisfied or exhausted":* Riesman and Glazer, "The Intellectuals," p. 79.

39 *"All social classes":* Russell Lynes, *Surfeit of Honey,* p. 49.

39 *Increasingly, middle-class girls:* Barbara Miller Solomon, *In the Company of Educated Women* (New Haven: Yale University Press, 1985), pp. 63–64.

40 *Nearly 60 percent of the nation's college-educated young women:* Computed by Phil Steinberg from U.S. Bureau of the Census statistics, 1960.

40 *Russian women ... "building ... [a] huge dam":* Bruno Bettelheim, "The Commitment Required of a Woman Entering a Scientific Profession in Present-Day American Society," in Jacqueline A. Mattfeld and Carol G. Van Aken, eds., *Women and the Scientific Professions,* (Cambridge: MIT Press, 1965), pp. 6–7.

40 *"particularly suited to the capacities of feeble-minded girls":* Betty Friedan, *The Feminine Mystique* (New York: Norton, 1963), p. 255.

41 *"Why is it never said":* pp. 206–7. *"frightening passivity":* pp. 282, 285.

42 *"a massive affliction":* Galbraith, *Affluent Society,* p. 323.

42 *"We seem to have suddenly awakened":* Dwight MacDonald, "Our Invisible Poor," *New Yorker,* January 19, 1963, p. 82.

43 *"88 percent of the families":* "Poverty U.S.A.," *Newsweek,* February 17, 1964, p. 19.

43 *U.S. News and World Report was so impressed:* "Sudden Drive on 'Poverty'—Why?" *U.S. News and World Report,* January 20, 1964, p. 36.

43 *poverty probably wouldn't have been discovered:* Edmund K. Faltermayer, "Who Are the American Poor?" *Fortune,* March 1964, p. 118. Herman Miller is quoted in the same article.

44 *"Would they be missed?":* "The Poor Amidst Prosperity," *Time,* October 1, 1965, pp. 34–35.

44 *"Certainly the goal":* Schlesinger, *Politics of Hope,* p. 82.

44 *"a feeling of revulsion":* Hirschman, *Shifting Involvements,* p. 5.

45 *The "ultimate dimension":* Sargent Shriver, "The War on Poverty Is a Move-

ment of Conscience," in Marvin E. Gettleman and David Mermelstein, eds., *The Great Society Reader* (New York: Random House, 1967), p. 209.

45 *"I just can't hold on to money":* Quoted in Robert A. Liston, *Sargent Shriver: A Candid Portrait* (New York: Farrar, Straus, 1964), p. 202.

45 *The "real test":* Sargent Shriver, foreword to George H. Dunne, ed., *Poverty in Plenty* (New York: Kennedy, 1964), p. 10.

46 *College students in particular:* Sargent Shriver, *The Point of the Lance* (New York: Harper and Row, 1964), p. 113.

47 *Kennedy's way out:* Frances Fox Piven and Richard A. Cloward, *Poor People's Movements: Why They Succeed, How They Fail* (New York: Vintage Books, 1979), p. 270.

47 *"the impoverished are people too":* "Poverty U.S.A.," p. 19.

48 *the poor were less threatening:* See Elinor Graham, "The Politics of Poverty," in Gettleman and Mermelstein, *Great Society Reader*, p. 225.

48 *"If you just enlist a person":* Shriver, "War on Poverty," pp. 210–11.

49 *"There is, in short, a language":* Michael Harrington, *The Other America: Poverty in the United States* (New York: Macmillan, 1962), p. 17.

49 *University of Michigan study:* Greg J. Duncan, with Richard D. Coe, Mary E. Corcoran, Martha S. Hill, Saul D. Hoffman, and James N. Morgan, *Years of Poverty, Years of Plenty* (Ann Arbor: University of Michigan Press, 1984).

49 *"fatalism, helplessness, dependence":* Oscar Lewis, "The Culture of Poverty," in Louis A. Ferman, Joyce L. Kornbluh, and Alan Haber, eds., *Poverty in America: A Book of Readings* (Ann Arbor: University of Michigan Press, 1969), p. 411.

50 *"The culture of poverty" had become coterminous with poverty:* Oscar Lewis, *La Vida: A Puerto Rican Family in the Culture of Poverty* (New York: Random House, 1965), p. xlii.

50 *"Those pockets of poverty":* Robert Coles, "Psychiatrists and the Poor," in Arthur I. Blaustein and Roger R. Wood, eds., *Man Against Poverty: World War III* (New York: Random House, 1968), p. 105.

51 *"Living in the present":* Lewis, "Culture of Poverty," p. 415.

52 *"It is hard to recognize":* S. M. Miller and Frank Riessman, *Social Class and Social Policy* (New York: Basic Books, 1968), pp. 54–55.

52 *Historian Donald Meyer has described the consumer personality:* Donald Meyer, *The Positive Thinkers: A Study of the American Quest for Health, Wealth, and Personal Power from Mary Baker Eddy to Norman Vincent Peale* (New York: Doubleday, 1965), p. 205.

53 *"The poor have become":* "Who the Poor Are," editorial, *New Republic*, February 15, 1964, pp. 4–5.

54 *"The lower-class individual":* Edward C. Banfield, *The Unheavenly City: The Nature and Future of Our Urban Crisis* (Boston: Little, Brown, 1968, 1970), p. 53. *"The lower-class forms":* p. 211. *"Improvements in sanitation":* p. 213. *"Not nearly enough therapists":* p. 224. *"At a very early age":* p. 229. *"As a matter of logic":* p. 231. *"Such persons could be cared for"* p. 236.

55 *"A set of production goals":* Shriver, "War on Poverty," p. 207.


## TWO: THE MIDDLE CLASS ON THE DEFENSIVE

57 *"Sleep was impossible":* Diana Trilling, *We Must March, My Darlings* (New York: Harcourt Brace Jovanovich, 1977), p. 87.

58 *"A faculty wife":* p. 96.

60 *"The personal, moral, and intellectual offense":* Trilling, *We Must March*, pp. 131–32.

61 *The story of the student left:* See, for example: Todd Gitlin, *The Sixties: Years*

*of Hope, Days of Rage* (New York: Bantam Books, 1987); Kirkpatrick Sale, *SDS* (New York: Vintage Books, 1974); James Miller, *Democracy Is in the Streets* (New York: Simon and Schuster, 1987).

62 *"Dad looked at his house"*: Jerry Rubin, quoted in *The Sixties Papers: Documents of a Rebellious Decade*, Judith Clavir Albert and Stewart Edward Albert, eds. (New York: Praeger, 1984), pp. 439–40.

63 *"In the period until 1968"*: Winni Breines, *The Great Refusal: Community and Organization in the New Left, 1962–1968* (New York: Praeger, 1982), p. 20.

64 *"Touch a university"*: Trilling, *We Must March*, p. 80.

65 *Bettelheim likened the student rebels to Nazis*: Bruno Bettelheim, "Disturbing Student Parallels," *New York Times*, March 23, 1969 (excerpted from his statement before the House Special Subcommittee on Education).

65 *"The new Fascisti"*: Quoted in "Campus Protest Takes New Shape," *New York Times*, November 20, 1967.

65 *Glazer compared them not only to Hitler but to Lenin and Stalin*: Breines, *Great Refusal*, p. 3.

65 *"impelled not to innovation"*: Daniel Bell, quoted in Breines, *Great Refusal*, p. 2.

65 *"rebels without a cause"*: Irving Kristol, "A Different Way to Restructure the University," in Daniel Bell and Irving Kristol, eds., *Confrontation: The Student Rebellion and the Universities* (New York: Basic Books, 1968, 1969), p. 150.

65 *"Nihilistic perversions"*: Eugene Genovese, quoted in Breines, *Great Refusal*, p. 2.

65 *"Romantic primitivism"*: Irving Howe, quoted in Breines, *Great Refusal*, p. 3.

65 *Sidney Hook organized*: *New York Times*, March 23, 1969.

65 *"They are the most selfish people"*: William Appleman Williams, quoted in "Campus Protest."

66 *"of course, the German student rebels"*: Bettelheim, "Disturbing Student Parallels."

67 *"the traits of elitism, suicidalism"*: Lewis S. Feuer, *The Conflict of Generations: The Character and Significance of Student Movements* (New York: Basic Books, 1969), p. viii.: *"the Cruel, Heartless, Impersonal Father"*: p. 445. *"Their fruitless rebellions"*: p. 467. *"the self-destructive ingredient"*: p. 420. *"Their indignation"*: p. 471.

68 *Christopher Jencks argued*: "Is It All Dr. Spock's Fault?" *New York Times Magazine*, March 3, 1968, p. 17.

68 *Yet the* Times *titled*: Christopher Jencks, personal communication, December 17, 1986.

68 *"the permissive doctrines"*: David Truman, quoted in "Columbia Starts to Discipline 500 for Campus Sit-In," *New York Times*, May 20, 1968.

68 *"unrelenting and excessive permissiveness"*: Rabbi Emmanuel Rackman, quoted in "Permissive Role in Society Scored," *New York Times*, November 10, 1968.

68 *"a uniquely indulged generation"*: Edward Shils, "Dreams of Plenitude, Nightmares of Scarcity," in Seymour Martin Lipset and Philip G. Altbach, eds., *Students in Revolt* (Boston: Houghton Mifflin, 1969), p. 15.

69 *"massive doses of affection"*: Robert Nesbit, "Knowledge Dethroned," *New York Times Magazine*, September 28, 1975, p. 34.

69 *"Dr. Yes"*: "Chicago's 'Dr. Yes,' " *Time*, July 5, 1968, p. 49.

69 *Rebellious youth*: Bruno Bettelheim, quoted in "Student Protests Tied to Guilt Idea," *New York Times*, March 21, 1969.

69 *I have known mothers*: Bruno Bettelheim, "Children Must Learn to Fear," *New York Times Magazine*, April 13, 1969, p. 125.

70 *"it is only through effort"*: George F. Kennan, *Democracy and the Student Left* (Boston: Atlantic Monthly Press, 1968), p. 11.

70 *"the motivation toward hard intellectual pursuits"*: Nesbit, *Knowledge Dethroned.*

70 *Pampered as babies:* Bettelheim, "Children Must Learn to Fear."

70 *Spiro Agnew made permissiveness:* "Agnew Develops His Father Image," *New York Times,* October 13, 1968.

71 *"the true responsibility"*: Spiro Agnew, quoted in Jules Witcover, *White Knight: The Rise of Spiro Agnew* (New York: Random House, 1972), pp. 331–32. *"spoiled brats"*: p. 264. *"a society which comes to fear"*: p. 290.

71 *global in scope:* Dr. Fred Brown, quoted in "Parents Excused in Youth Revolt," *New York Times,* May 12, 1968.

71 *Flacks's surveys:* Richard Flacks, "Who Protests: Social Bases of the Student Movement," in Julian Foster and Durward Long, eds., *Protest!: Student Activism in America* (New York: William Morrow, 1970), p. 134.

73–74 *"I am"* . . . *"a member"*: Midge Decter, *Liberal Parents, Radical Children* (New York: Coward, McCann, and Geoghegan, 1975), p. 16. *"From one end of this country"*: p. 23. *"We refused to assume"*: p. 36. *"As children of this peculiar enlightened class"*: p. 27. *One former radical:* p. 25. *"pushcart vendors"*: p. 31.

75 *"The member of the upper class"*: Margaret Mead, *And Keep Your Powder Dry!* (New York: Morrow, 1942, 1965), p. 54.

76 *"There is less energy"*: Kenneth Keniston, *Youth and Dissent: The Rise of a New Opposition* (New York: Harcourt Brace Jovanovich, 1971), p. 113.

77 *"There is much in the professor-student relationship"*: Seymour Martin Lipset and Gerald M. Schaflander, *Passion and Politics: Student Activism in America* (Boston: Little, Brown, 1971), p. 34.

77 *"Schools exploit you"*: Jerry Farber, *The Student as Nigger* (New York: Pocket Books, 1969, 1971), p. 28.

77 *"The idea that there is a measure of inequality"*: Shils, *Dreams of Plenitude,* p. 18.

78 *If students and professors were to be "coequal"*: Robert Brustein, "The Case for Professionalism," in Immanuel Wallerstein and Paul Starr, eds., *The University Crisis Reader,* vol. 1, *The Liberal University Under Attack* (New York: Vintage Books, 1971), p. 546.

78 *The period in which the professions arose:* see Robert H. Wiebe, *The Search for Order, 1877–1920* (New York: Hill and Wang, 1967); and, more recently, John H. Ehrenreich, *The Altruistic Imgination: A History of Social Work and Social Policy in the United States* (Ithaca, N.Y.: Cornell University Press, 1987), chapter 2.

78 *"the 'art of rising in life' "*: Samuel Haber, "The Professions and Higher Education in America: A Historical View," in Margaret S. Gordon, ed., *Higher Education and the Labor Market* (New York: McGraw-Hill, 1974), p. 241.

79 *"We are lucky"*: William Osler, quoted in Barbara Ehrenreich and Deirdre English, *For Her Own Good: 150 Years of the Experts' Advice to Women* (New York: Doubleday/Anchor, 1978), p. 89.

80 *"My very simple point"*: Robert Brustein, replying to Eric Bentley, in "Case for Professionalism," p. 557.

82 *"There is no blinking the fact"*: Brustein, "Case for Professionalism," p. 552.

83 *"contagious, highly diffuse anxiety"*: David Riesman, with Nathan Glazer and Reuel Denney, *The Lonely Crowd: A Study of the Changing American Character* (New Haven: Yale University Press, 1961), p. 48. *"For in their uneasiness"*: p. 51. See also Urie Bronfenbrenner, "Socialization and Social Class Through Time and Space," in Paul Bromberg, ed., *The Impact of Social Class* (New York: Crowell, 1972), pp. 381–409.

85 *"subjected earlier"*: Francis E. Merrill and H. Wentworth Eldredge, *Society and Culture: An Introduction to Sociology* (New York: Prentice Hall, 1952, 1958), p. 313.

85 *"The result is the producing"*: Albert K. Cohen, quoted in James H. S. Bossard

and Eleanor Stoker Boll, *The Sociology of Child Development* (New York: Harper and Row, 1948, 1966), p. 243.

85 *"Eating a thing because it tastes good"*: Winfield S. Hall, Ph.D., M.D., "The Nutrition of Children Under Seven Years," in *The Child in the City*, papers presented at the conference held during the Chicago Child Welfare Exhibit, 1911, published by the Chicago School of Civics and Philanthropy, 1912, p. 85.

85 *"never cries"*: John B. Watson, *Psychological Care of Infant and Child* (New York: Norton, 1928), pp. 9–10. *"Never hug and kiss"*: pp. 81–82.

86 *"strong and dangerous impulses"*: Martha Wolfenstein, "Fun Morality: An Analysis of Recent American Child-Training Literature," in Margaret Mead and Martha Wolfenstein, eds., *Childhood in Contemporary Cultures* (Chicago: University of Chicago Press, 1955, 1960), pp. 168–77.

86 *One widely cited study*: Allison Davis and R. J. Havighurst, quoted in Urie Bronfenbrenner, "Socialization and Social Class Through Time and Space," in Paul Blumberg, ed., *The Impact of Social Class* (New York: Crowell, 1972), pp. 381–409.

87 *Lower-class women could no longer be trusted*: Ehrenreich and English, *For Her Own Good*, chapters 5 and 6.

87 *"Play and singing"*: Quoted in Wolfenstein, "Fun Morality," p. 172.

87 *Which class was doing what*: Bronfenbrenner, "Socialization and Social Class," p. 381.

87–88 *The middle class had actually surpassed*: Bronfenbrenner, "Socialization and Social Class."

88 *"We may think"*: David M. Potter, *People of Plenty: Economic Abundance and the American Character* (Chicago: Phoenix Books, 1954), p. 204.

89 *As* Infant Care *told mothers*: Quoted in Wolfenstein, "Fun Morality," p. 176.

89 *Most experts were renouncing "overpermissiveness"*: Ethel Kawin, *Parenthood in a Free Nation*, vol. 1, *Basic Concepts for Parents* (New York: Macmillan, 1967, 1954), p. 14.

89 *"At his mercy"*: Quoted in Wolfenstein, "Fun Morality,"p. 177.

89 *"seems to be* much *commoner"*: Benjamin Spock, quoted in Ehrenreich and English, *For Her Own Good*, p. 254.

89 *"the . . . techniques"*: Bronfenbrenner, "Socialization and Social Class," p. 409.

90 *" 'Permissiveness' "*: Philip Slater, *The Pursuit of Loneliness: American Culture at the Breaking Point* (Boston: Beacon Press, 1970), p. 57.

92 *"By the mid-fifties"*: J. Ronald Oakley, *God's Country: America in the Fifties* (New York: Dembner Books, 1986), pp. 267–90.

93 *"the perverse appeal"*: Richard Rovere, quoted in William E. Leuchtenberg, *The Troubled Feast: American Society Since 1945* (Boston: Little, Brown, 1973), pp. 32–33.

94 *It was the music of the movement*: See Gitlin, *The Sixties*, chapter 2.

## THREE: THE DISCOVERY OF THE WORKING CLASS

97 *"huge, crude astonishment"*: Nora Sayre, *Sixties Going on Seventies* (New York: Arbor House, 1973), p. 311.

98 *"Most of us"*: Joseph Kraft, quoted in Godfrey Hodgson, *America in Our Time: From World War II to Nixon* (Garden City, N.Y.: Doubleday, 1976), p. 375.

98 *Vowed never to be "out-niggered"*: Seymour Martin Lipset and Earl Raab, *The Politics of Unreason: Right-Wing Extremism in America, 1790–1970* (New York: Harper and Row, 1970), p. 342.

99 *"the news profession"*: Chet Huntley, quoted in Hodgson, *America in Our Time*, p. 372.

99 *"I was stunned"*: Shad Northshield, quoted in Edith Efron, "The 'Silent Majority' Comes into Focus," *TV Guide*, September 27, 1969, p. 6.

100 *"The blue- and white-collar people"*: Fred Freed, quoted in Efron, " 'Silent Majority.' "

100 *"The liberal academic"*: Robert Wood, quoted in Richard Lemon, *The Troubled American* (New York: Simon and Schuster, 1969), p. 139.

100 *"fear [that] haunts all elites"*: Hodgson, *America in Our Time*, p. 382.

101 *The Ford Foundation*: Donald I. Warren, *The Radical Center: Middle Americans and the Politics of Alienation* (Notre Dame, Ind.: University of Notre Dame Press, 1976), p. xx.

102 *"Now the pendulum of public attention"*: "The Troubled American," *Newsweek*, October 6, 1969, p. 29.

102 *The "Middle Americans" were " 'discovered' "*: "Man and Woman of the Year: The Middle Americans," *Time*, January 5, 1970, p. 10.

102 *"The common man"*: "Revolt of the Middle Class," *U.S. News and World Report*, November 24, 1969, p. 52.

102 *28 percent of the people polled*: Lemon, *Troubled American*, pp. 238–39.

104 *The disgruntlement of Middle America*: "Troubled American," *Newsweek*, p. 46.

104–5 *It was an "investment advisor"*: Lemon, *Troubled American*, p. 33.

105 *The* Nation *observed*: "Spiro and 'Middle America,' " *Nation*, November 10, 1969, p. 492.

105 *Other critics from the left*: Lewis Chester, Godfrey Hodgson, and Bruce Page, *The American Melodrama: The Presidential Campaign of 1968* (New York: Viking Press, 1969), p. 164.

106 *"Paint your face black"*: *Newsweek*, "Troubled American," p. 52.

106–7 *Affluent "liberals"*: "Revolt of the Middle Class," p. 53.

107 *One of the injured*: Homer Bigart, "War Foes Attacked by Construction Workers," *New York Times*, May 9, 1970.

107 *"Stereotypical Image"*: Joseph Bensman and Bernard Rosenberg, *An Introduction to Sociology: Mass, Class, and Bureaucracy* (New York: Praeger, 1976), p. 177.

108 *Poor black women*: Daniel Patrick Moynihan, *The Negro Family: The Case for National Action* (Washington, D.C.: U.S. Department of Labor, Office of Family Planning and Research, 1965).

108 *Working-class women*: See, for example, William Simon and John Gagnon, "Working-Class Youth: Alienation Without an Image," in Louise Kapp Howe, *The White Majority: Between Poverty and Affluence* (New York: Vintage Books, 1970), pp. 45–59.

110 *"Acceptance of the norms"*: Seymour Martin Lipset, "Working-Class Authoritarianism," in *Political Man: The Social Bases of Politics* (Baltimore, Md.: Johns Hopkins University Press, 1959, 1981), p. 114.

110 *At least some sociologists rejected*: See S. M. Miller and Frank Riessman, "Working-Class Authoritarianism, A Critique of Lipset," *British Journal of Sociology*, September 1961, p. 272.

110 *Nazism was not a movement of the "masses"*: Richard F. Hamilton, *Who Voted for Hitler?* (Princeton, N.J.: Princeton University Press, 1982).

110 *no significant or consistent evidence*: Richard F. Hamilton, *Class and Politics in the United States* (New York: Wiley, 1972), pp. 399–506.

110–12 *"deep-rooted hostilities"*: Lipset, "Working-Class Authoritarianism," p. 114. *"limit the source of information"*: Quoted on p. 114. *"The fact that the movement's ideology"*: p. 123. *"isolationist sentiments"*: p. 481.

112 *"More ethnocentric"*: Leonard Broom and Philip Selznick, *Sociology: A Text with Adapted Readings* (New York: Harper and Row, 1977), p. 173.

112 *"reluctant to meet new people"*: Albert K. Cohen and Harold M. Hodges, quoted in Harold M. Hodges, Jr., *Conflict and Consensus: An Introduction to Sociology* (New York: Harper and Row, 1971), p. 244.

112 *"appears reluctant to accept new ideas":* Paul B. Horton and Chester L. Hunt, *Sociology* (New York: McGraw-Hill, 1976), p. 254.

113 *"He usually has little ability":* Arnold W. Green, *Sociology: An Analysis of Life in Modern Society* (New York: McGraw-Hill, 1972), p. 183.

114 *"It seems likely that such perceptual distortion":* Hamilton, *Class and Politics in the United States,* pp. 456–57.

118 *"an exploited and degraded proletariat":* Robin Wood, *Hollywood: From Vietnam to Reagan* (New York: Columbia University Press, 1986), p. 91.

120 *"embodiment of the out-of-fashion pure-at-heart":* Pauline Kael, *When the Lights Go Down* (New York: Holt, Rinehart, and Winston, 1980), p. 214.

120 *the lowest stage of "consciousness":* Charles Reich, *The Greening of America* (New York: Random House, 1970), pp. 228–29.

122 *"Long hair":* Stanley Aronowitz, *False Promises: The Shaping of American Working-Class Consciousness* (New York: McGraw-Hill, 1973), p. 31.

122 *Workers . . . were staying home on Mondays:* See Aronowitz, *False Promises.*

123 *"As psychologists and social researchers have confirmed":* "The Blue-Collar Worker's Lowdown Blues," *Time,* November 9, 1970, p. 68.

123 *Blue-collar workers had been splitting their votes:* Kevin P. Phillips, *The Emerging Republican Majority* (New Rochelle, N.Y.: Arlington House, 1969), p. 30.

124 *"Fears that a Republican administration":* Phillips, *Emerging Republican Majority,* p. 464.

124 *"The 'elite' ":* Richard M. Scammon and Ben J. Wattenberg, *The Real Majority: An Extraordinary Examination of the American Electorate* (New York: Coward-McCann, 1970), pp. 62–63.

125 *wanted stricter laws on obscenity:* Scammon and Wattenberg, *Real Majority,* pp. 74–75. *increases in the number of Americans who "often feel bad":* p. 75.

125 *a willingness to vote for a black presidential candidate:* Hodgson, *America in Our Time,* p. 486.

125 *"Can a former truck driver":* Kenneth Lamott, " 'It Isn't a Mirage They're Seeing,' Says George Wallace," *New York Times Magazine,* September 22, 1968, p. 32.

125 *25 percent of the nation's union members:* Lipset and Raab, *Politics of Unreason,* p. 363.

125 *Some polls suggested:* See Lipset and Raab, *Politics of Unreason;* and Jody Carlson, *George Wallace and the Politics of Powerlessness: The Wallace Campaigns for the Presidency, 1964–1976* (New Brunswick, N.J.: Transaction Books, 1981), p. 265.

126 *"Even in our well-educated society":* Samuel A. Mueller, "Busing, School Prayer, and Wallace: Some Notes on Right-Wing Populism," *Christian Century,* April 19, 1972, p. 451.

126 *Only in the South:* Hamilton, *Class and Politics in the United States,* pp. 460–61.

126 *"there was no reliable Wallace backing":* Phillips, *Emerging Republican Majority,* p. 462.

126 *Polls showed that Wallace voters:* See Carlson, *George Wallace.*

126 *Among Wallace supporters:* Hamilton, *Class and Politics in the United States,* pp. 462–63. *"downright pink":* p. 72.

127 *"True conservativism":* Quoted in Lipset and Raab, *Politics of Unreason,* p. 348. *"He is talking about poor people":* Quoted on p. 349. *Pollster Sam Lubell:* Quoted on p. 364.

127 *"I don't believe there is a backlash":* George C. Wallace, *Hear Me Out* (Anderson, S.C.: Drake House, 1968), p. 11.

128 *"The over-educated ivory-tower folks":* Quoted in Lipset and Raab, *Politics of Unreason,* p. 350.

128 *"The liberals, intellectuals, and long-hairs":* George Wallace, quoted in Wil-

liam E. Leuchtenberg, *The Troubled Feast: American Society Since 1945* (Boston: Little, Brown, 1973), p. 211.

128 *"Intellectual morons":* Wallace, *Hear Me Out*, p. 78.

128 *along with their briefcases:* Leuchtenberg, *Troubled Feast*, p. 211.

128 *survey of blue-collar Wallace supporters in Gary:* Thomas F. Pettigrew, Robert T. Riley, and Reeve D. Vanneman, "George Wallace's Constituents," *Psychology Today*, February 1972, p. 47.

128 *Spiro Agnew:* Quoted in Jules Witcover, *White Knight: The Rise of Spiro Agnew* (New York: Random House, 1972), p. 305.

129 *real earnings were declining:* Richard Parker, "Those Blue-Collar Worker Blues," *New Republic*, September 23, 1972, p. 16.

129 *Not middle-class suburban liberals:* The definitive book on the mix of class and racial antagonisms arising from court-ordered school integration is surely J. Anthony Lukas's *Common Ground: A Turbulent Decade in the Lives of Three American Families* (New York: Knopf, 1985).

130 *The highest levels of intolerance:* Hamilton, *Class and Politics in the United States*, pp. 415–16.

130 *a schoolteacher from a blue-collar family:* Quoted in Robert Coles, *The Middle Americans: Proud and Uncertain* (Boston: Little, Brown/Atlantic Monthly Press, 1971), p. 12.

130–31 *"Their mothers are too busy":* Quoted in "Troubled American," *Newsweek*.

131 *A 43-year-old steamfitter:* Quoted in Coles, *Middle Americans*, p. 6.

131 *54 percent of college graduates agreed:* "Troubled American," *Newsweek*, p. 35.

131 *"Campus* sans-culottes": Leuchtenberg, *Troubled Feast*, p. 199.

132 *"fatiguing and monotonous":* John Kenneth Galbraith, *The Affluent Society* (Boston: Houghton Mifflin, 1958), p. 341.

133 *"In the experience of most people":* John Lippert, "Fleetwood Wildcat," *Radical America*, vol. 11, no. 5, September/October 1977, p. 7.

133 *In strike after strike:* This summary is from John Ehrenreich's discussion of the rise of the professional-managerial class in *The Altruistic Imagination: A History of Social Work and Social Policy in the United States* (Ithaca, N.Y.: Cornell University Press, 1985), p. 25.

133 *"the site of two of the most violent labor conflicts":* Reeve Vanneman and Lynn Weber Cannon, *The American Perception of Class* (Philadelphia: Temple University Press, 1987), p. 27.

134 *They could be "Americanized":* See Stuart Ewen, *Captains of Consciousness: Advertising and the Social Roots of the Consumer Culture* (New York: McGraw-Hill, 1977).

134 *Almost every profession:* Barbara Ehrenreich and Deirdre English, *For Her Own Good: 150 Years of the Experts' Advice to Women* (Garden City, N.Y.: Anchor/Doubleday, 1979), chapter 3.

134 *New class of professional experts:* Robert H. Wiebe, *The Search for Order, 1877–1920* (New York: Hill and Wang, 1967), chapter 5.

134 *"administrators, legislators":* Fredrick Jackson Turner, quoted in Richard Hofstadter, *Anti-Intellectualism in American Life* (New York: Knopf, 1963), p. 200.

135 *"turn over the defense of society":* Edward A. Ross, quoted in Otis L. Graham, *The Great Campaigns* (New York: Prentice Hall, 1971), p. 237.

135 *The profession of management was born:* See Harry Braverman, *Labor and Monopoly Capital* (New York: Monthly Review Press, 1975); and, for richer historical detail, David Montgomery, *The Fall of the House of Labor* (Cambridge: Cambridge University Press, 1987).

135 *"The shop was really run by the workmen":* Frederick Winslow Taylor, quoted in Montgomery, *Fall of the House of Labor*, p. 189.

136 *Social workers and teachers:* See John Ehrenreich, *Altruistic Imagination*,

chapter 2; Ehrenreich and English, *For Her Own Good*, chapter 5; Samuel Bowles and Herbert Gintis, *Schooling in Capitalist America* (New York: Basic Books, 1975).

136 *This was a dubious "reform"*: Ehrenreich and English, *For Her Own Good*, chapter 3; Frances E. Kobrin, "The American Midwife Controversy: A Crisis of Professionalization," *Bulletin of the History of Medicine*, July–August 1966, p. 350.

136 *Public-health officials:* Barbara Ehrenreich and Deirdre English, *Complaints and Disorders: The Sexual Politics of Sickness* (New York: Feminist Press, 1973).

137 *Chemical workers:* Quoted in David Halle, *America's Working Man: Work, Home, and Politics Among Blue-Collar Property Owners* (Chicago: University of Chicago Press, 1984), pp. 206–7.

138 *"Trust was finally established":* Richard Sennett and Jonathan Cobb, *The Hidden Injuries of Class* (New York: Vintage Books, 1972), p. 38.

138 *Mike Lefevre:* Quoted in Studs Terkel, *Working* (New York: Pantheon Books, 1972, 1974), p. xxxiii.

138 *a forty-one-year-old garment worker and a young steelworker:* Quoted in Sandy Carter, "Class Conflict: The Human Dimension," in Pat Walker, ed., *Between Labor and Capital: The Professional Managerial Class* (Boston: South End Press, 1979), p. 112.

139 *vastly different notions:* Hope Jenson Leichter and William E. Mitchell, *Kinship and Casework* (New York: Russell Sage Foundation, 1967).

139 *working-class respondents felt:* Sennett and Cobb, *Hidden Injuries*, p. 38.

139–140 *a forty-six-year-old mother of three:* Quoted in Carter, "Class Conflict," p. 112.

140 *"Often fails to realize":* Francis E. Merrill and H. Wentworth Eldridge, *Society and Culture: An Introduction to Sociology* (New York: Prentice Hall, 1957), p. 318.

140 *"In the land of the media":* Quoted in "The Blue-Collar Worker's Low-Down Blues," *Time*, November 9, 1970, p. 68.

141 *A report: Work in America: Report of a Special Task Force to the Secretary of Health, Education, and Welfare* (Cambridge: MIT Press, no date), pp. 34–35.

141–42 *A fireman's wife:* Quoted in Coles, *Middle Americans*, p. 134. *a gas station owner's wife:* Quoted on p. 103. John, a Polish-American machinist: Quoted on p. 45.

## FOUR: THE "NEW CLASS": A BLUDGEON FOR THE RIGHT

144 *"It's the ultimate triumph:* Kevin Phillips, quoted in "Poppy the Populist," *Newsweek*, November 7, 1988, p. 58.

146 *Introducing these "neoconservatives":* Quoted in Peter Steinfels, *The Neoconservatives* (New York: Simon and Schuster, 1979), p. 4.

147 *an entirely new . . . social class:* Actually, the idea that there might be a third class, of bureaucrats and "mental workers," had been around a long time, even longer—among certain prescient anarchists—than the Soviet Union itself. David Bazelon, who wrote what is undoubtedly the best American book on the subject in 1967, later described the tangled lineage of the New Class idea before it fell into the hands of New York Trotskyist leader Max Schachtman in the 1940s:

> He [Schachtman] took some of this from Bruno Rizzi after refracting it through Trotsky's *The Revolution Betrayed*, who probably borrowed a piece here and there from Max Nomad, who of course inherited it all from Jan Waclaw Machajski [a Polish Bolshevik], who may

very well have lifted some from Louis Boudin, after that one came across it in Michael Bakunin. I think somebody also stole something from Robert Michels, but who knows. Daniel Bell has traced the original ownership of this Maltese Falcon back to Henri, Comte de Sainte-Simon. [David Bazelon, "How Now 'The New Class'?" *Dissent*, Fall 1979, p. 443.]

148 *"For a long time":* Milovan Djilas, *The New Class: An Analysis of the Communist System* (New York: Praeger, 1957), p. 47.

149 *"The New Class covers":* Michael Novak, "Needing Niebuhr Again," *Commentary*, September 1972, p. 60.

149 *"the new intelligentsia":* Seymour Martin Lipset and Herman Kahn, contributions to "America Now: A Failure of Nerve," *Commentary*, July 1975, pp. 49–58.

150 *"Repelled by the sight":* Norman Podhoretz, "The Adversary Culture," in B. Bruce-Briggs, ed., *The New Class?* (New Brunswick, N.J.: Transaction Books, 1979), pp. 19–31.

150 *"Scientists, teachers":* Irving Kristol, *Two Cheers for Capitalism* (New York: Basic Books, 1978), p. 27. *"In any naked contest":* p. 145.

151 *"represented itself":* Norman Podhoretz, *Breaking Ranks* (New York: Harper and Row, 1979), p. 288.

151 *a very different kind of group:* By including only those occupations deemed to be liberal, the neoconservatives eliminated the majority of the professional middle class, or "new class," as defined by David Bazelon, Alvin Gouldner, and others. The most generous estimate of the "liberal" wing of the professional middle class would include all public-sector employees, all private non-profit–sector employees (many of them employed in by-no-means liberal religious organizations), all teachers at all levels, and all media and entertainment workers. Using 1980 census figures, Phil Steinberg found that this generous estimate still accounts for only 44 percent of the professional and managerial workers who can be reasonably counted as "new class" members. A more cautious estimate would eliminate from the "liberal" wing all teachers below the college level—a group which the neoconservatives did not regard as a liberal threat anyway. With the schoolteachers out of the way, the "liberal" element accounts for only 27 percent of the new class. See Barbara Ehrenreich and John Ehrenreich, "The Professional-Managerial Class," in Pat Walker, ed., *Between Labor and Capital* (Boston: South End Press, 1979); Alvin Gouldner, *The Future of Intellectuals and the Rise of the New Class* (New York: Seabury/Continuum, 1979); and David Bazelon, *Power in America* (New York: New American Library, 1967).

152 *"The group is . . . best labeled":* Charles Murray, *Losing Ground: American Social Policy, 1950–1980* (New York: Basic Books, 1984), p. 42.

153 *"aura of massiveness":* Peter Steinfels, *The Neoconservatives* (New York: Simon and Schuster, 1979), p. 57.

153 *"The New Class was using":* Podhoretz, *Breaking Ranks*, pp. 288–89.

155 *"the professionalization of reform":* Daniel Patrick Moynihan, "The Professionalization of Reform," in Marvin E. Gettleman and David Mermelstein, eds., *The Great Society Reader* (New York: Random House, 1967), pp. 459–75.

155 *"a new strategy":* David Bazelon, interview, December 31, 1986.

156 *Even the concept of "scientific management":* See Ehrenreich and Ehrenreich, "Professional-Managerial Class," pp. 22–23; and Gouldner, *Future of Intellectuals*, pp. 16–17.

157 *"A more positive step":* Irving Kristol, *Two Cheers*, p. 145. Originally published as "On Corporate Philanthropy," *Wall Street Journal*, March 21, 1977.

158 *"Intellectual attacks":* Bruce-Briggs, *New Class?*, p. 207. *"What a quintessential New Class activity!"* and *"He sees politics":* Quoted on p. 207.

159 *"above all, the political voice":* William E. Simon, *A Time for Truth* (New York: Reader's Digest Press, 1978), p. 195.

159 *"concept of the New Class":* Robert L. Bartley, "Business and the New Class," in B. Bruce-Briggs, *New Class?*, pp. 57–66.

160 *Moynihan and Nixon:* Quoted in Alonzo L. Hamby, *Liberalism and Its Challengers: FDR to Reagan* (New York: Oxford University Press, 1985), p. 326.

162 *Angry constituencies of Middle Americans:* See Robert J. Hoy, "Lid on a Boiling Pot," in Robert W. Whitaker, ed., *The New Right Papers* (New York: St. Martin's Press, 1982), pp. 84–103.

163 *"We talk about issues":* Richard Viguerie, quoted in Connie Paige, *The Right-to-Lifers: Who They Are, How They Operate, Where They Get Their Money* (New York: Summit Books, 1983), p. 135.

163 *the Illuminati:* Quoted in Seymour Martin Lipset and Earl Raab, *The Politics of Unreason: Right-Wing Extremism in America, 1790–1970* (New York: Harper and Row, 1970), p. 258.

164 *even President Eisenhower:* Quoted by John B. Judis, *William F. Buckley: Patron Saint of the Conservatives* (New York: Simon and Schuster, 1988), p.193.

164 *secret system:* Sydney Blumenthal, *The Rise of the Counter-Establishment: From Conservative Ideology to Political Power* (New York: Times Books, 1986), pp. 6–7.

164–65 *Slowly but surely:* Kevin P. Phillips, *Post-Conservative America: People, Politics, and Ideology in a Time of Crisis* (New York: Random House, 1982), p. 34.

165–66 *A wealthy, Yale-educated attorney:* Alan Crawford, *Thunder on the Right: The "New Right" and the Politics of Resentment* (New York: Pantheon Books, 1980), p. 186.

166 *The existence of the "working poor":* Michael Harrington, *Who Are the Poor?* (New York: Democratic Socialists of America, 1987), p. 3.

166 *"The great central fact that looms":* William A. Rusher, "The New Elite Must Be Curbed," *Conservative Digest*, September 1975, p. 26.

166 *The goal of the New Class:* William A. Rusher, *The Making of the New Majority Party* (New York: Sheed and Ward, 1975), pp. 98–100.

166–67 *"Mr. Rusher is right":* William Murchison, "Bury the Hatchet," *Conservative Digest*, October 1975, pp. 10–11.

167 *"The producers of America":* Rusher, "The New Elite," p. 26.

168 *"an Establishment culture":* George Gilder, quoted in Jack Kemp, "Wide Support for the Populist Revolution," *Conservative Digest*, October 1982, pp. 8–9.

168 *"If there ever was a time":* Jerry Falwell, *Strength for the Journey* (New York: Simon and Schuster, 1987), p. 362.

168 *"Hedonism is the spirit of the age":* Patrick J. Buchanan, "Liberalism's Anti-Catholic Bias," *Conservative Digest*, July 1978, p. 43.

169 *"judicial permissiveness":* Phillips, *Post-Conservative America*, p. 22. *"permissiveness, homosexuality":* p. 23. *in education:* p. 159. *in mainstream churches:* p. 182. *"permissivism of various . . . hues":* p. 31. *Will and Ariel Durant:* p. 86.

169 *Washington:* John Chamberlain, "We Did Not Begin as a Permissive Society," *Conservative Digest*, July 1975, p. 32.

170 *specifically sexual connotations:* R. W. Burchfield, *A Supplement to the Oxford English Dictionary*, vol. 3 (Oxford: Clarendon Press, 1982), pp. 388–89. Uses of "permissiveness" in a sexual context can be found in the early sixties; see, for example, John D'Emilio and Estelle B. Freedman, *Intimate Matters: A History of Sexuality in America* (New York: Harper and Row, 1988), p. 264. But the word gains sexual overtones more generally only in the late sixties.

170 *"The permissiveness that currently pervades":* See, for example, "Advertising's Creative Explosion," *Newsweek*, August 18, 1969, p. 66.

170 *"hate, depravity":* Theodore H. White, *The Making of the President, 1968* (New York: Atheneum Books, 1969), p. 228.

170 *Agnew quoted Walter Laqueur:* Spiro T. Agnew, *Frankly Speaking: A Collec-*

*tion of Extraordinary Speeches* (Washington, D.C.: Public Affairs Press, 1970), p. 83.

170 *"The total permissive atmosphere":* Quoted in Jules Witcover, *White Knight: The Rise of Spiro Agnew* (New York: Random House, 1972), p. 265.

171 *"the lifestyles of Easterners":* Crawford, *Thunder on the Right,* p. 171.

171–72 Kevin P. Phillips, *Mediacracy: American Parties and Politics in the Communications Age* (Garden City, N.Y.: Doubleday, 1975), p. 34.

172–73 *the New Right's insights:* Samuel T. Francis, "The Message from MARS: The Social Politics of the New Right," in Whitaker, *New Right Papers,* p. 66. *"These lifestyles, values, and ideals":* p. 81.

174 *Became more "adult":* "The Shock of Freedom in Films," *Time,* December 8, 1967, p. 66.

174 *A "war on smut":* See William L. O'Neill, *Coming Apart: An Informal History of America in the 1960's* (Chicago: Quadrangle Books, 1971), pp. 202–77.

174 *Unlike the "marriage manuals":* See Barbara Ehrenreich, Elizabeth Hess, and Gloria Jacobs, *Re-Making Love: The Feminization of Sex* (Garden City, N.Y.: Doubleday, 1986), chapter 3.

175 *"Modern capitalism":* Daniel Bell, "The New Class: A Muddled Concept," in Bruce-Briggs, *New Class?,* p. 189.

175 *"The ads":* Stephen Fox, *The Mirror Makers: A History of American Advertising and Its Creators* (New York: Morrow, 1984), p. 264.

175 *Mary Wells:* Fox, *Mirror Makers,* p. 268.

176 *a Connecticut commuter:* "Advertising's Creative Explosion," *Newsweek,* August 18, 1969, p. 62.

176–77 *"a new sex life":* Fox, *Mirror Makers,* p. 271.

177 *the Websters indulge:* Walt Harrington, "What's Wrong with America?" *Washington Post Magazine,* July 26, 1987, p. 10.

178 *a residue of "disappointment":* Albert O. Hirschman, *Shifting Involvements: Private Interest and Public Action* (Princeton, N.J.: Princeton University Press, 1982).

178–79 *the number of Americans living alone* and *George Drapeau III:* "19 Million Singles," *U.S. News and World Report,* February 21, 1983, p. 53.

179 *"We're bullish":* Michael Singer, "Living Alone: The Urban Lifestyle of the 80s," Pacific News Service, 1979.

179 *Those goods and services included:* "19 Million Singles," p. 53.

179 *"What will this trend mean":* E. B. Weiss, "Flight from the Private Home Is New Pattern in U.S. Living," *Advertising Age,* July 28, 1969, p. 50.

179 *Investing in houses:* "Rise in Never-Marrieds Affects Social Customs and Buying Patterns," *Wall Street Journal,* May 28, 1986.

180 *ad for* Psychology Today: *New York Times,* October 24, 1975.

181 *"suburban pastoralism":* Allen Hunter, "The Role of Liberal Political Culture in the Construction of Middle America," *University of Miami Law Review,* vol. 42, no. 1, September 1987, p. 93.

181 *"A number of the Thomas Road Church members":* Frances FitzGerald, *Cities on a Hill: Journeys Through Contemporary American Cultures* (New York: Simon and Schuster, 1986), p. 135.

181–82 *"Purchasing for the home":* Elaine Tyler May, *Homeward Bound: American Families in the Cold War Era* (New York: Basic Books, 1988), p. 162.

183 *Welfare was a flagrant example:* See, for example, Lawrence Mead, *Beyond Entitlements* (New York: Free Press, 1986).

183 *Even Barry Goldwater:* Crawford, *Thunder on the Right,* p. 116.

183–84 *New Right ideologue:* George Gilder, *Wealth and Poverty* (New York: Basic Books, 1981), p. 101.

184 *"intelligentsia":* Charles Murray, *Losing Ground: American Social Policy, 1950–1980* (New Yorker: Basic Books, 1984), pp. 42–44.

*184 "Mario Cuomo's incessant invocations":* "Buchanan Labels Cuomo a 'Reactionary Liberal,'" *New York Times,* June 16, 1985.

*184 War on Poverty:* R. Emmett Tyrrell, Jr., *The Liberal Crack-Up* (New York: Simon and Schuster, 1984), p. 49.

*184 "Sometimes the government":* Tyrrell, *Liberal Crack-Up,* p. 227.

*185 National Review editorial:* Quoted in Rusher, *Making of the New Majority Party,* p. 322.

*185 "resignation and rage":* Gilder, *Wealth and Poverty,* p. 115.

*185 "fragile assumption . . . that adults are responsible":* Murray, *Losing Ground,* p. 45.

*186 largely deceptive:* Robert Greenstein, "Losing Faith in Losing Ground," *New Republic,* March 25, 1985, pp. 12–17.

*186 "Divorce, alcoholism, drug abuse":* Tyrrell, *Liberal Crack-Up,* p. 51.

*186 a report from the Reagan administration:* "U.S. Report Asserts Administration Halted Liberal 'Anti-Family Agenda,'" *New York Times,* November 14, 1986.

*187 the real value of AFDC benefits was declining:* Greenstein, "Losing Faith."

*187 There was no state:* Barbara Ehrenreich and Frances Fox Piven, "Women and the Welfare State," in Irving Howe, ed., *Alternatives: Proposals for America from the Democratic Left* (New York: Pantheon Books, 1984), pp. 41–60.

*187 A highly respected 1986 study:* David T. Ellwood and Mary Jo Bane, "The Impact of AFDC on Family Structure and Living Arrangements," *Research in Labor Economics,* vol. 7, 1986, pp. 137–207.

*187 Nor have any studies found:* Frances Fox Piven and Richard A. Cloward, "Sources of the Contemporary Relief Debate," in *The Mean Season: The Attack on the Welfare State,* Fred Block, Richard A. Cloward, Barbara Ehrenreich, and Frances Fox Piven (New York: Pantheon Books, 1987), pp. 45–108.

*187 A recent government study:* "Welfare Reform: Projected Effects of Requiring AFDC for Unemployed Parents Nationwide," General Accounting Office, March 22, 1987.

*187–88 Most European capitalist nations:* Robert Kuttner, *The Economic Illusion: False Choices Between Prosperity and Social Justice* (Boston: Houghton Mifflin, 1984), p. 246.

*188 yet have lower rates:* For comparative crime rates, see Elliott Currie, *Confronting Crime: An American Challenge* (New York: Pantheon Books, 1985). On teenage pregnancy, see Lena Williams, "Teen-Age Sex: New Codes Amid the Old Anxiety," *New York Times,* February 27, 1989. While there is no reliable comparative information on drug abuse, the United States certainly leads the West in drug-related crime.

*188 "wild Irish slums":* Daniel Patrick Moynihan, quoted in Frances Fox Piven and Richard A. Cloward, "Sources of the Contemporary Relief Debate," p. 76.

*188 "The welfare state":* Tyrrell, *Liberal Crack-Up,* p. 36.

*189 less than 15 percent of the total budget:* Military Domestic Education Project, *From the Poor to the Pentagon* (Washington, D.C.: Center on Budget and Policy Priorities and the Defense Budget Project, 1983), p. 51.

*189 the administration even inflated the deficit:* David A. Stockman, *The Triumph of Politics: Why the Reagan Revolution Failed* (New York: Harper and Row, 1986). See also Daniel Patrick Moynihan, "Reagan's Inflate-the-Deficit Game," *New York Times,* July 21, 1985.

*189* Murray, *Losing Ground,* pp. 227–28.

*189* Seymour Martin Lipset, "The Elections, the Economy, and Public Opinion, 1984," *PS: The Journal of the American Political Science Association,* vol. 18, no. 1, pp. 28–38.

*189 Even the most stigmatized programs:* Vicente Navarro, "The 1984 Election and the New Deal: An Alternative Interpretation," *Social Policy,* vol. 15, no. 4, 1985, pp. 3–10.

190 *The immediate, net effect of Reaganomics* and *only 60 percent of the money required:* "Poverty: Toll Grows Amid Cutbacks," *Los Angeles Times,* July 31, 1985.

190 *As Frances Fox Piven and Richard Cloward have shown:* Frances Fox Piven and Richard A. Cloward, *The New Class War* (New York: Pantheon Books, 1982).

191 *"Democrats will be as reflexive":* Morton Kondracke, "A Doubtful New Order," *New Republic,* November 15, 1980, pp. 11–13.

191 *"The most striking aspect":* Randall Rothenberg, *The Neoliberals: Creating the New American Politics* (New York: Simon and Schuster, 1984), p. 17.

192 *"historic, bipartisan breakthrough":* Robert Kuttner, "The Welfare Strait," *New Republic,* July 6, 1987, pp. 20–25.

192 *Describing the "repackag[ed]," "post-industrial" liberal:* Dennis Farney and Jeffrey H. Birnbaum, "Democrats Repackage Liberalism," *Wall Street Journal,* April 25, 1988.

192 *"The last official count":* Russell Baker, "Some Liberal Thinking," *New York Times Magazine,* January 12, 1986, p. 14.

192 *A 1985* New York Times/CBS News *Poll:* "A Liberal by Any Other Name May Get More Votes," *New York Times,* November 24, 1985.

193 *Ronald Reagan:* Sar Levitan, quoted in "A Defender of the Welfare System," *New York Times,* July 31, 1985.

193 *"dilemma of liberalism":* Fred Siegel, "Populism, Persuasion, and Accountability," *Present Tense,* Winter 1986, pp. 28–33.

194 *Charles Murray, for example, was nurtured:* Chuck Lane, "The Manhattan Project," *New Republic,* March 25, 1985, pp. 14–15.

195 *"The ideological spoilsmen":* Sidney Blumenthal, *The Rise of the Counter-Establishment: From Conservative Ideology to Political Power,* (New York: Times Books, 1986), p. 7.

## FIVE: THE YUPPIE STRATEGY

196 *"Yuppie is now understood":* Hendrik Hertzberg, "The Short Happy Life of the American Yuppie," *Esquire,* February 1988, p. 100.

197 *the yuppie eagerness:* "The Year of the Yuppie," *Newsweek,* December 31, 1984, p. 14.

198 *Only about 5 percent of their generation:* "The Big Chill (Revisited), or, Whatever Happened to the Baby Boom?" *American Demographics,* vol. 7, September 1985, pp. 22–25.

199 *A commentator in the* New Republic: Alex Heard, "Yuppie Love," *New Republic,* January 28, 1985, p. 10.

201 *"categories" of Americans:* "Beatniks, Preppies, and Punkers: The Love Affair with Labels," *U.S. News and World Report,* September 16, 1985, p.63.

201 *Since then, in a sharp reversal:* See Bennett Harrison and Barry Bluestone, *The Great U-Turn: Corporate Restructuring and the Polarizing of America* (New York: Basic Books, 1988), p. 5. See also Stephen J. Rose, *Social Stratification in the U.S.* (Baltimore: Social Graphics, 1983).

202 *the top fifth of American families:* David Wessel, "U.S. Rich and Poor Increase in Numbers: Middle Loses Ground," *Wall Street Journal,* September 22, 1986, p. 1. See also Barbara Ehrenreich, "Is the Middle Class Doomed?" *New York Times Magazine,* September 7, 1986, p. 44.

202 Upward *redistribution of wealth:* Ehrenreich, "Is the Middle Class Doomed?" See also Isabel V. Sawhill and Charles F. Stone. *Economic Policy in the Reagan Years* (Washington, D.C.: Urban Institute, 1984).

203 *"They are people like Glen Whitbeck":* "American's Hidden Poor," *U.S. News and World Report,* January 11, 1988, p. 18.

*203 Top executives earned:* "Best-Paid Executive: $12.7M," *Newsday,* April 26, 1986, p. 9.

*204 "The kind of salary reported":* Daniel F. Cuff, "Those Well-Paid Executives," *New York Times,* May 2, 1984.

*204 a party thrown by Malcolm Forbes:* Patricia Leigh Brown, "By Air and Land, They Got to the Forbeses'," *New York Times,* May 30, 1987.

*205 A sharp deterioration in the prospects:* See Phillip Longman, "The Mortgaged Generation: Why the Young Can't Afford a House," *Washington Monthly,* April 1986, pp. 11–15.

*205 "a typical wage-earner":* Frank S. Levy and Richard C. Michel, "The Economic Future of the Baby Boom," report prepared for the Joint Economic Committee of the U.S. Congress, December 7, 1985.

*205 The big news:* The first article to make this point was Robert Kuttner's "The Declining Middle," *Atlantic Monthly,* July 1983, p. 60.

*205 The fraction of families with middle-range incomes:* Katherine L. Bradbury, "The Shrinking Middle Class," *New England Economic Review,* September/October 1986, p. 41.

*205n economist Stephen J. Rose:* Robert Pear, "Middle Class Shrinks as Poverty Engulfs More Families, Two Studies Show," *New York Times,* December 11, 1983. *Katherine L. Bradbury:* "The Shrinking Middle Class," p. 45. *Bureau of Labor Statistics:* "The Middle Class Moves Higher Up the Economic Ladder," *Newsday,* June 21, 1988.

*206 The blue-collar working class was skidding:* See "The Debate Is On: Does College Pay?" *USA Today,* November 29, 1984.

*206 The gap is almost as large:* Louis Uchitelle, "Making a Living Is Now a Family Enterprise," *New York Times,* October 11, 1987.

*206 "the deindustrialization of America":* Barry Bluestone and Bennett Harrison, *The Deindustrialization of America: Plant Closings, Community Abandonment, and the Dismantling of Basic Industry* (New York: Basic Books, 1982).

*207 Only 60 percent were able to find new jobs:* Kenneth B. Noble, "Millions Who Lost Plant Jobs Lose Pay in Shift to Services," *New York Times,* February 7, 1986.

*207 laid-off steelworkers in Chicago:* "Former Steelworkers' Income Falls by Half," *New York Times,* October 31, 1984.

*207 Throughout America's industrial "rust belt":* See David Bensman and Roberta Lynch, *Rusted Dreams* (New York: McGraw-Hill, 1987).

*207 Employers launched a fierce initiative:* See Harrison and Bluestone, *Great U-Turn,* p. 113.

*207–8 Two Queens factory workers:* Personal communication from Gary Stevenson, Director of Organizing, AFSCME, District Council 1707.

*209 In 1968, only 6 percent of new PhD's:* Richard B. Freeman, cited in Thomas A. Lyson and Gregory D. Squires, "Some Planned to Be Sociologists: The Changing Fortunes of New PhD's in Today's Academic Labor Market," paper presented at the 29th Annual Meeting of the Society for the Study of Social Problems, Boston, September 1979.

*209 "Gary Rodgers, 44, is a PhD":* "A Warning to Academia," *Boston Globe,* March 30, 1985.

*209 More . . . jobs for American managers:* This is true at least in the industries studied by Saskia Sassen-Koob in New York City. See *The Mobility of Labor and Capital* (New York: Cambridge University Press, 1988), pp. 150–52.

*209 "A new mood on campus":* Bernard Wysocki, "A Corporate Recruiter Searches the Campuses for 'The Right People,'" *Wall Street Journal,* March 27, 1979.

*210 The number of students receiving bachelors' degrees in English:* Gene I. Maeroff, "Shifting Away from the Liberal Arts," *New York Times,* March 26, 1985.

210 *The social sciences:* Andrew Hacker, "The Decline of Higher Learning," *New York Review of Books,* February 13, 1986, p. 35.

210 *An engineering graduate student:* "More Foreigners Are Seeking Ph.D.'s in the U.S.," *New York Times,* July 20, 1988.

210 *A young woman interviewed by* Newsweek: "The Year of the Yuppie," p. 19.

211 *A record 73 percent of students:* "More College Freshmen Plan to Teach," *New York Times,* January 12, 1987.

211 *Only 49 percent believed abortion:* "Students Are Taking Care of Business," *USA Today,* December 10, 1984.

211 *"posters of Miss Piggy":* Peter Carlson, "Getting High on Miss Piggy and Lee Iacocca," *Washington Post Magazine,* December 7, 1986, p. 36.

212–13 *Ad for* Psychology Today: *New York Times,* September 24, 1976.

213 *Most American men no longer earned enough:* Alvin L. Schorr, "Family Wage: Gone," *New York Times,* December 12, 1983.

214 *Objectivity, scientific rationality:* Barbara Ehrenreich and Deirdre English, *For Her Own Good: 150 Years of the Experts' Advice to Women* (Garden City, N.Y.: Anchor/Doubleday, 1978), chapter 3.

214–15 *The president of the American Medical Association:* Quoted in Richard Harrison Shryock, *Medicine in America: Historical Essays* (Baltimore: Johns Hopkins University Press, 1966), p. 185.

215 *Ellen Richards:* Robert Clarke, *Ellen Swallow: The Woman Who Founded Ecology* (Chicago: Follett, 1973).

215 *Feminists simultaneously demanded:* See Barbara Ehrenreich and Deirdre English, *Witches, Midwives, and Nurses: A History of Women Healers* (New York: Feminist Press, 1972) and *Complaints and Disorders: The Sexual Politics of Sickness* (New York: Feminist Press, 1973).

216 *In medicine, only 9 percent:* Perri Klass, "Are Women Better Doctors?" *New York Times Magazine,* April 10, 1988, p. 32.

216 *In business, only 4.9 percent:* Cathy Trost, "The New Majorities," *Wall Street Journal,* March 24, 1986.

217 *A 1976 study:* Grace Kleinbach, "Social Class and Medical Education," Department of Education, Harvard University, 1976; and quoted in Vicente Navarro, *Medicine Under Capitalism* (New York: Prodist, 1976), p. 144.

217 *The proportion of women construction workers:* See Molly Martin, ed., *Hard-Hatted Women* (Seattle: Seal Press, 1988).

218 *the traditional masculine ideal:* Barbara Ehrenreich, *The Hearts of Men: American Dreams and the Flight from Commitment* (New York: Doubleday/Anchor, 1983).

218 *if women were tired:* Herb Goldberg, *The New Male: From Self-Destruction to Self-Care* (New York: Morrow, 1979).

218 *the "new man" did not rule out marriage:* interviews conducted for Barbara Ehrenreich," Is There a New Man?" *New York Times Magazine,* May 15, 1984. I thank Harriet Bernstein for conducting most of the interviews for this article.

219 *"A pairing-off":* David Bloom, quoted in "Is the Middle Class Shrinking?" *Time,* November 3, 1986, p. 55.

219 *office romance was "flourishing":* Ellen Graham, "My Lover, My Colleague," *Wall Street Journal,* March 24, 1986.

220 *"progressive demoralization":* Betty Friedan, *The Feminine Mystique* (New York: Norton, 1963) p. 377.

221 *the birthrate among the educated:* Ben J. Wattenberg, *The Birth Dearth* (New York: Pharos, 1987).

221 *But the real issue:* For a story of a journalist who abandoned her career because a child was doing poorly in school, see Mary Fay Bourgoin, "You Can't Be a Mother and 'Have It All,'" *Washington Post,* November 27, 1983.

222 *"Our aim":* Betty Friedan, *The Second Stage* (New York: Summit Books, 1981), pp. 27–28.

222 *A far larger number of women remained:* See Ruth Sidel, *Women and Children Last: The Plight of Poor Women in Affluent America* (New York: Viking Press, 1986), chapter 3.

222–23 *"eccentric in focus":* Catherine R. Stimpson, "Fretting Together," *Nation,* February 7, 1987, pp. 149–50.

223 *On the campuses:* Suzy Bolotin, "Voices from the Post-Feminist Generation," *New York Times Magazine,* October 17, 1982.

223 *a startling 56 percent of American women:* Barbara Ehrenreich, "The Next Wave," *Ms.,* July/August 1987, p. 166.

224 *Sales of luxury goods boomed:* "Despite Collapse of Stocks, Luxury Sales Bounce Back," *New York Times,* June 7, 1988.

224 *The 5 percent of Americans:* Stephen J. Rose, *Social Stratification in the U.S.,* pp. 35–36.

225 *compensatory spending:* Michael Kinsley, "Arise, Ye Yuppies!" *New Republic,* July 9, 1984, p. 4.

225 *A study by the Stanford Research Institute:* Quoted in David E. Shi, *The Simple Life: Plain Living and High Thinking in American Culture* (New York: Oxford University Press, 1985), p. 269.

226 *Voluntary simplicity:* See T. Jackson Lears, *No Place of Grace: Antimodernism and the Transformation of American Culture, 1880–1920* (New York: Pantheon Books, 1981), chapter 2.

226 *"quiet revolution":* Quoted in Shi, *Simple Life,* pp. 268–69.

228 *The mass market disappeared:* Bruce Steinberg, "The Mass Market Is Splitting Apart," *Fortune,* November 28, 1983, p. 76.

229 *"There is a consumer out there":* "Where Sears Has Stumbled," *New York Times,* June 5, 1986.

230 *a largely predictable list:* "What's Hot, What's Not," *Miami Herald,* January 13, 1985.

230 *"new cultural style":* Deborah Silverman, *Selling Culture* (New York: Pantheon Books, 1986), p. 11.

231 *"New Upper Classes":* Benita Eisler, *Class Act* (New York: Franklin Watts, 1983), p. 274.

232 *"He would like to marry someday":* "The Year of the Yuppie," p. 18.

233 *centered in the upwardly mobile middle class:* See Barbara Ehrenreich, "Is There a New Man?"

237 *The rise and fall of the word:* Hertzberg, "Short Happy Life," p. 101.

237 *A 1985 Roper poll:* Cited in Hertzberg, "Short Happy Life," p. 102.

237 *yuppies placed third:* Bill Barol, "The Eighties Are Over," *Newsweek,* January 4, 1988, p. 44.

238 *a simple quiz:* Stevie Pierson, "Are You a Yuppie?" *Metropolitan Home,* April 1985, p. 60.

239 *A self-described "young urban professional writer":* Heard, "Yuppie Love," p. 10.

239 *a writer in Glamour:* Janice Harayda, "It's Time People Stopped Putting Down Yuppies," *Glamour,* October 1987, p. 40.

241 *"A couple of years ago":* Peter Baida, "Confessions of a Reluctant Yuppie," *American Scholar,* Winter 1985–86, p. 45.

242 *"conspicuous consumption is passé":* Joanne Lipman, "The Going Gets Tough and Madison Avenue Dumps the Yuppies," *Wall Street Journal,* December 9, 1988.

242 *"Had it with pride":* Pete Hamill, "Doing Good," *New York,* October 13, 1986, p. 35.

242 *"signs of increased altruism":* Barol, "The Eighties Are Over," p. 48.

243 *"There is a lot of pent-up idealism":* Arthur Schlesinger, Jr., quoted in Barol, "The Eighties Are Over," p. 48.

## SIX: THE NEXT GREAT SHIFT

*244 My wife and I are baby-boomers:* Paul S. Hewitt, "Something's Gone Terribly Wrong with Being 'Rich,' " *Los Angeles Herald Tribune,* January 7, 1989.

*245 A young family earning $600,000:* Brooke Kroeger, "Feeling Poor on $600,000 a Year," *New York Times,* April 26, 1987.

*246 A growing cadre of celebrity pundits:* James Fallows, "The New Stars of Washington," *New York Review of Books,* June 12, 1986, p. 41.

*249 the Democratic Party:* Thomas Byrne Edsall, *The New Politics of Inequality* (New York: Norton, 1984), pp. 60–62.

*251 a weird pile of liberal shit:* Mark Rudd, quoted in Barbara Ehrenreich and John Ehrenreich, "The Professional-Managerial Class," in Pat Walker, ed., *Between Labor and Capital* (Boston: South End Press, 1979), p. 38.

*253 they are sanctified:* George Gilder, *Wealth and Poverty* (New York: Basic Books, 1981).

*254 a casino society:* Anthony Bianco, "Playing with Fire: As Speculation Replaces Investment, Our Economic Future Is at Stake," *Business Week,* September 16, 1985, pp. 78–90.

*254 "Rarely have so few,":* Robert B. Reich, "Leveraged Buyouts: America Pays the Price," *New York Times Magazine,* January 29, 1989, p. 32.

*255 A few recent books:* See Lewis H. Lapham, *Money and Class in America: Notes and Observations on a Civil Religion* (New York: Weidenfeld and Nicholson, 1987); and Vance Packard, *The Ultra-Rich: How Much Is Too Much?* (Boston: Little, Brown, 1989); Nelson W. Aldrich, Jr., *Old Money: The Mythology of America's Upper Class* (New York: Knopf, 1988).

*257 the decline of labor coverage:* See Jo-Ann Mort, "The Vanishing Labor Beat," *Nation,* November 21, 1987, pp. 588–90.

*258 A kind of language barrier:* See, for example, Michael Harrington, *The Long-Distance Runner* (New York: Henry Holt, 1988). College-educated left-wing intellectuals, he writes, have little trouble conversing with self-taught "labor intellectuals," who often turn out to be labor leaders. However, in his own experience, "that same ease did not exist with the rank and file, and particularly the black rank and file. . . . [I]n most cases, there is simply not that shared language" (p. 49).

*259 "critical discourse":* Alvin Gouldner, *The Future of Intellectuals and the New Class* (New York: Seabury Continuum, 1979), p. 29.

*261 "For some":* John Kenneth Galbraith, *The Affluent Society* (Boston: Houghton Mifflin, 1958), pp. 341–42.

# INDEX

Note: The abbreviation *pmc* stands for "professional middle class"

## ABOUT THE AUTHOR

Barbara Ehrenreich is the author of numerous books, including *The Hearts of Men* (hailed as "brilliant" by the *New York Times*). Her essays and articles have appeared in the *Washington Post*, the *New York Times Magazine*, the *Atlantic*, the *Nation*, and the *New Republic*, and she is currently a regular columnist for *Ms.* magazine and *Mother Jones*. She lives on Long Island with her husband and two children.